THE B.C. HANDBOOK FOR *Action* ON CHILD ABUSE AND NEGLECT

1998

Published by:

Ministry for Children and Families

Compiled by:

Ministry of Attorney General
Ministry for Children and Families
Ministry of Education, Skills and Training
Ministry of Health
Ministry of Women's Equality

The ministries wish to thank the community agencies and organizations which helped to develop the handbook.

The handbook is available on the Ministry for Children and Families'
web site:

   http://www.mcf.gov.bc.ca

Additional copies may be purchased from:

  Crown Publications
  521 Fort Street
  Victoria BC V8W 1E7

  phone: (250) 386-4636
  fax: (250) 386-0221
  e-mail: crown@pinc.com
  web site: http://www.crownpub.bc.ca

To order, please quote stock number 643.

Canadian Cataloguing in Publication Data
Main entry under title:
The B.C. handbook for action on child abuse & neglect

  "This version replaces the 1988 Inter-ministry
child abuse handbook."—Introduction.
 ISBN 0-7726-3268-8

  1. Child abuse - British Columbia - Prevention -
Handbooks, manuals, etc. 2. Child sexual abuse -
British Columbia - Prevention - Handbooks, manuals,
etc. 3. Abused children - Services for - British
Columbia. 4. Child abuse - Law and legislation -
British Columbia. . I. British Columbia. Ministry
of Attorney General. II. British Columbia.
Ministry for Children and Families. III. Title:
Inter-ministry child abuse handbook.

HV6626.54.C3B74 1998   362.7(68(09711   C98-960033-5

Contents

Part Three - Support and Intervention Services

Part Four - Collaborative Planning and Information Sharing

Part Five - Promoting Well-being and Preventing Abuse and Neglect

Part Six - Appendices

PART I - INTRODUCTION

Welcome to the handbook

You should read this handbook in conjunction with existing laws, policies and procedures. That way, you can get more detail and stay current with new laws or policies put in place after this handbook was published.

This handbook is intended for service providers – those who work regularly with children and/or families. It summarizes the key principles, laws and policies dealing with the abuse and neglect of children in B.C. These policies are intended to prevent child abuse and neglect, and to lessen the harm to children and families when they do occur.

Service providers have a special responsibility and are an important part of British Columbia's child protection system – a network of professionals, including child care providers, law enforcement officials, social workers, doctors and other health care providers, educators, mental health workers, child and youth workers, residential care providers, government employees, and volunteers, with the overriding goal of ensuring the safety and well-being of British Columbia's children.

That means working together to prevent child abuse and neglect whenever possible – and, when it happens, reporting it.

Our responsibility to report child abuse and neglect is backed up in law. The *Child, Family and Community Service Act* requires every person who has a reason to believe that a child has been or is likely to be abused or neglected, or may need protection, to promptly report the matter to a child protection social worker.

Under the *Criminal Code*, physical assault, sexual assault and other sexual offences involving children are crimes, as are abandoning a child and failing to provide the necessities of life.

This handbook covers:

- how to recognize abuse and neglect;
- how to respond to a disclosure of abuse or neglect from a child;
- how to report abuse and neglect and intervene;
- how investigations are undertaken, and the possible role of service providers;
- the rules governing the sharing of information among service providers;
- the importance of collaboration among all those working with children and families;

- what services are available to help children and families;

- how to promote child well-being and prevent abuse and neglect; and

- how to advocate for children or make a complaint about service.

The purposes of the handbook

The handbook aims to:

- ensure that efforts in British Columbia to respond to child abuse and neglect are effective, consistent and sensitive to the needs of children;

- promote collaboration among service providers responding to child abuse and neglect;

- ensure that service providers are aware of how they are accountable for their responses to child abuse and neglect;

- provide an overview of the law and the government's policies relating to child abuse and neglect;

This version replaces the 1988 *Inter-Ministry Child Abuse Handbook* and reflects changes that have taken place since then in the legislation, policy and structure of participating ministries. Changes to the system, such as the development of the new Ministry for Children and Families, are also reflected in this handbook.

It discusses the integrated roles of all involved service providers, and reflects the perspectives of specific ministries. This approach supports collaborative work practices among those who serve children.

Because all elements of the response to child abuse and neglect – from prevention to intervention – are covered here, it is important to read the handbook in its entirety, and not to read sections in isolation from one another. Reading the entire handbook will give you an appreciation of the breadth of action needed to address child abuse and neglect, and the role that collaboration plays in enhancing the delivery of services to children and their families.

General principles

Ensuring the safety and well-being of children requires us to:

- put children's needs first;
- work together; and
- be accountable for our actions.

The following principles offer guidance on how to ensure an effective response. They reflect many of the principles contained in the *United Nations Convention on the Rights of the Child*, the *Child, Family and Community Service Act*, and the policy and legislation of various ministries that serve children and their families.

Responding to the needs of children

- The safety and well-being of children is paramount.

- Children are entitled to protection from abuse, neglect, harm and the threat of harm.

- Interventions to ensure a child's safety should be those that are the most effective in keeping the child safe and the least disruptive to the child.

- While all children are vulnerable, some are more vulnerable than others. Children with disabilities and very young children may not be able to protect themselves, and are particularly dependent on adults for their safety and well-being. Service providers should be especially vigilant in preventing, detecting and intervening in cases of abuse and neglect involving such children.

- Children's need for privacy and confidentiality should be respected. This is particularly important when a child may have been abused or neglected.

- Children should have their views considered and be involved when decisions relating to them are made.

- Children should be provided with prevention information and skills that will help them resist or avoid abuse, when possible, and report abuse or neglect.

The responsibilities and needs of a family

- As long as the child's safety and well-being can be assured, a child's family is the preferred environment for the child's care and upbringing, and the responsibility for the care and protection of the child rests primarily with the parent(s).

- Parents should have their views considered and, wherever possible, participate in working towards the best interests of the child.

- Families and children should be informed of the services available to them and be assisted in obtaining those services.

Service delivery

- Service providers who work with children do so in a position of trust, and their conduct should reflect this trust.

- Services should be planned and provided in ways that are sensitive to the needs and the cultural, racial and religious heritage of those receiving the services.

- All people and agencies providing services for children should work in a collaborative way.

- Services for children should be sensitive to the child's developmental stage, capacity and temperament.

- Communities should participate in the planning and, where possible and appropriate, in the delivery of services to families and children.

- The sharing of information, within the rules governing confidentiality and disclosure of information, is essential for service providers.

The role of aboriginal communities

First Nations, aboriginal and Metis communities have very specific needs and face particular challenges. Children from these communities grow up in a unique social and cultural context. This handbook recognizes:

- the importance of preserving a child's aboriginal identity, and

- the specific role of aboriginal communities in ensuring the safety and well-being of aboriginal children.

First Nations, aboriginal and Metis communities continue to assert their right to control decisions affecting them, and especially decisions about the welfare of their children. In doing so, they are building on their cultural strengths, and building their capacity to become more involved in child and family services. In keeping with the development of this capacity, non-aboriginal service providers working with aboriginal children should make every effort to involve aboriginal communities in areas such as

- acquiring information to help assess levels of risk in the child's family;

- identifying services that will reduce these risks;

- planning and delivering services that are culturally appropriate and accessible;

- participating in developing and implementing plans that will preserve the child's cultural identity;

- reuniting aboriginal children who have been removed from their culture, extended family and community;

- identifying and developing appropriate out-of-home placement resources; and

- participating as an equal party at protection and continuing custody hearings involving aboriginal children.

A number of aboriginal communities already have a well-developed network of child protection services. Some have aboriginal child welfare agencies whose employees provide family support and child protection services in their communities by authority delegated from the director, under the terms of the *Child, Family and Community Service Act*. (See Appendix B for a list of First Nations child welfare agencies which have employees with delegated authority).

Other aboriginal communities are in various stages of developing this capacity. Also, several First Nations are participating in the treaty process, which may include child welfare in the model of self-government.

A Guide to Aboriginal Organizations and Services in British Columbia, a resource booklet published annually by the Ministry of Aboriginal Affairs, is available from:

Ministry of Aboriginal Affairs
PO Box 9100, Stn Prov Govt
Victoria BC V8W 9B1

Phone: (250) 356-0330

PART II - RECOGNIZING, REPORTING, INVESTIGATING AND DEALING WITH ABUSE AND NEGLECT

Understanding what child abuse and neglect are and knowing how to take appropriate action are critical in ensuring the safety and well-being of children.

Defining child abuse and neglect

The following definitions will help you respond to child abuse and neglect. Some are modifications of definitions given in a variety of sources. Every effort has been made to use plain language. While recognizing that one profession may use a particular term somewhat differently than another profession, the definitions below are intended to support the work of all service providers.

Child

A person under 19 years of age.

Physical abuse

A deliberate, non-accidental physical assault or action by an adult or significantly older or more powerful child that results or is likely to result in physical harm to a child. It includes the use of unreasonable force to discipline a child or to prevent a child from harming him/herself or others. The injuries sustained by the child may vary in severity and range from minor bruising, burns, welts or bite marks to major fractures of the bones or skull, and, in its most extreme form, the death of a child. Physical assault is a crime.

Sexual abuse

Sexual abuse generally means any sexual use of a child by an adult or a significantly older or more powerful child. There are many criminal offences related to sexual activity involving children. *The Criminal Code* prohibits:

- any sexual activity between an adult and a child under the age of 14 – a child under 14 is incapable in law of consenting to sexual activity (s. 150.1 of the *Criminal Code*). The criminal law recognizes that consensual "peer sex" is not an offence in the following situation: if one child is between 12 and 14 years and the other is 12 years or more but under the age of 16, less than two years older, and not in a position of trust or authority to the other.

- any sexual activity between an adult in a position of trust or authority towards a child between the ages of 14 and 18 years

- any sexual activity without the consent of a child of any age. (Depending on the activity, non-consensual sexual activity may constitute the criminal offence of sexual assault.)

- use of children in prostitution and pornography.

The Ministry for Children and Families states that sexual abuse is any behaviour of a sexual nature toward a child, including one or more of the following:

- touching or invitation to touch for sexual purposes, or intercourse (vaginal or anal)

- menacing or threatening sexual acts, obscene gestures, obscene communications or stalking

- sexual references to the child's body or behaviour by words or gestures

- requests that the child expose their body for sexual purposes

- deliberate exposure of the child to sexual activity or material.

The Ministry for Children and Families states sexual exploitation includes permitting, encouraging or requiring a child to engage in:

- conduct of a sexual nature for the stimulation, gratification, profit or self-interest of another person who is in a position of trust or authority, or with whom the child is in a relationship of dependency

- prostitution

- production of material of a pornographic nature.

Sexual aspects of organized or ritual abuse should be considered a form of sexual exploitation.

Sexual activity between children or youth may constitute sexual abuse if the difference in age or power between the children is so significant that the older or more powerful child is clearly taking sexual advantage of the younger or less powerful child. This would exclude consensual, developmentally appropriate sexual activity between children where there is no significant difference in age or power between the children.

Emotional abuse

Emotional abuse is the most difficult type of abuse to define and recognize. It may range from habitual humiliation of the child to withholding life-sustaining nurturing. It can include acts or omissions by those responsible for the care of a child or others in contact with a child, that are likely to have serious, negative emotional impacts. Emotional abuse may occur separately from, or along with, other forms of abuse and neglect.

Emotional abuse can include a pattern of

- scapegoating;
- rejection;
- verbal attacks on the child;
- threats;
- insults; or
- humiliation.

Emotional harm

When emotional abuse is persistent and chronic, it can result in emotional damage to the child. A child is defined by the *Child, Family and Community Service Act* as emotionally harmed if they demonstrate severe:

- anxiety;
- depression;
- withdrawal; or
- self-destructive or aggressive behaviour.

If a child is emotionally harmed by the parent's conduct, as demonstrated by these severe behaviours, the child is in need of protection. This must be reported to a child protection social worker.

Neglect

Neglect involves an act of omission on the part of the parent or guardian that results or is likely to result in physical harm to the child. It generally refers to situations in which a child has been, or is likely to be physically harmed through action or inaction by those responsible for care of the child. This may include failure to provide food, shelter, basic health care, or supervision and protection from risks, to the extent that the child's physical health, development or safety is harmed or is likely to be harmed. This also includes failure to thrive (see p. 13). Not always intentional, neglect may be a result of insufficient resources or other circumstances beyond a person's control.

The Child, Family and Community Service Act states that a child needs protection if the child has been, or is likely to be, physically harmed due to neglect by the child's parent.

Failing to provide the necessities, abandoning a child and corrupting a child are crimes.

Recognizing indicators of possible child abuse and neglect

Anyone who provides service to children should watch for signs of possible abuse or neglect. While many indicators, particularly those of a behavioural nature, may be signs of other problems, a series or cluster of indicators observed over a period of time may be cause for concern regarding abuse or neglect. These signs or indicators often happen in combinations or as dramatic changes from normal behaviour. They may be the child's reaction to abuse or neglect, and can be a way of communicating that he or she has been, or is being, abused or neglected.

By themselves, these signs do not prove abuse or neglect. But they do tell us we need to know more about the child's circumstances. They can be the result of phenomena such as divorce, separation, death of a significant person or the arrival of a new sibling. That's why indicators must be assessed by professionals. The important thing to know is what the signs are, and how to report them if a child may need protection.

Possible Indicators of Physical Abuse

Physical Indicators

- injuries (bruises, welts, cuts, burns, bite marks, fractures, etc.) that are not consistent with the explanation offered (e.g. extensive bruising to one area)
- presence of several injuries (3+) that are in various stages of healing
- repeated injuries over a period of time
- injuries that form a shape or pattern that may look like the object used to make the injury (e.g. buckle, hand, iron, teeth, cigarette burns)
- facial injuries in infants and pre-school children (e.g. cuts, bruises, sores, etc.)
- injuries not consistent with the child's age and development
- bald patches on child's head where hair may have been torn out
- repeated poisonings and/or accidents

Behavioural Indicators

- runaway attempts and fear of going home
- stilted conversation, vacant stares or frozen watchfulness, no attempt to seek comfort when hurt
- describes self as bad and deserving to be punished
- cannot recall how injuries occurred, or offers an inconsistent explanation
- wary of adults or reluctant to go home
- often absent from school/child care
- may flinch if touched unexpectedly
- extremely aggressive or withdrawn
- displays indiscriminate affection-seeking behaviour
- abusive behaviour and language in play
- overly compliant and/or eager to please
- poor sleeping patterns, fear of the dark, frequent nightmares
- sad, cries frequently
- drug/alcohol misuse
- depression
- poor memory and concentration
- suicide attempts

Possible Indicators of Sexual Abuse

Physical Indicators

- fatigue due to sleep disturbances
- sudden weight change
- cuts or sores made by the child on the arm (self-mutilation)
- recurring physical ailments
- difficulty in walking or sitting
- unusual or excessive itching in the genital or anal area due to infection(s)
- torn, stained or bloody underwear
- sexually transmitted disease(s)
- pregnancy
- injuries to the mouth, genital or anal areas (e.g. bruising, swelling, sores, infection)

Behavioural Indicators

In a younger child
- sad, cries often, unduly anxious
- short attention span
- inserts objects into the vagina or rectum
- change or loss of appetite
- sleep disturbances, nightmares
- excessively dependent
- fear of home or a specific place, excessive fear of men or women, lacks trust in others
- age-inappropriate sexual play with toys, self, others (e.g. replication of explicit sexual acts)
- age-inappropriate, sexually explicit drawings and/or descriptions
- bizarre, sophisticated or unusual sexual knowledge
- reverts to bedwetting/soiling
- dramatic behavioural changes, sudden non-participation in activities
- poor peer relationships, self-image
- overall poor self-care

In an older child
- sudden lack of interest in friends or activities
- fearful or startled response to touching
- overwhelming interest in sexual activities
- hostility toward authority figures
- fire setting
- need for constant companionship
- regressive communication patterns (e.g. speaking childishly)
- academic difficulties or performance suddenly deteriorates
- truancy and/or running away from home
- wears provocative clothing or wears layers of clothing to hide bruises (e.g. keeps jacket on in class)
- recurrent physical complaints that are without physiological basis (e.g. abdominal pains, headache, nausea)
- lacks trust in others
- unable to "have fun" with others
- suicide attempts
- drug/alcohol misuse
- poor personal hygiene
- promiscuity
- sexual acting out in a variety of ways

Possible Indicators of Emotional Abuse

Physical Indicators	Behavioural Indicators
• bedwetting and/or diarrhea • frequent psychosomatic complaints, headaches, nausea, abdominal pains	• mental or emotional development lags • behaviours inappropriate for age • fear of failure, overly high standards, reluctance to play • fears consequences of actions, often leading to lying • extreme withdrawal or aggressiveness, mood swings • overly compliant, too well-mannered • excessive neatness and cleanliness • extreme attention-seeking behaviours • poor peer relationships • severe depression, may be suicidal • runaway attempts • violence is a subject for art or writing • complains of social isolation • forbidden contact with other children

Possible Indicators of Neglect

Physical Indicators	Behavioural Indicators
• abandonment • lack of shelter • unattended medical and dental needs • consistent lack of supervision • ingestion of cleaning fluids, medicines, etc. • consistent hunger • inappropriate dress for weather conditions • poor hygiene • persistent conditions (e.g. scabies, head lice, diaper rash, or other skin disorders) • developmental delays (e.g. language, weight) • irregular or non-attendance at school or child care • not registered in school • not attending school	• depression • poor impulse control • demands constant attention and affection • lack of parental participation and interest • delinquency • misuse of alcohol/drugs • regularly displays fatigue or listlessness, falls asleep in class • steals food, or begs for food from classmate(s) • reports that no caregiver is at home • frequently absent or tardy • self-destructive • drops out of school (adolescent) • takes over adult caring role (of parent) • lacks trust in others, unpredictable • plans only for the moment

Possible Indicators of Failure to Thrive

Physical Indicators

- a child who has stopped growing and/or has experienced significant weight loss may be suffering from failure-to-thrive syndrome. Medical assessment is necessary to determine whether the syndrome is organic or non-organic in origin.
- the following physical characteristics are often present in failure-to-thrive children:
  - child appears pale, emaciated, has "sunken cheeks"
  - child's body fat ratio is extremely low (e.g. wrinkled buttocks)
  - skin may feel like parchment paper as a result of dehydration
  - prolonged vomiting and/or diarrhea
  - child has not attained significant developmental milestones within their age range (e.g. cannot hold head up at six months of age, cannot walk at 18 months, etc.)

Behavioural Indicators

- appears lethargic and undemanding (e.g. cries very little)
- uninterested in environment or surroundings
- displays little or no movement (e.g. lies in crib motionless)
- is unresponsive to stimulation from strangers
- shows little stranger anxiety (e.g. is indifferent to attention received from strangers)

When You Suspect a Child May Have Been Abused or Neglected

Children do not always tell us about their abuse or neglect and sometimes the indicators are not that obvious. When talking to children about possible abuse and/or neglect, the following points may be helpful:

- choose your approach carefully as the child may be fearful or reluctant to talk about what happened;

- be relaxed and casual because if you appear anxious or exhibit strong feelings the child may withdraw;

- make sure you have enough time and a private setting where there is little chance for interruptions;

- in a neutral and objective manner express your concerns to the child and seek or ask their explanation for the indicators that you have observed; and

- be a good listener and express your confidence in the child as this shows your genuine concern for their safety and well-being.

Handling disclosures - How children tell us about being abused or neglected

Sometimes children will tell you directly that they are being abused or neglect. Sometimes they use indirect ways to tell you - through art, writing or hints. These are all known as disclosures. There are two ways a disclosure of abuse or neglect may take place:

1. Direct disclosures

Sometimes children tell others directly that they are being abused or neglected. They may start with a small example and watch how you react. Research indicates that children tell their story many times before action is taken. You should respond to a child's disclosure of abuse or neglect with an open mind and a willingness to believe them.

Bear in mind that the child will be formally interviewed for investigative purposes once a report is made to a child protection social worker and/or the police.

2. Indirect disclosures

Sometimes children do not tell others directly, but use indirect methods of communicating about their abuse or neglect. These include their behaviours, emotions, art, writing, appearance, inquiries or discussion of fears, concerns or relationships. Children also divulge information through indirect statements, statements made with conditions ("promise not to tell anyone"), or third party statements. Appendix E gives examples of these kinds of approaches and how best to respond. Leading questions should not be used because they contain an answer, which can result in inaccurate information. Use open-ended questions when talking to a child about possible abuse and/or neglect.

When a child discloses abuse
1. Stay calm and listen
2. Go slowly
3. Reassure them that they have not done anything wrong
4. Be supportive
5. Gather essential facts
6. Tell the child what will happen next
7. Report
8. Make notes

When A Child Discloses Abuse or Neglect

1. Stay calm

An abused or neglected child needs to know that you are calm and available to help them. Reactions of shock, outrage, or fear may inhibit the child and make them feel more anxious or ashamed. A calm response not only allows the child to tell their story, it also provides the reassurance that what has happened is not so bad that it cannot be talked about and worked through calmly.

2. Go slowly

It is normal to feel inadequate or unsure about what to do or say when a child tells you about their abuse. As a result, there is a tendency to rush things. Frequently, too much is asked too quickly. Proceed slowly. Gentle questions such as: "Can you tell me more about what happened?" are helpful. Avoid questions that begin with "why".

3. Reassure the child that they have not done anything wrong

Any questions that are asked are usually associated in the child's mind with getting into trouble. Avoid using "why" questions. For example: "Why did he/she hit you?" suggests indirectly that the child may have done something wrong and increases the child's reluctance to discuss the matter.

4. Be supportive

Children need support and reassurance when discussing their abuse or neglect. It is helpful to let the child know that:

- they are not in trouble;

- they are safe with you;

- you are glad that they have chosen to tell you about this;

- they have done the right thing telling about this;

- you are sorry that they have been hurt or that this has happened to them;

- you will do everything you can to make sure they are not hurt again; and

- you know others who can be trusted to help solve this problem.

5. Get only the essential facts

If this is the first time the child has disclosed abuse or neglect, a full investigation will be necessary. The child will be interviewed in depth by a child protection social worker and, if there is a criminal investigation, by the police. To avoid the child having to endure multiple interviews, limit your discussion to finding out generally what took place. When you have sufficient information and reason to believe that abuse and/or neglect has occurred, gently stop gathering facts and be supportive.

6. Tell the child what will happen next

Children who disclose their abuse feel anxious and vulnerable about what people think of them and what will happen next. It is important, however, to avoid making promises to the child about what may or may not happen next. For example, avoid promises that the alleged perpetrator won't get into trouble. Provide only reassurance that is realistic and achievable. Discuss with the child what you think will happen next and who will be involved.

7. Report to the child protection social worker

Report disclosures of abuse or neglect immediately to a child protection social worker for follow-up and investigation. Express your willingness to help the child through the steps which will follow, if appropriate.

8. Make notes

Make notes of all comments made by the child about abuse or neglect using the child's exact words where possible. Save all drawings and artwork. This information needs to be shared with the child protection social worker, the police and Crown counsel, if appropriate.

Reporting Child Abuse or Neglect

In some ways, this is the simplest yet the most urgent aspect of responding to child abuse or neglect. If you have reason to believe a child has been or is likely to be abused, neglected, or in need of protection, you *must* report the matter immediately to a child protection social worker. The law is set out in legislation called the *Child, Family and Community Service Act*.

Report to a child protection social worker in either a Ministry for Children and Families office, or a First Nations child welfare agency that provides child protection services.

- If you are in Vancouver call 660-4927. From elsewhere in B.C., call 1-800-663-9122.

    or

- Call the Helpline for Children: Dial 0 and ask the operator for Zenith 1234.

If a child is in immediate danger, police should be called. Dial 911, or call the operator and ask for police assistance.

CALL HELPLINE
- ZENITH 1234
Tell children help is just a phone call away. They can reach the Helpline for Children by dialing 0 and asking the operator for Zenith 1234. It doesn't cost anything to call, and a child protection social worker is always there to listen and help, 24 hours a day, seven days a week. For more information see the reporting summary inside the front cover of this handbook.

Legal Duty to Report

Everyone who has a reason to believe that a child has been or is likely to be physically harmed, sexually abused or sexually exploited, or needs protection due to the specific circumstances outlined in the *Child, Family and Community Service Act*, is legally responsible under that act to report the matter to a child protection social worker. In British Columbia, a child is anyone under the age of 19.

The duty to report applies to everyone, including service providers, family members and the general public – in short, anyone who is aware of circumstances that should be reported.

- It doesn't matter if you believe someone else is reporting the situation, you still have to report.

- It doesn't matter if you're aware that a child protection social worker is already involved with the child, you still have to report the matter. All new incidents must be reported as well.

- The legal duty to report overrides any duty of confidentiality, except a solicitor-client relationship.

- Time is of the essence in ensuring the safety and well-being of children. Report immediately.

- If you have reason to believe that a child has been or is likely to be abused or neglected, then the responsibility for making a report to a child protection social worker legally rests with you.

- Do not contact the alleged perpetrator. This is the responsibility of the police, or the child protection social worker.

- If an employer needs to contact the alleged perpetrator in order to protect children under their authority, this should be coordinated with the police and child protection social worker.

Many agencies and ministries have developed internal reporting procedures requiring that reports be made to supervisory personnel as well as to a child protection social worker. All internal reporting procedures must conform with the legal duty to report to a child protection social worker.

When to Report that a Child Needs Protection

The *Child, Family and Community Service Act* sets out the circumstances under which you must report - that is, when you have reason to believe that a child "has been, or is likely to be, physically harmed, sexually abused or sexually exploited by a parent or by another person and the parent is unwilling or unable to protect the child, or if the child has been or is likely to be physically harmed because of neglect by the child's parent," or if:

- the child is emotionally harmed by the parent's conduct;

- the child is deprived of necessary health care;

- the child's development is likely to be seriously impaired by a treatable condition and the child's parent refuses to provide or consent to treatment;

- the child's parent is unable or unwilling to care for the child and has not made adequate provision for the child's care;

- the child is or has been absent from home in circumstances that endanger the child's safety or well-being;

- the child's parent is dead and adequate provision has not been made for the child's care; and

- the child has been abandoned and adequate provision has not been made for the child's care.

How to Report

All child abuse and neglect concerns must be reported to a Ministry for Children and Families child protection social worker or a First Nations child welfare agency that provides child protection services. This applies even if a report has been made to the police.

There are three ways to reach a Ministry for Children and Families child protection social worker:

- **Ministry for Children and Families – local district office,** Monday to Friday 8:30 a.m. to 4:30 p.m. (listed in the blue pages of your phone book).

- **After Hours Lines** for Vancouver, North Shore, Richmond: 604-660-4927 Lower Mainland (Burnaby and Delta in the west to Maple Ridge and Langley in the east): 604-660-8180 Anywhere else in B.C.: 1-800-663-9122

- **Helpline for Children** – dial 0 and ask the operator for Zenith 1234. This toll-free service operates 24 hours a day.

What to Report

In most circumstances, the identity of the person who makes a report will not be revealed without consent unless the child protection social worker is required to give their name for the purposes of a court hearing.

The report should include the reporter's name, telephone number and relationship to the child. It should also provide as much of the following information as possible:

- the name and location of the child;
- any immediate concerns about the child's safety;
- any information as to why you believe the child is at risk;
- any statements or disclosures made by the child;
- the age and vulnerability of the child;
- information on the family, parents and alleged offenders;
- information on siblings or other children who may be at risk;
- knowledge of any previous incidents or concerns regarding the child;
- information about other persons or agencies closely involved with the child and/or family;
- information about other persons who may be witnesses or may have information about the child;
- information on the nature of the child's disabilities, if any, his or her mode of communication, and the name of a key support person;
- any other relevant information concerning the child and/or family, such as language or culture.

Don't delay making a report just because you don't have all this information. Contact the child protection social worker immediately with the information you do have.

You don't have to report when it is clear that an injury or other harm is accidental and is a result of circumstances outside the control of the parent or other person responsible for the child in, for example, a playground injury.

Informing the police

Police play an important role in protecting children. They can respond quickly to protect children in immediate danger.

- If a child is in immediate danger, every person aware of it must call the police right away, then report to a child protection social worker as soon as possible.
- If a child is not in immediate danger, report to a child protection social worker. They will call police if they believe a criminal offence is occurring or may have occurred.

Child protection social workers understand the need to involve police immediately where it is evident that a criminal offence has occurred or is occurring. This is particularly important in matters such as sexual assault where it is critical to the investigation that evidence be obtained immediately. *Prompt action can prevent further harm and help police catch the perpetrator.*

Police are responsible for conducting a criminal investigation which can include obtaining witness statements, arranging to obtain medical forensic evidence where appropriate, protecting the crime scene and maintaining the continuity of evidence.

Informing a superintendent of schools in the case of a public school or a senior authority in the case of other educational institutions

When child abuse or neglect is believed to have occurred in a public school or in an educational institution, or during school activities sponsored by the school or institution, the child protection social worker will notify the school superintendent, in the case of a public school, or the senior authority, in the case of other educational institutions.

If a case comes to the attention of an employee of a public school or an educational institution, the employee must report it to a child protection social worker and to the superintendent or senior authority.

The school board, superintendent of schools or senior authority of an educational institution has the responsibility of ensuring the safety of children in educational settings, and has the authority to suspend or dismiss employees, and suspend or expel students.

If a child is in immediate danger and requires police assistance, police should be notified without delay so they can protect the child.

When abusive behaviours between children occur at school, school personnel should immediately notify the principal, who is responsible for student conduct. The principal also has a duty to report promptly to a child protection social worker if he/she has reason to believe a child has been or is likely to be abused or neglected. The report of school personnel to the principal does not replace his/her duty to report to a child protection social worker.

Informing a medical health officer

When child abuse or neglect is believed to have occurred in a child care facility that is or should be licensed, the child protection social worker will notify the medical health officer. Child care facility licensees are also required to inform the medical health officer.

These facilities include

- preschools;

- special needs child care (also known as supported child care);

- group day care;

- emergency care;

- family child care;

- child minding;

- out-of-school care;

- residential care for children and youth; and

- occasional child care, for example at a ski hill or resort.

Informing a director of a youth custody (containment) centre

Youth custody centres are legislated by the *Young Offenders Act* as places of detainment and detention. When abuse or neglect is believed to have occurred in a youth custody centre, or while participating in centre activities, the child protection social worker will notify the director of the youth custody centre.

If a case comes to the attention of an employee at the youth custody centre, the employee must report it to a child protection social worker and to the director of the youth custody centre.

The director of the youth custody centre is responsible for taking the necessary steps to ensure that children in the facility are safe. It should be noted that children cannot be removed from the youth custody centre unless permitted by provisions of the *Young Offenders Act* and relevant provincial legislation.

Other reporting considerations

Child sexual exploitation
If you suspect that a child is being coerced to perform sexual activities or may be involved in pornography, contact the police immediately. Children in residential programs are particularly vulnerable as are children living on the street. Children may be coerced into providing sexual services in exchange for a place to sleep, food, a shower or for money. It is the responsibility of the police and a child protection social worker to determine the type of intervention necessary and whether criminal offences have occurred. Children involved in the sex trade are victims of sexual abuse and not criminals.

Abusive behaviour between children

Abusive behaviour between children, including sexual behaviour, generally involves an imbalance of power. For example, one child may be significantly older than the other, or one of the children may be more vulnerable for other reasons.

This kind of behaviour has many different causes and occurs along a continuum of severity. Responses to the children's behaviour will therefore vary. A sensitive, collaborative approach and careful analysis by service providers, parents and the community are key components of any effective response.

The decision as to whether to report to a child protection social worker is made on a case-by-case basis. There is no need to report:

- normal sexual play or exploration between children of similar ages;

- minor altercations or aggression between children; and

- any other activity that is in the bounds of normal childhood behaviour.

Factors to be considered when deciding to report include:

- the seriousness of the behaviour;

- the existence of a power imbalance between the children;

- whether the behaviour resulted in harm to the child(ren); and

- the willingness and ability of the involved children's parents to respond appropriately.

In deciding whether to report to a child protection social worker, ask yourself:

- are the children behaving inappropriately for their age?;

- are they being coercive or exploitive?;

- is their behaviour impulsive or premeditated?;

- is there a pattern of domination, force, aggression (actual or threatened) or intimidation which endangers the physical or psychological well-being of another child?

The child protection social worker may contact the parents of the affected children (both abused and aggressor) to decide whether their behaviour is an indicator of abuse or neglect. The child protection social worker may also:

- need to determine whether the parent(s) will take appropriate action to prevent further abuse; and

- where appropriate, speak to the children with the consent of the parent(s).

The child protection social worker consults with others involved with the child to decide whether an investigation into the child's need for protection should commence. A report will be made to police if it is believed that a criminal offence may have occurred or is occurring.

The child protection social worker shares the results of his or her assessment with the parent(s), when appropriate, and with the person in authority where the abusive behaviour occurred. It is important for the child protection social worker to work with other service providers to develop and implement a community safety plan, where appropriate, and to ensure that counselling services are arranged as needed for the affected child(ren) and family/families.

Police should be called if a child needs immediate police assistance or if a criminal offence has occurred or is occurring.

A child under 12
Where a child under 12 has killed, assaulted or endangered another person, police must report to a child protection social worker. Where police receive a report of a child under 12 who has committed a less serious offence, they may report the circumstances to a child protection social worker.

Historical abuse
If a child discloses past abuse to you, you must report it to a child protection social worker.

If a child discloses past abuse to you, you must report it to a child protection social worker.

An adult who was abused as a child may be in a position to know if their abuser could be abusing other children. If they have reason to believe this is happening, they have a legal duty to report this belief to a child protection social worker.

A service provider who has reason to believe that a child has been or is likely to be abused by an alleged past abuser also has a duty to report this belief to a child protection social worker.

When working with adults who were abused as children inform them of their legal duty to report any current belief that a child has been or is likely to be physically or sexually abused. It may not be easy for them to report and they may need your support.

In addition to receiving the report, a child protection social worker or any service provider can advise the adult of the services or remedies that may be available through the police, the Criminal Injury Compensation Program, victim services and civil litigation.

Reporting child fatalities

Under the *Coroners Act*, you must notify a coroner or police if you become aware of a child fatality that is sudden and unexpected. Most reports under the act are made by police and hospital personnel. However, other individuals may call a coroner if they are not sure whether a report has been made, or if they want to know the status of the coroner's investigation.

A child protection social worker who becomes aware of the death of a child in care, or a child otherwise known to them, files a report under the *Child, Family and Community Service Act* to the director, who in turn notifies the chief coroner and the Children's Commission.

The Children's Commission reviews all child fatalities and investigates those it determines warrant investigation. The commission, in consultation with a multidisciplinary team, may make recommendations about services delivered to the child or their family, or about any other issue related to the death of the child. These recommendations are forwarded to relevant ministries, agencies and individuals, and are outlined in public reports.

Failing to Report or Knowingly Making a False Report

Sometimes people don't make a report because they think they need proof to back it up. This is not true. All that is required is reason to believe that a child has been, is, or is likely to be physically harmed, sexually abused, sexually exploited, or in need of protection.

The person making the report is not responsible for determining whether the abuse and/or neglect actually happened or is likely to happen. That is the job of the child protection social worker.

Remember, reporting can be the beginning of a positive change, and can keep the child and perhaps other children from harm. *Reporting can save lives.*

Failing to promptly report suspected abuse or neglect to a child protection social worker is a serious offence under the *Child, Family and Community Service Act*. So is knowingly making a false report. Both offences carry a maximum penalty of a $10,000 fine, or six months in jail, or both. No action for damages may be brought against a person for reporting information under the *Child, Family and Community Service Act* unless the person knowingly reported false information.

When a child protection social worker learns that someone may have failed to report child abuse or neglect, or has knowingly made a false report, they assess this information. If they believe there has been a failure to report, or that false information was reported, they inform the police, who may investigate and recommend charges under the *Child, Family and Community Service Act*.

Investigating Child Abuse and Neglect

The child protection social worker, police and any other person involved in an investigation (e.g. the medical health officer or the superintendent of schools) all share responsibility for ensuring the safety of children. They must immediately clarify the roles and responsibilities of each participant, collaborate and cooperate throughout the investigation(s), since an investigation into reported abuse or neglect has to be done quickly.

There are several types of investigations related to child abuse or neglect. They may occur simultaneously, requiring a cooperative approach. An agency's role and responsibilities will vary, depending on the purpose of the investigation.

If the primary purpose is to...	▶ then the person or organization primarily responsible for the investigation is...
determine if a child needs protection	▶ a child protection social worker
determine whether a criminal offence has occurred	▶ police, who become involved in all investigations when a criminal offence may have occurred
investigate as an employer or controller of student discipline where there has been a report of child abuse or neglect by an employee, contracted service provider, volunteer or student at an educational institution	▶ the superintendent of schools or appropriate senior authority of the educational institution
review the status of a facility's licence when there is a report of child abuse or neglect in a facility that is or should be licensed under the *Community Care Facility Act*, such as a child care facility	▶ the medical health officer
investigate as an employer or controller when there is a report of child abuse or neglect in other settings (e.g. hospitals, youth custody centres, volunteer organizations such as athletic teams, etc.)	▶ the head of the organization
investigate abusive behaviour between children	▶ varied depending on where the abuse took place, the nature of the abuse, and the authorities that need to be involved
investigate as an employer or controller of resident discipline where there has been a report of child abuse or neglect by an employee, contracted service provider, volunteer or resident at a youth custody centre	▶ the director of the youth custody centre
investigate professional conduct of a member belonging to a regulated profession	▶ the registrar of the regulated profession

As with every other aspect of protecting the well-being and safety of children, various people conducting investigations must work closely together and share information when they are legally permitted. Your priorities should be to treat the child sensitively, keep the number of interviews to a minimum, provide plenty of support, and limit the emotional impact on the child as much as possible.

Initial response by a child protection social worker

The child protection social worker's main initial task upon receiving a report is to assess the information in it. The purpose of the assessment is to decide how to respond to the report.

Child protection social workers may speak to parents and others before deciding whether to investigate, so that needs and problems can be clarified and services provided without waiting until the situation reaches a critical point. At this stage, social workers can work to support families even in the absence of clear protection concerns.

Decision about whether to investigate.
A child protection social worker may investigate if:

- they have reason to believe that the child may need protection and an investigation is required; and

- the report concerns a matter that is within their jurisdiction.

If, based on their assessment of the information, the child protection social worker does not have reason to believe that the child needs protection, they may consider the following alternatives to investigation:

- offering support services to the family;

- referring the child and/or family to a community agency; or

- taking no further action.

Initial response by police

Police should respond promptly to reports of alleged criminal offences related to child abuse or neglect. If the alleged offence did not occur recently and the child's safety has been ensured by a child protection social worker, an immediate response by the police may not be required.

The attending officer should inform the child and/or parent(s) of the availability of victim services. Where these services do not exist, the officer will make every effort to ensure that follow-up services are provided to meet the information and support needs of the child and family. Where appropriate, the officer involves a child protection social worker and other service providers as soon as possible.

Where a police officer has reasonable grounds to believe that a child's health or safety is in immediate danger, and there are no other means available to ensure the child's health or safety, the officer may take charge of the child under the *Child, Family and Community Service Act*. The officer must notify the child protection social worker immediately after taking charge of the child. The child protection social worker will speak with the parent and the child if possible, and will make arrangements with the police to ensure that the child is safe. This may include:

- returning the child to the parent at a place of safety;

- taking the child to a safe place identified by the parent (such as the home of a relative or family friend); or

- taking the child to another place of safety.

When a child under 12 breaks the law, police have the authority, under the *Child, Family and Community Service Act*, to take charge of the child and deliver the child to their parent(s) as defined in that act. Police report such circumstances, where appropriate, to a child protection social worker.

General considerations in investigations

Interviewing a child

Child protection social workers and police are authorized to interview a child for child protection or criminal investigations respectively.

Responding to a child's needs

Treating the child sensitively is a priority. The interview should take place as soon as possible following the disclosure or report, and the number and duration of interviews should be kept to a minimum. Joint interviews should be conducted whenever possible.

Special techniques may be needed to communicate with children who are very young or who have certain disabilities. Where the child has difficulty communicating, the interviewers should make arrangements to have a competent and unbiased interpreter or communication specialist, or a person skilled in communicating with the particular child, present for the interview. Court registries have lists of approved language interpreters.

It is important for the child to be interviewed in a place that is likely to be perceived by the child as safe and non-threatening and, if the child has a disability, a room that is physically accessible to them. If interviews are to be conducted in an adult setting, such as a police station, the interviewing room should be made as comfortable and child-friendly as possible.

A support person may be present if appropriate. The investigator should brief the support person on his or her role before the interview, so that the interview process is not jeopardized.

A support person can assist in an interview by

- attending to the child's need for privacy during the interview and getting to or from the interview;

- being a quiet presence to help the child feel safe and secure;

- helping to make the interview space comfortable;

- responding to external and other interruptions (e.g. accompanying the child to the bathroom);

- providing for physical needs (e.g. facial tissue, water, a favourite toy).

Assistance from service providers

Service providers, such as health care and education personnel and child care providers, may assist with the interview by:

- providing the interviewer with access to the child;

- providing an appropriate place to interview the child;

- being present during an interview to support the child if requested and if it will assist the investigation;

- providing the interviewer with any relevant information about the child, including the child's culture, developmental level, family circumstances and emotional state; and/or

- providing other assistance (e.g. an interpreter or equipment for children whose first language is not English, or who have a communication disability).

Supporting the child and family during investigations

Child protection social workers and police should, at the earliest opportunity, support the child and family, as appropriate, and explain the investigation process. In criminal investigations, where victim services are not already involved, police should advise the child and/or family of the availability of victim services.

Investigators should provide the following information for the child and family:

- phone numbers and addresses for support services for parents and children;

- police case file number;

- investigator's name and telephone number;

- steps that will be taken in the case;

- what to expect during the investigative process; and

- how to obtain information about the progress of the case.

Other service providers who are involved with the family and who become aware of the investigation should also be prepared to offer support during an investigation, which is a time when a family may feel particularly vulnerable. This may include:

- letting the child and/or family know you are available if they would like to talk with someone;

- checking on how they are doing as the case progresses;

- offering to accompany them to court to provide emotional support; and

- encouraging them to seek professional help, if that is what seems to be needed.

Supporting other people affected by the abuse or by the investigation
In cases where several children may have been abused or neglected (e.g. in a school or child care setting), other people are often affected. Critical stress debriefing or other appropriate support should be arranged for all those affected, and coordinated in a way that does not interfere with the investigation process.

Responding to child protection reports during custody and access disputes
Reports of child abuse and neglect that are made by one party against the other in a custody and access dispute are to receive the same careful consideration as all other types of reports. The fact that the report occurs during a custody and access dispute is one of several factors to consider (e.g. dynamics in the parents' relationship), but is not in itself a reason for not investigating.

If a family court counsellor, or anyone else directed by the court to carry out a custody and access investigation, receives an allegation of abuse or neglect, they must report the allegation to a child protection social worker and generally await the outcome of the investigation before taking any further action on the custody and access issues. If there are more than two parties involved, the custody and access investigation of non-accused parties can continue. Measures are available to keep the child safe while awaiting the outcome of the investigation. The parties may wish to obtain legal advice.

The child protection investigation

Timing of the investigation

An investigation must begin when a child protection social worker assesses a report and believes that a child may need protection. The purpose of the investigation is to determine:

- whether there are reasonable grounds to believe that a child needs protection and, if so;
- what action is necessary to protect the child.

The investigation must be undertaken immediately if the child's health or safety is in immediate danger or the child is particularly vulnerable because of age or developmental level.

In any other case, the investigation must be undertaken within five working days of assessing the report, and completed within 30 days, wherever possible.

Steps in a child protection investigation

A child protection social worker may take one or more of the following steps in completing a child protection investigation:

- decide whether a child is in immediate danger of harm and, if so, develop and implement a plan for immediate safety to protect the child;
- report the matter to the police immediately:
  - in those cases where a criminal offence may have occurred or is occurring; or
  - as soon as it becomes evident that the abuse or neglect may constitute an offence under the *Criminal Code*; and
  - where the abuse or neglect may constitute a criminal offence, coordinate with the police, who are responsible for ensuring that medical evidence is obtained;
- coordinate with other investigators, as applicable, and observe relevant protocols;
- identify any involved aboriginal agencies, Indian bands, or foster parents;

- review other information available, including current and closed records in the Ministry for Children and Families, and records from other professionals or agencies that may be involved with the family;

- contact the parent(s) before interviewing the child, unless the parent(s) cannot be located or contact would interfere with the investigation;

- interview the child, siblings and other children in the home;

- interview the parent(s);

- interview other people who know the family, or are a resource to the family, and who may have additional information about the situation;

- ensure that the child undergoes a medical examination in the appropriate circumstances (e.g. in cases where alleged physical or sexual abuse may have occurred or where there has been severe or persistent neglect);

- obtain an immediate assessment by a mental health professional in the appropriate circumstances (e.g. in cases where a child is suicidal or self-mutilating);

- conclude the investigation by deciding whether or not there are reasonable grounds to believe that the child needs protection;

- unless reporting would cause emotional or physical harm to any person or endanger the child's safety, or if a criminal investigation is under way or contemplated, report the results of the investigation to:

  - the parent who is apparently entitled to custody;

  - the person who reported;

  - the child who is capable of understanding the information;

  - other service providers, as necessary, to ensure the safety and well-being of the child.

- maintain records of the child protection investigation, including written reasons why actions were taken or not taken.

The role of other service providers in a child protection investigation

Police may be called upon to:

- investigate allegations of a criminal offence;

- conduct a joint or parallel investigation;

- take charge of a child who is in immediate danger;

- assist in entering the premises, by force if necessary;

- assist the child protection social worker in removing a child; or

- assist in enforcing an order giving a child protection social worker access to a child to complete a child protection investigation.

Suspected Child Abuse and Neglect (SCAN) Teams

- *provide diagnostic and psychosocial assessments;*
- *provide education and training/orientation on child abuse and neglect for hospital personnel; and*
- *serve as a link to community resources.*

British Columbia's Children's Hospital provides consultation to other hospitals wishing to develop their own SCAN teams.

Health professionals, particularly physicians, hospital-based social workers and nurses, and public health nurses, may be called upon to:

- provide a safe and supportive environment while a medical examination is taking place in a hospital, clinic or practitioner's office;

- prepare the child for examination;

- provide comprehensive consultative services to child protection social workers and other service providers, particularly where medical or developmental issues are of importance;

- determine a child's capacity to consent to health care; and,

- conduct a medical examination, especially when the child protection social worker

  - believes the child may have suffered non-accidental physical harm or injuries;

  - is not satisfied that the parent's explanation of the injury is consistent with the harm the child has suffered;

  - believes the child may have been sexually abused;

  - believes a child's development is likely to be seriously impaired by a treatable condition, and the parent(s) refuses to provide or consent to treatment; or

  - believes the child is being deprived of necessary medical care.

Physicians who do not feel they have the expertise to conduct examinations for child abuse and neglect should refer these cases to physicians with specialized expertise in this area when available.

Many larger hospitals have Suspected Child Abuse or Neglect (SCAN) Teams who may assist the child protection social worker in coordinating the investigation. The child protection social worker, police and hospital or other health personnel should coordinate medical examinations to prevent the child from having to be examined more than once.

As a provincial resource, B.C.'s Children's Hospital child protection unit provides assessments of children who have been abused or neglected, and consultation to, and training of, physicians in British Columbia.

Support from other service providers

A child who has been abused or neglected may continue to feel the effects long after the crisis of disclosing this information is over. The child needs to be in a safe environment and to be given respect, understanding, guidance and support.

Because many children spend much of their time in child care facilities, schools and recreational programs, staff are in key positions to provide support for a child who has been abused or neglected. The facility should be a safe and nurturing place. Above all, the child needs to be regarded and treated as one of the group or class, and not singled out.

Plans to support the child should be made by staff in consultation with the child and the child's parent(s), and should be appropriate to the child's age and developmental stage.

Interviewing the parent(s)

The intent of the child protection social worker's interview with the parent(s) is to obtain the parent(s)' view and perspective, and to assist in assessing the parent(s)':

In cases where a criminal offence may have occurred, and both the police and child protection social worker need to interview the parent(s), they should collaborate to make the appropriate arrangements.

- involvement in the abuse or neglect;

- ability and willingness to protect the child;

- willingness to believe the child's account of events;

- ability and willingness to support the child;

- own need for support.

Where interviews of the parent(s) or other adult witnesses are likely to be required by both police and a child protection social worker, police should collaborate with the child protection social worker in scheduling these interviews.

Deciding whether a child needs protection

The decision about whether a child needs protection under the *Child, Family and Community Service Act* rests solely with the child protection social worker. This decision can be based on information from others involved in the investigation, such as police, teachers, public health nurses, physicians, cultural or social service agencies, child care providers or, where the child is aboriginal, a designated representative of the aboriginal community.

The decision requires a careful assessment of all the facts, evidence and professional opinions obtained during the investigation, as well as the child's views and the ability and willingness of family members or others close to the child to protect the child.

Outcomes of the child protection investigation

If, after investigating, the child protection social worker does not have reason to believe that the child is in need of protection, the child protection social worker may, in consultation with the family and service providers who work with the child and/or family, arrange support services for the family as needed. If these services are not required, the child protection social worker will take no further action.

If, after investigating, the child protection social worker has reasonable grounds to believe the child needs protection, the child protection social worker is directed by the *Child, Family and Community Service Act* to take those available measures that are least disruptive to the child, unless the child is in immediate danger. If there is reason to believe that the child needs protection and is in immediate danger, the child protection social worker may remove the child.

If there is reason to believe that the child needs protection but is not in immediate danger, the child protection social worker must not remove the child if other available measures are less disruptive to the child and meet their need for protection. These may include:

- support services
- a court order for essential health care;
- a temporary provision to take charge of a lost, runaway or unattended child;
- arrangements for a child to reside outside the home (e.g. with relatives or friends) with the consent of the parent; or
- agreements or court orders to enable the removal of an offending person from a child's home or to prohibit contact or interference with the child.

If no other measures are available or adequate to keep the child safe, the child protection social worker removes the child.

Criminal investigation

General steps in the police investigation

Police conduct an investigation to determine whether there are reasonable and probable grounds to believe that a criminal offence related to child abuse or neglect has been committed. This includes cases that do not immediately appear likely to proceed to prosecution. For example, a case may have to proceed without the child's testimony due to age, communication, difficulty or reluctance on the part of the child and/or family.

The investigation involves gathering evidence in order to establish the facts, and preparing for criminal proceedings where appropriate. This includes:

- preserving the crime scene;
- obtaining the child's account of events;
- obtaining a statement from the alleged offender;
- obtaining statements from other witnesses;
- arranging to obtain and preserve any physical evidence;
- obtaining medical and other expert opinions if needed;
- determining the need to arrest a suspect; and
- submitting a report to Crown counsel where criminal charges are being recommended.

Obtaining medical forensic evidence

Where police require a medical examination of the child for the purpose of obtaining forensic evidence, and a child protection investigation is also underway, police should collaborate with the child protection social worker in making arrangements for the medical examination.

Where the alleged offence involves very recent sexual assault or serious physical injury, police should make every effort to ensure that the child is immediately examined by an appropriate health care practitioner. In other cases where a medical examination is required, police should make arrangements with the child and/or parent(s) to have the child examined as soon as possible.

Police should discuss with the health care practitioner and, where involved, the child protection social worker, the type of forensic evidence that needs to be collected. The medical examination should be conducted and evidence collected in a way that is least intrusive to the child. Police should ensure that the child and parent(s) are aware of their options to consent to all or parts of the medical examination, and how the prosecution may be affected if consent is not given. Where police attend the hospital or health care facility with the child, they should consult with medical personnel to ensure that the storage of forensic evidence satisfies evidentiary requirements.

Victim services

Throughout the criminal justice process police will inform the child and/or parent(s) about the availability of services that support victims of child abuse or neglect and their families. In communities where they exist, specialized victim services that serve children will normally be the primary victim service provider. Where there are no victim services in the community, police, in collaboration with the child protection social worker and community agencies, will ensure that follow-up services are made available to the child and family.

Investigations in public schools and other educational institutions

If child abuse or neglect is believed to have occurred in a public school or in another educational institution or during school activities, the investigation is conducted in a coordinated manner through the following activities:

- the child protection social worker assesses the report to decide how to respond to it, and commences an investigation if there is reason to believe that a child may need protection;

- the police conduct an investigation to determine if a criminal offence may have been committed; and

- the superintendent of schools or the senior authority of an educational institution investigates as part of his/her legal responsibilities.

The superintendent of schools or the senior authority is responsible for coordinating investigations that occur in a public school to:

- ensure that the child is safe from harm during the investigations;

- assist the investigators in clarifying their respective roles, mandates and responsibilities in responding to the report of abuse or neglect;

- ensure that required investigations are not interfered with or compromised by persons under the superintendent of schools' authority;

- assist parents in obtaining information about the investigation and its results from the appropriate authority;

- document the results of any investigation performed at the direction of the superintendent; and

- collaborate with other professionals to develop follow-up plans to support the alleged victim and others, both children and staff, who may be affected by the disclosure or investigation (e.g. critical incident debriefing, counselling, referrals, etc.).

The school superintendent is authorized, under the *School Act*, to investigate reports that a child is not registered with a school or is not receiving an educational program. If the superintendent has a reason to believe that a child needs protection, they must report this matter to a child protection social worker.

The school principal is responsible for the safety of children while they are attending school and/or participating in school activities. Parents are entitled to be informed of their child's behaviour in school. School staff may contact parents to ensure that they are aware when abusive behaviour between students occurs at school or at an authorized school function.

The *School Act* provides authority for a school board to dismiss, suspend or otherwise discipline an employee for just and reasonable cause. If a superintendent of schools believes the welfare of students is threatened by the presence of an employee, the superintendent may suspend the employee. The school board has the power to confirm, vary or revoke that suspension. School boards must report to the College of Teachers, without delay, the reason for any teacher's dismissal, suspension, or disciplinary action and any resignation in which circumstances are such that it is in the public interest to do so.

Within the independent school system, teachers are certified under either the *Teaching Profession Act* or the *Independent School Act*. Under the *Independent School Act*, the Inspector of Independent Schools has the authority to issue teacher certification restricted to independent schools and to suspend or revoke certification for cause. Independent school authorities must report, without delay, the reason for any teacher's dismissal, suspension or disciplinary action and any resignation in which circumstances are such that it is in the public interest to do so. All such reports are directed to the Inspector of Independent Schools, and to the College of Teachers when the teacher involved is a college member.

Investigations in community care facilities

When a report of child abuse or neglect in a licensed child care facility is received by a child protection worker, medical health officer or the police, each should promptly notify the other two. (Note: The medical health officer also has responsibility for investigations in facilities which are operating without a required license).

The following investigations are then conducted in a coordinated manner:

- the child protection social worker assesses the report to decide how to respond and investigates if the child may need protection;
- the police conduct an investigation to determine if a criminal offence may have been committed;
- the medical health officer (or delegated licensing officer) conducts a licensing investigation to determine if:
  - any immediate action needs to be taken to ensure the health and safety of the children in the facility (e.g. attach conditions to or suspend the licence);
  - the licensee has contravened the *Community Care Facility Act* or regulations and decide what, if any, the consequences will be for the licensee (e.g. attach conditions to, cancel or suspend the licence);
  - any action needs to be taken to prevent an unlicensed facility from operating.

A medical health officer conducting a licensing investigation may request that the Ministry for Children and Families second a child protection social worker to provide assistance in interviewing the allegedly abused child and other children.

The facility operator is responsible for taking the necessary steps to ensure that all children in the facility are safe during the investigation. If the medical health officer has reasonable grounds to believe the health or safety of the children is at risk, they may attach terms or conditions to, or suspend, a licence.

Investigations in youth custody (containment) centres

If child abuse or neglect is believed to have occurred in a youth custody centre, while participating in custody centre activities or on authorized absences, the investigation is conducted in a coordinated manner through the following activities:

- the child protection social worker assesses the report to decide how to respond and commences an investigation if there is reason to believe that a child may need protection;

- the police conduct an investigation to determine if a criminal offence may have been committed; and

- the director of the custody centre investigates as part of his or her legal responsibilities.

The director of the custody centre is responsible for coordinating investigations that occur in the youth custody centre to:

- ensure that the child in the custody centre is safe from harm during the investigation;

- assist investigators in clarifying their respective roles, mandates and responsibilities in responding to the report of abuse or neglect;

- ensure that required investigations are not interfered with or compromised by persons under the director's authority;

- ensure that children are not interviewed more than necessary;

- assist parents or guardians in obtaining information about the investigation and its results from the appropriate authority subject to any legal requirements or limitations;

- document the results of any investigations performed at the direction of the director; and

- collaborate with other professionals to develop follow-up plans to support the alleged victim(s) and others, both children and staff, who may be affected by the abuse or investigation. (e.g. counselling, referrals, critical incident debriefing, etc.).

After the investigation - child protection legal proceedings

Child protection proceedings must occur whenever a child is removed from their home, and may include three stages of hearings:

- presentation hearing;

- child protection hearing;

- continuing custody hearing.

Some child protection proceedings can also occur without removal if the child protection social worker has reason to believe the child needs protection but removal is not necessary to make the child safe (e.g. if the alleged abuser resided in the home but is ordered by the court to leave, i.e. protective intervention order).

Service providers closely involved with the child and family may have a role to play in supporting the child and family during the legal process. You may also be asked to appear in court as a witness or to give expert testimony.

Service providers and other professionals who have been in contact with the child and/or the child's parent(s) may be asked, or required by subpoena, to be witnesses in court proceedings. You have the right to contact your own lawyer to discuss your role and obligations as a witness.

You may also want to contact a lawyer to discuss your rights, obligations and legal options in responding to a court application or order related to your agency's or organization's records.

The presentation hearing
The first court hearing following removal is the presentation hearing. This is generally a short hearing where a child protection social worker reports on the reasons why the child was removed. Information from the reporter or others who may be involved with the child may be part of the child protection social worker's report.

The court may order that the child remain in the director's custody, or be returned to the parent(s), with or without supervision by the director.

The protection hearing
If an order is made giving the director interim custody of the child, or if the child is returned home under an interim supervision order, a protection hearing begins within 45 days of the conclusion of the presentation hearing. This allows time for further assessment of the child's circumstances and the development of a comprehensive plan of care for the child.

During this period, the child protection social worker may return the child to the parent(s) and withdraw from the proceeding, provided that arrangements are adequate to keep the child safe.

At the protection hearing, the court must determine whether the child needs protection, as defined in the *Child, Family and Community Service Act*, and who should have custody of the child. If the court finds that the child needs protection, it must make one of the following orders in the child's best interests:

- that the child be returned or remain with the parent(s) from whom the child was removed (a supervision order must accompany this order);

- that the child be placed in the temporary custody of another person under the supervision of the director;

- that the child be placed in the temporary custody of the director; or

- that the child be placed in the continuing custody of the director.

Criminal proceedings

Physical assault, sexual assault and other sexual offences involving children are crimes. Abandoning a child and failing to provide the necessities of life are crimes. Police determine whether there are grounds for a criminal investigation and, if necessary, conduct an investigation. A summary of *Criminal Code* offences is found in Appendix D.

Keeping the child and/or parent(s) informed - the *Victims of Crime Act*
The *Victims of Crime Act* provides that victims can request and obtain information about a case as it proceeds through the criminal justice system, including information about:

- the status of the police investigation;

- decisions regarding charges, court dates and outcomes;

- release of the accused/offender and conditions of release.

Information can be obtained from police, victim services, court registries, the Court Services Branch, Criminal Justice Branch or Corrections Branch of the Ministry of Attorney General.

In cases where the child's safety may be at risk because of changes in the status of the accused/offender (e.g. release from custody, changes to bail order), the child and/or parent(s) will be advised as soon as possible.

Consistency and continuity of approach
Each component of the justice system strives for a consistent approach to child abuse and neglect cases, from initial contact through to disposition of the case. When different personnel are involved with a case, communication among them is important in order to ensure continuity of planning and services.

Victim services

Trained victim service workers are able to provide emotional support, court orientation, information and referrals, and court accompaniment for children and their families as they go through the criminal justice system. In addition to justice related support, specialized victim services in some communities may also provide counselling service for children who have been abused or neglected.

Arrest and recommending charges

Public interest considerations often apply in favour of arrest in order to secure the suspect's attendance in court, and prevent the repetition of the offence or the commission of other offences such as interfering with the administration of justice and intimidation of witnesses.

Where the suspect is arrested and released from police custody, police should notify the child and/or parent(s), child protection social worker and victim services (if involved) of the release and any condition attached to it.

Where there are reasonable grounds to believe that an offence has been committed, and a suspect has been identified, police should forward a report to Crown counsel recommending a charge.

Laying of charges, case preparation and bail hearing

Given the serious nature of criminal offences related to child abuse and neglect, the prosecution of such offences is almost always in the public interest. Therefore:

- Crown counsel should take steps to expedite the processing of child abuse and neglect cases, in recognition of the importance of timeliness to children;

- if there is a substantial likelihood of conviction, charges should normally be approved; and

- diversion from the formal justice system of persons charged with a *Criminal Code* offence related to physical or sexual abuse or neglect of children will rarely be approved by Crown counsel, and only after consultation with the regional Crown counsel or the Assistant Deputy Attorney General.

It is crucial that Crown counsel explain the court processes to the child and parent(s), and prepare the child for testifying in court. To assist the child in giving evidence, Crown counsel may, depending on the circumstances, request the judge to:

- allow the child to testify outside the courtroom or behind a screen (s. 486 (2.1) of the *Criminal Code*)

- exclude the public from the courtroom (s. 486 (1) of the *Criminal Code*)

- allow a child under 14 to have their support person of choice present and close to the child while they are testifying (s. 486 (1.2) of the Criminal Code).

Where Crown counsel has approved charges for a criminal offence of child physical assault, sexual assault or other sexual offences involving children, or neglect, Crown counsel will routinely inform the accused's employer or "governing body" of the name of the accused and the nature of the charge(s) laid, having considered any publication bans and the requirements of the *Freedom of Information and Protection of Privacy Act*.

Where Crown counsel has approved charges for an offence(s) of child physical or sexual abuse or neglect including an offence(s) of sexual exploitation, Crown counsel is required by the *Criminal Records Review Act* to inform the accused's "employer" or "governing body" of the name of the accused and the nature of the charge(s) laid.

Where Crown counsel is aware that a child protection social worker is involved with a case of child abuse or neglect, Crown counsel should inform them of the decision concerning charges.

Bail hearing

Crown counsel policy provides that throughout the bail process, Crown counsel should consider the protection and safety of the child and any witnesses, and seek as appropriate either detention or protective bail conditions.

If the accused is released, Crown counsel should advise the child and/or parents and any other person protected by the bail conditions of the release of the accused on bail, and the conditions of that release.

Policy provides that Crown counsel should generally apply for a publication ban pursuant to section 486 of the *Criminal Code* which protects the child from the publication of any information which would identify them as a complainant in a sexual assault case.

Corrections Branch and Youth Probation Officers

Bail supervision

Given the serious nature of child abuse and neglect, the bail supervisor should closely monitor all accused persons released on bail, in liaison with the child protection social worker (where involved).

The bail supervisor should advise the following people of the protective conditions in the order, and how and to whom they should report breaches of those conditions:

- the child victim and/or parent(s);
- any other persons protected under the order;
- the child protection social worker; and
- where appropriate, other persons in close contact with the accused.

Community release and supervision

Where an offender is released on probation or with a conditional sentence order containing protective conditions, court registry staff should provide a copy of the order to the investigating police department as soon as possible after the order is signed.

All offenders are subject to a criminal risk needs assessment, which determines the appropriate level of supervision. At the time of intake, the probation officer should ensure that the child and/or parent(s) are aware of all conditions that apply to the offender, particularly any protective conditions.

The probation officer should, as needed, report to others involved with the child (e.g. child protection social worker, police, Crown counsel, school, child care centre) all known significant changes in the situation, status or the whereabouts of the offender.

Where the child's safety may be at risk, the probation officer should advise the child and/or parent(s), police and child protection social worker as soon as possible.

Custody and releases from custody

While the accused is in remand or sentenced custody, Corrections Branch staff and youth custody centre staff should ensure that current or previous no-contact orders (contact by telephone or letter) are adhered to.

Pursuant to request under the *Victims of Crime Act*, Corrections Branch staff or youth custody probation staff should notify the child and/or parents of relevant information regarding sentence offenders, including the criminal's custodial status, institutional transfers, temporary or conditional release, and date of discharge.

Corrections personnel should notify police of any offender released from custody who is at risk of committing a sexual offence or another offence involving violence.

PART III - SUPPORT AND INTERVENTION SERVICES

Some of the services described in this section help build or rebuild the strengths of children and families. Others help reduce risk factors for children, families and communities.

This section also describes intensive interventions, including treatment, required by children and families should chronic or severe emotional or behavioural problems appear.

Early support and early intervention services

Regardless of the support a family is receiving, if you have reason to believe that abuse or neglect has occurred or is likely to occur, or that a child needs protection, as in Part II, you must report the situation immediately to a child protection social worker.

Early support and early intervention activities are designed for children and families who may be experiencing difficulty in having healthy, nurturing relationships. Just because a child or family needs these services, however, does not necessarily mean there is a danger of abuse or neglect.

The sooner a child or family gets the support they need, the better. Early intervention and support can keep a situation from deteriorating, and dramatically increase a family's chances of achieving stability. As soon as a family is identified or self-identifies, support and information should be provided.

Service responses frequently used in this approach include:

- parenting education, including child development, positive discipline techniques and stress reduction;

- home support – working intensively with parents in the family home;

- professional assessment, counselling and support;

- parent-to-parent support;

- respite care for parents – providing brief or periodic care for a child;

- child care;

- school counselling;

- alternative measures programs for young offenders; and

- support for adult children of substance misusers.

Services available in educational settings

Schools and post-secondary settings may offer such services as:

- counselling programs;

- safe school programs;

- safe campus programs at colleges and universities;

- assistance for families from various cultural backgrounds by multicultural workers;

- school meal programs;

- young parent programs, delivered in a school or linked with the school to help young parents obtain academic and life skills training, with child care provided; and

- early intervention and referrals by school-based substance abuse prevention workers.

Family support services

Families can find a wide range of support services. In some cases, you can request service on behalf of a family. Services may include:

- child care support programs – support, resources and referral services for child care providers and parents;

- arranging for child care;

- parenting education;

- respite services;

- home support worker assistance;

- a one-on-one child and youth counsellor who works with the child and their family and consults with the child's school;

- family counselling;

- assistance for aboriginal families by aboriginal support workers;

- assistance for immigrant families by settlement workers.

Services for children with disabilities and chronic health difficulties

Before an infant or other child with special needs leaves a hospital, hospital personnel should ensure that the parents have been referred to treatment and support services for assistance and that they know what to do in an emergency.

There are a variety of services which may be appropriate for children with disabilities or chronic health problems, and children at risk of developing such conditions. You can find these services through child development centres, family physicians or pediatricians, public health nurses, hospitals and associations for people with disabilities in your community. They may include:

- infant development programs;
- medical treatment;
- therapy to prevent further disabilities;
- respite care;
- special education;
- life-skills training;
- fittings for adaptive equipment;
- family support.

Intensive support and intervention services

A child who has developed chronic or serious difficulties because of abuse or neglect may need intensive support and intervention services. Services may include:

- emotional support;
- life-skills training;
- alternate care for the child;
- counselling;
- specialized sexual abuse counselling;
- treatment; and
- rehabilitation.

Services for children with serious emotional and behavioural problems

There may be a serious mental health concern about a child when abuse or neglect has been particularly harmful, long-standing or traumatic, or caused by someone in a trusted relationship. There may also be such a concern when the child or family is having significant difficulties in other areas that affect their well-being.

In these cases, assessment, treatment and/or behavioural management are recommended, and may be provided through child and youth mental health professionals, contracted community agencies or special programs in schools.

Mental health professionals can assess emotional or behavioural disturbance and recommend and provide the appropriate treatment. In some cases, they will recommend consultation with service providers and caregivers, either in combination with treatment by a mental health professional or on its own.

Community agencies offer specialized assessment and treatment services for children who have experienced sexual abuse where there are serious emotional or behavioural concerns. Specialized services for young children with sexual behaviour problems are available in some communities. Both these services are available through agencies under contract to the Ministry for Children and Families.

Services for children who witness abuse

Transition houses and other community agencies provide specialized individual and group counselling for children through Children Who Witness Abuse programs. These services help children cope with the trauma they experience. Support is also provided for the parent (usually the mother) who has experienced abuse by a partner. Children Who Witness Abuse programs are designed to help break the intergenerational cycle of violence against women.

Services for street youth

While services for street youth tend to be concentrated in urban centres, a number of smaller communities have also undertaken initiatives for this population. Services may include:

- safe houses;
- efforts to reconnect children with their families;
- youth crisis lines;
- school- and street-based all-night recreation programs;
- street outreach workers;
- street outreach nurses;
- youth health clinics;
- needle exchange programs;
- programs for youth who have been sexually exploited; and
- pre-employment training programs.

Services for children and families experiencing substance misuse

Clinical and support services for adults who misuse alcohol and/or other drugs can help parents to strengthen their abilities to develop and sustain healthier families.

Substance misuse outpatient programs, which exist in most communities, assist those who wish to resolve problems related to their own or a family member's misuse of substances. Outpatient counsellors provide comprehensive assessment and treatment planning for individuals or family members, usually in the home community.

Many aboriginal communities are served by alcohol and drug counsellors employed by the band or tribal council through federal government funding. You can make referrals to residential treatment centres specifically operated for aboriginal clients through provincial or federal alcohol and drug counsellors.

Many workplaces provide Employee and Family Assistance Programs (EAPs or EFAPs) to help employees and their families resolve personal problems such as those related to substance misuse. Counsellors in these programs can refer their clients directly to specialized and residential programs, while maintaining case management responsibilities.

Services for young offenders

Youth forensic psychiatric services are available to young offenders between the ages of 12 and 17. Referrals can only be made through the youth courts, Crown counsel, youth probation services, or custody centres. While inpatient assessment services are only available in the Burnaby Inpatient Assessment Unit, you can find outpatient assessment and treatment services in most B.C. communities. These include outpatient clinics, contracted agencies, mental health professionals or visiting travelling clinics.

Additional counselling, treatment and supervision services are available in several communities for adolescent sexual offenders — many of whom are victims of abuse themselves — and for other offenders who have experienced family violence and are experiencing stress resulting from trauma.

Information for service providers

There are a variety of means through which service providers can increase their knowledge about responding to child abuse and neglect. They include:

- policies and manuals of various ministries and professional disciplines;

- child protection social workers;

- specialized interagency training for police, Crown counsel, victim services workers, child protection workers, educators and other service providers; and

- training for child care providers on prevention and responses to child abuse and neglect.

Contact your staff training personnel to find out what is available in your workplace.

PART IV - COLLABORATIVE PLANNING AND INFORMATION SHARING

Cooperating to address abuse and neglect

Service providers should listen to and work together with children and their families from the earliest opportunity, to establish goals and work toward their achievement. It is of critical importance that any agency's decisions regarding a child and family not be made in isolation from them or others involved with them. This collaborative approach should be taken as early as possible and continue as long as necessary.

Working together - who is involved in planning?

Everyone who is making decisions affecting the child and family – various professionals, advocates and community support agencies, as well as the child, family and others who provide care for the child – should be involved. They constitute the planning team.

If a child is aboriginal, the child protection social worker lets the parents know about services available through the aboriginal community. The social worker involves an aboriginal community in planning if:

- the parent or child with capacity asks for aboriginal community involvement;

- an aboriginal community is already involved; or

- the community is willing to become involved and the parent or child with capacity doesn't object.

If the parent or child with capacity objects to aboriginal community involvement, the child protection social worker does not involve the community if it would jeopardize an agreement with the family necessary to ensure the child's safety.

Everyone working with a child should work together, along with the child and family, to decide how to coordinate the services the child receives. When the issues the family faces fall mainly under the mandate of one particular program or organization, then you may decide to let that program or organization's representative take the lead. Of course, even if your organization has not taken the lead, you should still work closely with the others.

Your program or organization should develop local rules about:

- deciding who is responsible for child abuse and neglect cases;

- developing and implementing policies and procedures to be followed by all personnel, including requirements for reporting suspected abuse or neglect; and

- developing and maintaining clear lines of communication and responsibility with the other agencies involved, both in the immediate community and with referral institutions elsewhere.

The role of the planning team

As a member of the planning team, your job includes:

- helping assess any possible risks for the child;

- assessing the strengths and needs of the child and family;

- planning action, including services to be provided, to build on strengths and address needs;

- ensuring the delivery of those services and monitoring them to ensure they meet the needs of the child and family;

- identifying any gaps in service and addressing them as far as possible;

- evaluating services and, where appropriate, making recommendations for improvement; and

- deciding when and how to close or transfer the file of the child and family.

Factors in collaborative planning

The factors you consider when planning services can vary depending on circumstances. For instance, if there are no child protection concerns, planning will likely be different than when a child protection investigation is under way.

Information sharing, confidentiality and the law

Throughout this handbook, reference is made to the need for a collaborative response to child abuse and neglect. Sharing and coordinating information are vital parts of this response. This means that personal information (including confidential), whether recorded or not, may be shared among service providers, clients and various public bodies, under specific circumstances and in accordance with various statutes.

Information about children and families collected by most provincial government employees and public bodies is governed by the *Freedom of*

Information and Protection of Privacy Act. Along with the *Document Disposal Act*, which all ministries are subject to, the *Freedom of Information and Protection of Privacy Act* governs:

- when personal information can be collected and recorded;
- what the recorded personal information can be used for;
- when, to whom and for what purpose personal information in records can be disclosed;
- how personal information in records must be stored;
- when personal information in records can be disposed of.

If you have questions regarding confidentiality and disclosure of information consult with legal services or the appropriate government information and privacy branch. There may also be other provincial legislation that applies to information in the custody or control of a public body which must be read together with the *Freedom of Information and Protection of Privacy Act*.

Information collected by child protection social workers under the *Child, Family and Community Service Act* is not governed by the *Freedom of Information and Protection of Privacy Act*. Instead, the *Child, Family and Community Service Act* establishes its own laws about confidentiality and disclosure. These laws are intended to address the specific information concerns that arise in the context of child protection and preventive service work.

Information obtained as a result of the operation of, or court order under, the *Young Offenders Act* (Canada), is governed by that act.

Sharing of information obtained and retained by the RCMP is governed by the *Privacy Act* (federal) and personal information can be disclosed by RCMP personnel in accordance with that legislation, including when doing so is consistent with the purpose for which the information was gathered.

Information sharing by service providers

Information sharing is an important element of collaboration in the response to child abuse and neglect, and of providing integrated service to children and families. There are various ways that service providers can share information about children and families, including protocols developed in accordance with applicable legislation for this purpose.

Child protection reports and investigations

The *Child, Family, and Community Service Act* requires every person, whether or not they are part of a public body, who has a reason to believe that a child needs protection, to promptly report the matter to a child protection social worker.

The child protection social worker may report the results of a child protection investigation to the child, if they are capable of understanding the information, unless:

- a criminal investigation is underway or contemplated; or

- it is the director's opinion that providing the information would cause physical or emotional harm to any person or endanger the child's safety.

The *Child, Family and Community Service Act* requires child protection social workers to report the results of a child protection investigation to the parent apparently entitled to custody of the child and to the person who made the report, unless:

- a criminal investigation is underway or contemplated; or

- it is the director's opinion that providing the information would cause physical or emotional harm to any person or endanger the child's safety.

The child protection social worker may also advise others involved if necessary to ensure the safety and well-being of the child.

Information sharing by service providers who are within public bodies

(a) Child protection social workers' right to necessary information held by public bodies

Under the *Child, Family and Community Service Act*, child protection social workers have a right to information in the custody or under the control of public bodies if the information is necessary for the social worker to do their job. This right overrides the *Freedom of Information and Protection of Privacy Act* and any other provincial legislation. It does not override federal legislation, including the *Young Offenders Act*, or solicitor/client privilege.

Where possible, child protection social workers respect and comply with any concerns or recommendations from the public body about the use of and further sharing of the information.

(b) Information sharing with consent and involvement in decision making

In keeping with the principle that people should be encouraged to participate in decisions that affect them, it is preferred that information about people be shared with their consent. Involving people in decisions that affect them, whether at a case conference or in individual discussions, leads to better, more lasting decisions. Obtaining consent to disclose also provides an opportunity to verify the accuracy of information. Child protection social workers under the *Child, Family and Community Service Act* and public bodies under the *Freedom of Information and Protection of Privacy*

Act can release information about a person when that person consents and completes the proper form.

Under provincial legislation, certain children have the right to consent to disclosure of information about themselves:

- Under the *Child, Family and Community Service Act*, a child 12 years of age or over has a right of access to *Child, Family and Community Service Act* records that contain information about the child, and can consent to the disclosure of that information without anyone else's approval.

- Under the *Freedom of Information and Protection of Privacy Act*, a child with capacity has a right of access to his or her own personal information and can consent to the disclosure of that information without anyone else's approval.

- Both acts permit specified persons to consent to the disclosure on behalf of a child where the child lacks the capacity to do so.

(c) Sharing information without consent

In the context of a collaborative response to child abuse and neglect, the primary objective of sharing information about children and families is to ensure the safety and well-being of a child. There may be situations where seeking or obtaining consent to share information is not possible or appropriate. Where information is shared without the consent of the person involved, he or she should, where appropriate, be informed that the information has been shared.

The *Child, Family and Community Service Act* applies to child protection social workers. All other service providers who are within public bodies disclose information without consent under the *Freedom of Information and Protection of Privacy Act*.

Section 79(a) of the *Child, Family and Community Service Act* allows child protection social workers to disclose information to service providers without consent where it is necessary to ensure a child's safety or well-being.

Examples of information sharing necessary for ensuring the child's safety include circumstances where the child protection social worker is:

- assessing information in a report about child abuse or neglect;

- conducting a child protection investigation;

- taking charge of a child;

- providing police with information related to a criminal investigation involving child abuse or neglect;

- assisting another person in protecting a child;

- making or helping to make decisions about the care and custody of a child and about access to a child; or

- providing a family court counsellor with information required for the completion of a custody or access report.

Examples of information sharing necessary for ensuring the child's well-being include circumstances where the child protection social worker is:

- planning or participating in planning for a child in care; or

- developing or implementing a support services agreement to protect a child.

The child protection social worker determines whether to disclose and to what extent to disclose by considering the following:

- the child's view and sense of safety;

- the child's needs and circumstances;

- whether the disclosure will assist in protecting the child from abuse, neglect, harm or threat of harm; and

- whether it is possible to obtain consent in a timely manner.

Section 33(c) of the *Freedom of Information and Protection of Privacy Act* allows public bodies to disclose personal information without consent when disclosure is:

- for the purpose for which the information was obtained or compiled; or

- for a purpose that has a reasonable and direct connection to that purpose and is essential to the work of the public body that uses or discloses the information.

Other parts of Section 33 provide disclosure guidelines in other circumstances. In particular, Section 33(p) sets out the rules respecting the disclosure of information in compelling circumstances affecting anyone's health or safety, including that of a child.

Information sharing by service providers who are not within public bodies

Information held by service providers who are not public bodies is not subject to the *Freedom of Information and Protection of Privacy Act* unless required by the terms of a contract. Information sharing by these service providers may be governed by other legislation or by professional regulations (e.g. codes of ethics, codes of conduct or policies).

Service providers who are not public bodies and may not be subject to the *Freedom of Information and Protection of Privacy Act* may include, but are not limited to:

- most community-based service agencies (such as transition houses, sexual assault centres, specialized victim services, neighbourhood houses and family service agencies);
- child care providers;
- private psychologists; and
- physicians.

Service providers who are not public bodies should contact their regulatory body, association, contract manager or appropriate organization or network for further information about this topic.

Information sharing with aboriginal communities

Sharing information is a cornerstone of collaborative service delivery. In order for aboriginal people to have meaningful involvement in planning and delivering services for aboriginal children, it is important for child protection social workers to share information with representatives of aboriginal communities where provided for under the *Child, Family and Community Service Act*.

Where an aboriginal child is the subject of court proceedings under the *Child, Family and Community Service Act*, a designated representative of the child's Indian band or aboriginal community may become a party to the proceedings. This entitles the designated representative to receive information that is required to be disclosed in court proceedings under the *Child, Family and Community Service Act*.

In cases where a child protection social worker is providing services for an aboriginal child or family, information can be shared with the child's aboriginal community with consent (see *Information sharing with consent and involvement in decision making*).

In cases where seeking or obtaining consent is not possible or appropriate, the child protection social worker may share information with members of the child's aboriginal community where it is necessary to ensure the safety or well-being of a child (see *Sharing information without consent*).

In some areas of the province, the director has delegated authority to employees of First Nations child welfare agencies. (See Appendix B for a list of First Nations child welfare agencies which have employees with delegated authority). In these situations, the child protection social worker shares information with the delegated employee of the aboriginal agency in the same manner as for a child protection social worker within the Ministry for Children and Families.

All information shared with employees of aboriginal agencies with delegated authority is subject to the *Child, Family and Community Service Act*. Those employees, therefore, cannot share information except as provided for in the act.

In situations where employees of an aboriginal agency do not have delegated authority, the child protection social worker determines whether an agreement or protocol with the agency exists, and shares information based on that agreement or protocol, subject to the confidentiality provisions of the *Child, Family and Community Service Act*.

PART V - PROMOTING WELL-BEING AND PREVENTING ABUSE AND NEGLECT

There is no better way to deal with child abuse and neglect than to stop it before it happens. That way the harm to a child is never done and — especially when we promote healthy relationships — the family involved can become a stronger, more nurturing place in which to grow.

All parents face challenges from time to time in bringing up their children. That is when prevention services are of the most importance in helping families learn to cope with problems and issues.

To be effective, promotion and prevention activities acknowledge different needs and concerns children have at various ages and developmental stages. And, as with other responses to child abuse and neglect, promotion and prevention measures are most effective when they are developed and delivered in a collaborative manner, involving families and communities, as well as service providers from all sectors — education, health, justice, child care, social services and recreation.

Four principles that guide promotion and prevention initiatives area:

- support the building of capacities of individuals, families and communities;

- enable people to take control of their health and social well-being;

- focus on the underlying factors and conditions that affect health and social well-being; and

- develop policies that support the well-being and safety of all children.

We will look first at ways to promote children's well-being, and then at specific ways of preventing child abuse and neglect.

Promoting children's well-being

We can promote children's well-being on two levels: making society a better place for children, and making families and relationships healthier for children.

There is a wide range of activities. We can undertake to tackle society-wide causes of abuse and neglect through program development and activities such as programs to reduce child poverty, measures to stop discrimination, initiatives to strengthen a community's self-reliance and participation, and advocacy to persuade decision-makers to improve the services that help children and families.

We can also work at a more direct, immediate level to promote healthy relationships and encourage effective parenting skills. These activities focus on every stage of a child's development.

This kind of wellness promotion begins even before the child is born by providing information, community-based services and family-friendly environments to promote effective family planning, healthy pregnancies and early child care.

Other activities aim to increase the capacities of families to provide their children with a nurturing and caring environment through support activities for parents, such as child care, parent-to-parent support activities, and parent education activities.

People working with children aim to create environments in which all children have the opportunity to reach their potential and become lifelong learners and healthy productive citizens. And, as children grow toward adulthood, we can strive to promote the healthy development of youth with peer-involvement initiatives, social networks and opportunities for youth to participate in creating a healthy community.

Preventing child abuse and neglect

While we would all hope such programs could eliminate abuse and neglect, the reality is that more direct action is still needed - action that improves protection and decreases risk factors for children, families and communities.

Such direct prevention activity includes support activities, awareness raising, education, advocacy and ensuring children's safety in settings inside and outside the home. In order to be effective, these activities should:

- be collaborative and integrative;
- support and involve children and families;
- strengthen the environments in which children and families live; and
- be sensitive to the issues of diversity and inclusiveness.

Providing additional support

Some children and families need more support than others, often because of factors that increase the risk of abuse or neglect. Services and activities are available to help them cope. They include:

- providing support for children with a variety of needs, through such initiatives as infant development programs, supported child care, special educational services, counselling services, respite services and recreation services;

- helping ensure healthy babies by preventing problems such as poor prenatal nutrition or the misuse of alcohol or other drugs during pregnancy;

- helping parents with limited resources to find affordable housing, quality child care, recreational opportunities for their children, proactive counselling and preventive health services in their communities;

- providing respite and home care services for parents with few resources or little support; and

- encouraging the development of peer support groups and networks of parents, in order to build parents' capacity to provide caring and nurturing environments.

Developing awareness

Awareness and information can be powerful allies in fighting abuse and neglect. Prevention activities include raising awareness among children, parents, service providers and the public about:

- the difference between physical abuse and discipline, and between appropriate and inappropriate sexual behaviour;

- alternatives to corporal punishment;

- standards of care for children in Canada;

- ways to nurture healthy child development;

- the possible effects on children of all forms of sexual abuse and inappropriate sexual behaviour; and

- how to find resources to assist in parenting and promote the optimum healthy development of children.

Many kinds of parenting and child care classes and workshops are offered throughout the province by public health staff, child and youth mental health staff, school district staff, child care support programs and numerous community-based agencies, community colleges, and volunteer groups.

Children and youth

Many resources and programs are geared to developing the awareness and skills of children and youth. Police/school liaison officers deliver education programs designed to "street-proof" children and prevent child abuse and neglect.

Some programs are specialized; for example, helping children and youth with disabilities become more aware of healthy sexuality and sexual abuse prevention. Others examine issues around dating violence, provide youth with information on birth control, and offer a safe haven for children to help address "stranger danger".

School-based prevention education

British Columbia has mandatory personal safety curriculum for all students in the province, and it is a graduation requirement. *Personal Planning* (K-7) and *Career and Personal Planning* (8-12) are designed to help students acquire the knowledge, attitudes and skills needed to lead healthy and productive lives. Areas covered are:

- healthy living;
- mental well-being;
- family life education;
- child abuse prevention;
- substance misuse prevention; and
- safety and injury prevention.

Advocacy

Another way to prevent abuse and neglect is to advocate to try to ensure, on a case-by-case basis, that the children and families you are involved with get the services they need.

Service providers often advocate on behalf of children and their parents informally, for example, in team meetings, and in promoting the development of appropriate services.

As well, the following bodies provide advice to people seeking information or who have concerns about service:

- The *Child, Youth and Family Advocate* helps children, youth and families to advocate when they believe they cannot get the services they need, the service providers they deal with are not listening to them, or a service provider or professional has made a decision affecting them without consulting them.

- The *Ombudsman* responds to complaints that a decision affecting a child, youth or family made by a government worker seems unfair, illogical or against the rules.

- The *Public Trustee* responds to concerns by children or youth regarding the use of their assets by others, their rights in legal proceedings, and contracts being made on their behalf.

- The *British Columbia Family Advocate* appointed by the Attorney General under the *Family Relations Act* may intervene at any stage of a legal proceeding involving a child, to act as counsel for the interests and welfare of the child.

Reviews and Monitoring

- The *Children's Commissioner* carries out the following functions:
  - sets standards for the complaints processes of ministries and agencies of government;
  - reviews complaints about breaches of rights of children in care and about services to children not resolved by the Ministry for Children and Families;
  - monitors case planning for children who are in the continuing care of the Director of Child, Family and Community Service;
  - reviews child deaths and critical injuries and, after investigating, makes recommendations intended to prevent deaths and critical injuries;
  - reports to the public on how ministries and agencies of the government are doing in their service to children;
  - reviews all children's deaths, investigating those it determines warrant investigation, and making recommendations to caregivers and service providers to improve service and prevent further deaths;
  - reviews critical injuries of children in the care or charge of the Director of Child, Family and Community Service, to ensure that the circumstances under which a child was injured are known, and that any changes in practice or policy required to protect other children from similar circumstances are made; and
  - informs the people of British Columbia about the state of the province's child- and family-serving system through regular data collection, evaluation and reporting.

Conduct of service providers

The provincial government has recently taken measures under the *Criminal Records Review* Act to protect children. There are now procedures for reviewing the criminal records of people who have access to children as part of their employment with the provincial government or a provincial government agency, educational institution, child care setting, hospital or other agency that receives funding or licensing from the provincial government.

The goal is to reduce the likelihood that people with relevant criminal records could occupy positions of trust with children.

The province is also helping other employers to develop these procedures for employees who have unsupervised access to children. The act provides that any professional licensing body whose members provide services for children have a criminal record review as a condition of licensure.

Professional associations and regulatory bodies strive to prevent child abuse and neglect by their members through professional codes of conduct. Some government agencies provide information to their contracted service providers and other community-based organizations about safeguarding children through careful recruitment and monitoring of staff and volunteers.

Further information

You can find further information on promotion and prevention activities through the following resources:

- Affiliation of Multicultural Societies and Service Agencies of B.C.: (604) 718-2777

- British Columbia Council for Families: (604) 660-0675

- British Columbia Aboriginal Network on Disability Society: (250) 381-7303

- British Columbia Association of Aboriginal Friendship Centres: (250) 652-0210

- Criminal Records Review, Security Programs Division, Ministry of Attorney General: (250) 356-5486

- Enquiry B.C. (can transfer a call to the appropriate source for information on specific programs delivered or funded by the provincial government): (604) 660-2421 in Vancouver, (250) 387-6121 in Victoria, or 1-800-663-7867 from other locations in the province.

- First Nations Summit - Child Welfare Committee: (604) 990-9939

- Justice Institute of B.C. (for training programs for criminal justice, aboriginal, health, counselling and community agency staff) (604) 525-5422; TDD/TTY (604) 528-5655

- La Societé des Enfants Michif (Metis Family Services): (604) 584-6621

- Ministry for Children and Families After Hours Response Teams (for information on family support services and child protection):

  660-4927 in Vancouver (serving Vancouver, Richmond, West Vancouver, North Vancouver, Vancouver International Airport, Lions Bay and Bowen Island)

  660-8180 in the Lower Mainland (serving Aldergrove, Burnaby, Coquitlam, Delta, Ladner, Langley, Maple Ridge, New Westminster, Pitt Meadows, Port Coquitlam, Port Moody, Surrey and White Rock)

  1-800-663-9122 from other locations in the province

- National Clearing House on Family Violence, Family Violence Prevention Division, Health Canada, 1-800-267-1291 (publishers of Sexual Abuse Information Series for Children, Teens and for Partners of Sexual Abuse Victims)

- Prevention Source B.C. (prevention of alcohol and drug misuse): 874-8452 in the Lower Mainland, or 1-800-663-1880 from other locations in the province

- Provincial Prostitution Unit, Ministry of Attorney General, SAFE Line: 1-888-224-SAFE or 660-7233 in Vancouver

- Public health services — see listings in blue pages (for information from public health nurses on healthy child development, prevention, promotion and parenting support)

- Red Cross Abuse Prevention Services: (604) 709-6600

- Sexual Health Resource Network (material on sexuality education and sexual abuse, targeted to the needs of children and youth with disabilities): 434-1331, ext. 535 in the Lower Mainland, or 1-800-331-1533

- Society for Children and Youth of British Columbia, Resources on Children's Rights: (604) 433-4180

- Special Programs Branch, Ministry of Education, Skills and Training: (250) 356-2333, TTY (250) 356-7632

- Stopping the Violence Branch, Ministry of Women's Equality: (250) 387-3613

- Taking Care of Ourselves and Others, Total Respect of Ourselves and Others, Community Programs Branch, Ministry of Attorney General, 1-800-680-4264

- United Native Nations: (604) 688-1821

- Vancouver Aboriginal Child and Family Services Society: (604) 689-2402

- Vancouver Lower Mainland Multicultural Family Support Services Society: (604) 436-1025

- Victim Services Division, Community Justice Branch, Ministry of Attorney General, (604) 660-5199 (Child Sexual Abuse Victim Service Worker handbook)

Conclusion - looking ahead

The development of this handbook is part of the response to abuse and neglect embodied in the new child protection legislation which came into force in British Columbia in 1996, and the subsequent restructuring of government services for children and families.

If there is a single key theme to that reorganization, and to this handbook, it is the importance of collaboration.

Working together collaboratively builds better relationships among all those in contact with children, families and service providers. It means sharing appropriate information among child-serving agencies and organizations, as permitted by applicable legislation. It means cooperating in developing plans and providing services. And, it means the prompt reporting of suspected child abuse or neglect. We are all part of a coordinated province-wide effort aimed at reducing child abuse and neglect.

This kind of collaboration makes good sense for day-to-day operations. It knits together service providers in every part of British Columbia, from every discipline, into a supportive network to protect the children of this province.

Although it is challenging, there is a deep sense of satisfaction to be gained in overcoming challenges and delivering the best service possible to children and families.

There is reason for hope as we enter the next century. British Columbians are becoming more aware of how to prevent and intervene appropriately to stop child abuse and neglect. Our effective response can assist children in British Columbia to grow up safe and healthy.

Appendix A

Quick Reference:
General Directory for
Government Services

Quick Reference: General Directory for Government Services

Call Enquiry BC for any questions you may have regarding provincial government services.

In Victoria call. 387-6121

In Vancouver call 660-2421

From elsewhere in B.C. call 1-800-663-7867

Ministry for Children and Families After Hours Line:

For emergencies outside office hours (usually 8:30 a.m.-4:30 p.m.,
Monday to Friday), call the ministry's 24-hour After Hours Line:

In Vancouver, the North Shore and Richmond, call 660-4927

In the Lower Mainland from Burnaby and Delta in the west
to Maple Ridge and Langley in the east, call. 660-8180

From elsewhere in B.C. call 1-800-663-9122

Alcohol and Drug Information and Referral Service
Ministry for Children and Families

In the Lower Mainland call 660-9382

From elsewhere in B.C. call. 1-800-663-1441

Children's Commissioner

In the Victoria area call 356-8963

From elsewhere in B.C. call. 1-800-859-1441

Child Protection Services Unit
B.C.'s Children's Hospital

Call. . . . . (604)-875-3270

(Provides medical diagnosis and consultation to professionals in
cases of child abuse or neglect. Also provides crisis counselling
for parents and a follow-up clinic for abused children.)

Child, Youth and Family Advocate

In Vancouver call 775-3203

From elsewhere in B.C. call. 1-800-476-3933

Helpline for Children

To report abuse or neglect, dial 0 and ask the operator for Zenith 1234

Ombudsman

In the Victoria area call 357-5855

From elsewhere in B.C. call. 1-800-567-3247

Prevention Source Centre

Provides information on the prevention of alcohol and drug misuse.

In the Lower Mainland call 874-8452

From elsewhere in B.C. call 1-800-663-1880

Public Trustee

In Vancouver call 660-4444

From elsewhere in B.C. call 1-800-663-7867

Victims Information Line

Ministry of Attorney General

Call. 1-800-563-0808

First Nations Child, Family and Community Service Agencies

FIRST NATIONS CHILD, FAMILY AND COMMUNITY SERVICE AGENCIES

As of January 1, 1998 the following First Nations agencies have full child protection authorities delegated to their staff by the Director of Child, Family and Community Service.

- Lalum'utul Smun'eem Child and Family Services
  Phone: . . . . (250) 746-1002

- Nlha'7kapmx Child and Family Services
  Phone: . . . . (250) 455-2118

- Northern Shuswap Family and Children's Services
  Society (aka Knucwentwecw) Phone: . . . . (250) 392-2995

- Nuu-Chah-Nulth Community and Human Services
  Phone: . . . . (250)724-3232

- Scw'exmx Child and Family Services
  Phone: . . . . (250) 378-2771

- Xolhmi:lh Child and Family Services Program
  Phone: . . . . (604) 858-0113

As of January 1, 1998 the following First Nations agencies have partial authorities delegated to their staff by the Director of Child, Family and Community Service.

- Ayas Men Men Child and Family Services
  Phone: . . . . (604) 985-4111

- Lake Babine Family and Child Services
  Phone: . . . . (250) 692-4770

- Sechelt Child and Family Services
  Phone: . . . . (604) 885-9404

As of January 1, 1998 the following First Nations agencies have an agreement with the Director of Child, Family and Community Service to work towards delegated authority.

- Central Island Child and Family Services
  Phone: . . . . (250) 245-0008

- Nisga'a Family and Child Services
  Phone: . . . . (250) 633-2601

Summary of the Law with Respect to Child Abuse and Neglect

SUMMARY OF THE LAW WITH RESPECT TO CHILD ABUSE AND NEGLECT

The *Child, Family and Community Service Act*

Overview

This legislation emphasizes the primacy of children's entitlement to be safe from harm. The paramount consideration of the act is the safety and well being of children. The act recognizes that a family environment is preferred for child-rearing, as long as the child is safe. It also recognizes that parents are primarily responsible for protection of their children and authorizes government intervention when family protection breaks down. The act allows provincial authorities to intervene when a child may be in need of protection.

The *Child, Family and Community Service Act* not only applies to children under the age of 19 years who may be in need of protection, but also has special provisions that focus on the needs of youths between the ages of 16 and 19 and young adults between the ages of 19 and 24.

Determining when a child is in need of protection

The act states that a child needs protection:

    a. if the child has been, or is likely to be, physically harmed by the child's parent;

    b. if the child has been, or is likely to be, sexually abused or exploited by the child's parent;

    c. if the child has been, or is likely to be, physically harmed, sexually abused or sexually exploited by another person and if the child's parent is unwilling or unable to protect the child;

    d. if the child has been, or is likely to be, physically harmed, because of neglect by the child's parent;

    e. if the child is emotionally harmed by the parent's conduct;

    f. if the child is deprived of necessary health care;

    g. if the child's development is likely to be seriously impaired by a treatable condition and the child's parent refuses to provide or consent to treatment;

h. if the child's parent is unable or unwilling to care for the child and has not made adequate provision for the child's care;

i. if the child is or has been absent from home in circumstances that endanger the child's safety or well-being;

j. if the child's parent is dead and adequate provision has not been made for the child's care;

k. if the child has been abandoned and adequate provision has not been made for the child's care;

l. if the child is in the care of a director or another person by agreement and the child's parent is unwilling or unable to resume care when the agreements is no longer in force.

For the purpose of subsection (1)(e), a child is emotionally harmed if they demonstrate severe:

- anxiety;

- depression;

- withdrawal; or

- self-destructive or aggressive behaviour.

Administration of the act

The director is responsible for:

- assessing all reports;

- where required, investigating to determine whether a child may need protection;

- intervening when a child needs protection.

A director can delegate any or all of their powers under the act to child protection social workers. Under the act, police officers are authorized to provide various forms of assistance to the director in carrying out the child protection mandate.

Duty to report

The act imposes a duty on any person who has reason to believe that a child needs protection to promptly report the matter to a director or a person delegated by the director. Failure to report in these circumstances or knowingly reporting false information constitutes an offence under the act punishable by a fine of up to $10,000 or, imprisonment for up to six months, or both.

Response to a report

When the director receives a report, they must assess the information in the report and may offer support services to the child and family, refer the child and family to a community agency, or investigate the child's need for protection.

Some of the less disruptive options for the family available to the director are:

- agreements for support services or for the child to be cared for outside the home;

- applying to the court for an order prohibiting contact between the child and another person if there are reasonable grounds to believe that the other person would cause the child to need protection;

- obtaining an order for a child to receive essential health care;

- arranging for someone to look after the child for a period of up to 72 hours where the child is lost, has run away, or is found without adequate supervision

- providing homemaker services for a period of 72 hours where the child is found without adequate supervision

A director may remove a child if the child needs protection and there is no less disruptive means of protection, or if the child is in immediate danger. If a child is lost or has run away, a director may also take charge of a child and provide safety for a period of up to 72 hours.

Family participation

Throughout the act, family and, where applicable, the community is encouraged to take responsibility by making decisions and plans for children. The act provides for alternative dispute resolution mechanisms to try and agree on an arrangement that will protect the child. The legislation attempts to keep cases out of court by providing many options both before and after removal of children from their parents.

Accountability provisions

The act provides for accountability through an administrative review of the exercise of the director's powers, duties and function under the act. The *Children's Commission Act*, administered by the Attorney General, establishes a complaints resolution process which will include the determination of breaches of the rights of children in care as well as the review of decisions concerning designated services to children.

The *Freedom of Information and Protection of Privacy Act*

Public access to information

This act gives the public a right of access to records held by a public body, including personal information about themselves, and specifies the limited exceptions to these rights of access (e.g. where there would be an unreasonable invasion of another person's personal privacy). The act also gives individuals a right to request the correction of personal information about themselves, and prevents the unauthorized collection, use or disclosure of personal information by a public body.

Sharing information with the public

Increasingly, there are situations where a public body has information in its possession that it needs to disclose in order to protect children. The *Freedom of Information and Protection of Privacy Act* place limits on the ability of public bodies to disclose personal information. The ability to disclose personal information within a public body, to another public body or to the public will depend on the particular circumstances. For example, if there are compelling circumstances affecting a child's safety, or if disclosure of the information is for the purpose for which it was obtained for a consistent purpose, the *Freedom of Information and Protection of Privacy Act* allows disclosure. (Note that in cases of compelling circumstances, the act requires notice of the disclosure to the person the information is about, and in the case of disclosure for a consistent purpose, the *Freedom of Information and Protection of Privacy Act's* definition of "consistent use" must be met.)

Where a public body has information about a significant risk of harm to the safety of the public or a group of people, the *Freedom of Information and Protection of Privacy Act* imposes a duty on the head of that public body to disclose the information without delay to the public, the affected group of people, or an applicant. This overrides any consideration about privacy of individuals the information is about. This duty rarely arises, but could arise, for example, where a sexual offender is going to be released into the community and there is a significant risk that the individual will re-offend. (Here, too, there are notice requirements.)

Information held by federal government agencies such as the RCMP and Corrections Canada or information collected in the administration of federal acts such as the *Young Offenders Act* are governed by the federal *Privacy Act*.

Protecting the privacy of children

The act also provides for regulations that protect children's privacy. The right to access records and personal information can be exercised on behalf of a person under 19 years of age by the individual's parent or guardian, only if the individual is incapable of exercising those rights. This has been interpreted as restricting the access to information about a child to only the legal parent or guardian. In light of this regulation, then, in the case of a child without capacity who is in the legal care of the director under the *Child, Family and Community Service Act*, the child's natural parents would be unable to act in place of the child under the *Freedom of Information and Protection of Privacy Act* to obtain information about the child from a public body. However, the natural parents would be in the same position as any other applicant under the *Freedom of Information and Privacy Act* and may be able to obtain some information about the child from a public body if it would not be an unreasonable invasion of the personal privacy of the child, but this does not extend to child protection information held by the Ministry for Children and Families.

Relationship to the *Child, Family and Community Service Act*

The *Child, Family and Community Service Act* provides that the *Freedom of Information and Protection of Privacy Act* does not apply to a record made under the *Child, Family and Community Service Act* and in the custody or control of a director, or to information in that record. Accordingly, any information that is in the custody and control of a director and was made under the *Child, Family and Community Service Act* is not subject to the provisions of the *Freedom of Information and Protection of Privacy Act*. The *Child, Family and Community Service Act* provides a comprehensive scheme for access to information in the control of the director and protection of the confidentiality of this information.

The *Criminal Records Review Act*

This act is designed to prevent the physical and sexual abuse of children. Individuals who work with children or who may have unsupervised access to children in the course of employment and who are employed by the government, a school board or independent school, are members of a professional association listed in the act, or received operating funds from the government, must undergo a criminal records check. The act also requires a criminal record check for unlicensed child care providers. Individuals who have a criminal record for relevant offences listed in the act undergo an adjudication process to determine if they present a risk to children.

Legislation Governing Educational Settings
The *Teaching Profession Act*

The purpose of this act is to establish the College of Teachers and to enable it to set standards for teacher education and for teachers' professional conduct and competence. To ensure compliance, the college controls the certification of teachers and the issuance of teaching certificates. To teach in the public school system in British Columbia, a teacher must be a member of the college and hold a certificate of qualification issued by the college. School principals, vice-principals, directors of instruction, superintendents and assistant superintendents must also be college members and hold teaching certificates.

A person will not be admitted to membership unless they meet the standards of qualification and standards of fitness established by the college, and satisfy the college that they are of good moral character and otherwise fit and proper to be granted membership. If a person fails to authorize a criminal record check under the *Criminal Records Review Act*, the college will not admit that person to membership. If an adjudicator under the act has determined that a person presents a risk of physical or sexual abuse to children, the college must review the application or registration and take appropriate action. The college must also notify the registered member's employer.

The college has the jurisdiction to inquire into the conduct or competence of any member or former member where a complaint or report has been received by the college regarding that person. If a member is found to be incompetent or guilty of misconduct, the college can:

- reprimand the member;
- suspend the membership and certificate of qualification of the member; or
- terminate that person's membership and cancel his or her certificate of qualification.

If a former member is found guilty of misconduct, the college will take actions similar to those taken against a member.

The *School Act*

This act provides authority for a school board to dismiss, suspend or otherwise discipline an employee for just and reasonable cause. If a superintendent of schools is of the opinion that the welfare of students is threatened by the presence of an employee, the superintendent may suspend the employee. The school board has the power to confirm, vary or revoke that suspension. The College of Teachers must be notified immediately if a board dismisses, suspends or otherwise disciplines a member of the college. If an employee is a member of the College of Teachers and that person resigns, the school board must notify the college of the circumstances of the resignation, if the board feels it is in the interest of the public to do so.

The *School Act* also requires children between six and 16 years of age to be enrolled in school and to be participating in an educational program at a school. Alternatively, a child may be educated at home, but that child must be registered with a school. The superintendent of schools is required to investigate reports of home schoolers who are not registered with schools as home schoolers, and those who may not be receiving an educational program.

Individual school boards may make rules:

- establishing codes of conduct for students attending educational programs operated by or on behalf of the board;

- regarding the suspension of students and the provision of educational programs for suspended students;

- regarding attendance of students in educational programs.

Boards must continue to make an educational program available to students who have been suspended. An administrative officer of a school and a superintendent of schools have the authority to suspend a student in accordance with the rules established by a board.

The *Independent School Act*

Within the independent school system, teachers are certified under either the *Teaching Profession Act* or the *Independent School Act*. Under the *Independent School Act*, the Inspector of Independent Schools has the authority to issue teacher certification restricted to independent schools and to suspend or revoke certification for cause. Independent school authorities must report, without delay, the reason for any teacher's dismissal, suspension or disciplinary action and any resignation in which circumstances are such that it is in the public interest to do so. All such reports are directed to the Inspector of Independent Schools, and to the College of Teachers when the teacher involved is a member of the college. The provisions of the *Criminal Records Review Act* apply to independent school authorities.

The *College and Institute Act*

This act provides the province with the power to designate a college and university college and to designate a provincial institute. A college, university college and institute become a corporation upon designation. The province appoints the majority of the members to the boards to govern, manage and direct the affairs of the institutions. Each board must appoint a president, who is also the chief executive officer, to supervise and direct the staff of the institution. The president may, for just cause, suspend an employee or student of the institution. Where a suspension occurs, the president must make a report to the board immediately.

The *Institute of Technology Act*

This act establishes the British Columbia Institute of Technology (BCIT). BCIT is also governed by a board made up of a majority of provincially appointed members. A president is appointed and the duties of the president include the supervision of the staff of the institution. Where a suspension occurs, the president must make a report to the board within 48 hours.

The *Open Learning Agency Act*

This act establishes the Open Learning Agency as a corporation to collaborate with universities, institutions, school boards and other agencies concerned with education. The Open Learning Agency is governed by a provincially appointed board that appoints a president, who is also the chief executive officer of the agency. It is the responsibility of the president to appoint officers and hire employees.

Other legislation pertaining to post-secondary institutions

The *University Act*, the *Royal Roads University Act*, and the *University of Northern British Columbia Act* all govern the operation of the public universities in British Columbia. The governing structure of each university includes a president whose duties include recommending appointments, promotions and removal of professors, members of administrative staff and officers, and other employees of the university.

Exemption for post-secondary institutions

Post-secondary education institutions are exempt from the requirements of the *Criminal Records Review Act*.

The *Community Care Facility Act*

This legislation provides for the licensing of community care facilities including child care and child/youth residential facilities. The Director of Licensing or a delegated medical health officer may attach terms or conditions to or suspend or cancel the license of a community care facility where there are reasonable grounds to believe that the health or safety of persons cared for at the facilty is at risk. In addition, the Director of Licensing or delegate has authority to certify early childhood educators as well as suspend or cancel their certifications.

The Minister of Health or delegated health authority may, where there are reasonable grounds to believe that the health or safety of persons cared for at the facility is at risk because of an act or omission of staff, appoint an administrator to operate the facility for a specified period.

The medical health officer is required to investigate every application for a license to operate a community care facility and to investigate every complaint that a facility is being operated inappropriately. The investigation of complaints is usually delegated to a licensing officer who is sometimes assisted by a child protection social worker. The medical health officer is given a broad mandate to inquire into all matters concerning the facility, it employees and its guests, including any treatments or programs being carried out in the facility.

The *Victims of Crime Act*

Under this act, children who have been victims of a crime are entitled to receive information which includes:

- victim services available in the child's community;
- compensation under the *Criminal Injury Compensation Act*;
- how the criminal justice system works;
- the status of the police investigation and the court case;
- the administration of the offender's sentence;
- rights to privacy under the *Freedom of Information and Protection of Privacy Act*

Victims of crime will also be given the opportunity to provide the court with information about the effect of the crime. A child may be provided with legal representation upon request to the Attorney General under Section 3 of the act.

The *Family Relations Act*

While this act primarily deals with the determination of rights upon family breakdown, it provides for protection of children through a number of provisions. The *Family Relations Act* gives the court jurisdiction to make orders in relation to child custody, access and guardianship, and specifies that in making any of these orders, the court shall give paramount consideration to the best interests of the child. Section 2 of the act allows the Attorney General to appoint a family advocate who may intervene at any stage of a legal proceeding involving children in order to act as counsel for the interests and welfare of a child. Section 37 and Section 38 allow the court to make restraining orders and orders prohibiting interference with a child where issues of custody and access are before the court.

Part 3 of the act provides for the recognition and enforcement of extra-provincial custody and access orders. Section 45 allows the court to exercise its jurisdiction to make or vary custody or access order over a child from another province and Section 50 allows a B.C. court to supersede a custody order from another province where the court is satisfied that the child would suffer serious harm if he or she were returned to the parent entitled to custody in the other province.

Part 4 of the *Family Relations Act* deals with international child abductions and incorporates the provisions of the Hague Convention to assist in the return of children who have been unlawfully removed from their custodial parent.

Within Canada, under the criminal law, child abduction is dealt with in Section 280 through Section 285 of the *Criminal Code*.

The *Infants Act*

This act provides that children have the right to consent to health care without the necessity of obtaining their parents' or guardians' consent, provided the child has the capacity to give consent to such health care. The act also provides for involvement by the Public Trustee and, in some cases, the court to ensure that that rights of children are protected when they are involved in property issues, contracts, leases and litigation.

The *Child, Youth and Family Advocacy Act*

This act creates the office of the Child, Youth and Family Advocate. The advocate is appointed by the Lieutenant Governor in Council after receiving a recommendation from the legislative assembly. The advocate is an officer of the legislature.

While the advocate may not act as legal counsel, their office is responsible for ensuring that the rights and interests of children are protected and advanced, and that there is appropriate advocacy and support offered to children, youth and families dealing with government and community services. The advocate is specifically responsible for assisting children in the care of the director to bring alleged breaches of their rights to the complaint resolution process of the Children's Commission under the *Children's Commission Act*.

The advocate has the right to access any information that is in the custody and control of a public body as defined in the *Freedom of Information and Protection of Privacy Act* where such information is necessary for the performance of their duties. The advocate is also under a duty of confidentiality and cannot be compelled to disclose information obtained under this act except for the purposes of carrying out their duties and powers.

The *Criminal Code of Canada*

Whenever a child has been physically or sexually abused, abandoned or neglected, a crime may have been committed. Children who suffer abuse and neglect are also often victims of an offence under the *Criminal Code*, such as physical and sexual assault, sexual interference, sexual exploitation of a child, and failure to provide the necessities of life. The police are responsible for enforcing the criminal law. On receipt of a report of child abuse or neglect, the police will determine whether there are grounds for a criminal investigation, and will conduct an investigation where such grounds exist.

Generally, criminal investigations involving such matters will be done in cooperation or conjunction with an investigation by a social worker under the *Child, Family and Community Service Act*.

The *Young Offenders Act* (federal)

This act governs the application of the criminal justice system to young people over 12 but under 18 years of age. It establishes a special court known as the youth court, which has exclusive jurisdiction over any offence alleged to have been committed by a young person, including any sexual offences that are provided for in the *Criminal Code of Canada*. This act also provides for the disclosure and non-disclosure of youth court records (including police records pertaining to youths) and provides for the protection of the identity of young persons charged under this act.

An Order In Council issued under the authority of this act allows a record to be made available, on request, to designated authorities carrying out specific functions and duties related to youth.

The *Privacy Act* (federal)

The purpose of the *Privacy Act* is to protect the privacy of individuals with respect to personal information about themselves held by a federal government institution (including the RCMP and to provide individuals with a right of access to that information.

Section 8 provides that personal information under the control of a government institution shall not be disclosed without the consent of the individual to whom it relates, except in specified situations such as disclosure to specified investigative bodies for the purpose of carrying out lawful investigations or enforcing any law of Canada or a province. Further, the head of a government institution may disclose personal information without the consent of the person where the public interest in the disclosure clearly outweighs any invasion of privacy that could result from the disclosure.

The *Access to Information Act* (federal)

This act provides a right of access to information in records under the control of a federal government institution, in accordance with the principle that government information should be available to the public, that necessary exceptions to the right of access should be limited and specific, and that decisions on disclosure of government information should be reviewed independently of government. This act sets out the necessary exception to a right of access, and includes as exceptions records containing information pertaining to criminal investigations, and records that contain personal information except where permitted by the federal *Privacy Act*.

Summary of Relevent Criminal Code Offences

SUMMARY OF RELEVANT CRIMINAL CODE OFFENCES

Criminal Code of Canada

Introduction

The *Criminal Code of Canada* provides the key legislative mandate for the justice system response to criminal offences related to abuse and neglect of children. It establishes criminal offences, procedures for investigation and prosecution and sanctions for offenders. Enforcement of the criminal law as it applies to child victims of criminal offences is vital for the protection of children.

While service providers outside the justice system need not become experts on criminal law and procedure related to child abuse and neglect, it is important that people working with and for children, and the public in general, understand that most forms of child abuse, and some forms of neglect, constitute criminal offences.

Physical Abuse of Children

Criminal Code Offences

The *Criminal Code* contains numerous offences related to physical abuse of children, some of which apply to victims of all ages and others that are specific to children, including:

Offence(s)	Section(s)	Offence against
• assault and aggravated assault - excision (female genital mutilation)	265-268 268(3)	any person female child under 18
• causing bodily harm with intent	244-244.1	any person
• unlawfully causing bodily harm	269	any person
• administering a noxious thing	245	any person
• criminal negligence	219-221	any person
• murder	229-231	any person
• manslaughter	234	any person
• infanticide	233	child under one year
• killing an unborn child in the act of birth	238	unborn child
• homicide from injury before/during birth.	223(2)	child born alive who later dies

Other *Criminal Code* Provisions

- Where a person fears on reasonable grounds that another person will cause personal injury to him/her, his/her spouse or child, the *Criminal Code* (Section 810) provides a process where the court may order that the defendant enter into a "good behaviour" recognizance. A similar process applies where a person fears that another person will commit a serious personal injury offence against any person (Section 810.2).

- Section 43 of the *Criminal Code* - commonly referred to as the corporal punishment defence - excuses certain persons in authority vis-a-vis children (teachers, parents, or person standing in the place of a parent) from using "reasonable force" against a child under their care if such force is used "by way of correction".

Sexual Abuse of Children

Criminal Code Offences

Similar to offences related to physical abuse, the *Criminal Code* contains sexual offences that apply to victims of all ages as well as offences specific to children. In addition, there are significant differences in how offences in the former category apply to sexual activity among adults, between adults and children, and among children.

Offence(s)	Section(s)	Offence against/involving
• sexual interference	151	child under 14
• invitation to sexual touching	152	child under 14
• sexual exploitation (by adult in position of trust or authority)	153	child between 14 & 18
• sexual assault and aggravated sexual assault	271-273	any person - consent no defence when child under 14 with some exceptions (s.150.1)
• incest	155	any person - excludes from culpability a person who was under restraint, duress or fear
• anal intercourse	159	any person - not offence where it involves consenting adults 18 or over
• bestiality - in presence of or by a child	160 160(3)	any person - child under 14
• indecent acts - exposure (of genitals for sexual purpose)	173 173(2)	any person - child under 14
• corrupting morals (pornography) - child pornography	163 163.1	any person - child under 18
• procuring (prostitution) - person under 18	212 212(2), (2.1),& (4)	any person - child under 18
• procuring sexual activity (by parent/guardian)	170	child under 18
• householder permitting sexual activity	171	child under 18

Other *Criminal Code* provisions

- Where any person fears, on reasonable grounds, that another person will commit certain sexual offences against children, the *Criminal Code* provides a process where a court may order the defendant to enter into a recognizance prohibiting activities that involve contact with children under 14 and attendance at specified places where children under 14 are likely to be present (Section 810.1).

- To protect children from contact with convicted or accused sex offenders, the *Criminal Code* contains a vagrancy offence (Section 179(1)(b)) that applies to a person who has been convicted of certain sexual offences and, if "found loitering in or near a school ground, playground, public park or bathing area".

- Where a person is convicted of certain sexual offences against children under 14, or is accused of such an offence and released on conditions, the court may impose an order prohibiting the offender from attending certain places where children under 14 are likely to be present or obtaining paid/volunteer employment in a position of trust or authority with respect to children under 14 (Section 161).

Neglect of Children

Criminal Code Offences

While the *Criminal Code* does not establish a specific criminal offence of "child neglect", the criminal law recognizes the responsibility of parent/guardians to provide care and protection for children through several related offences, including:

Offence(s)	Section(s)	Offence against/involving
• failure to provide necessities of life - criminal negligence (re above)	215 219-221	child under 16
• abandoning child	218	child under 10
• neglect to obtain assistance in childbirth	242	child at time of birth
• corrupting children	172	child under 18

Emotional /Psychological Abuse of Children

Criminal Code Offences

The *Criminal Code* does not include specific offences concerning emotional or psychological abuse of children. What it does include are several offences, applicable to victims of all ages, with respect to threatening or intimidating behaviour by others.

Offence(s)	Section(s)	Offence against/involving
• criminal harassment	264	any person
• conveying threats	264.1	any person
• intimidation	423	any person
• making indecent or harassing telephone calls	372	any person
• extortion	346	any person
• culpable homicide (causing death by wilfully frightening)	222(5)	child or sick person

Kidnapping and Abduction of Children

Criminal Code offences

In addition to the general offences of kidnapping and forcible confinement, the *Criminal Code* establishes several offences specific to abduction of children of different ages and by parents/guardians or others.

Offence(s)	Section(s)	Offence against/involving
• kidnapping and forcible confinement	279	any person
• abduction of person under 14, under 16, by any person	280, 281	child under 14, child under 16
• abduction in contravention of custody order (by parent/guardian)	282(1)	child under 14
• abduction (by parent/guardian)	283	child under 14
• removal of child from Canada (for purpose of committing certain offences against the child)	273.3	different provisions for specified offences against children under 14, 14-18, and under 18

Other *Criminal Code* provisions

By virtue of Section 7(4.1) of the *Criminal Code*, sexual offences against children committed outside Canada by Canadian citizens or permanent residents are deemed to have been committed in Canada.

Measures to facilitate child witness testimony

In recognition of the trauma a child may experience from facing the accused in court and giving evidence in a public forum, Section 486 of the *Criminal Code* contains several provisions, subject to the discretion of the court, to facilitate child witness testimony. For example, it includes provisions for a child to testify behind a screen or outside the courtroom by means of closed-circuit television. It prohibits the accused from personally cross-examining the child witness. It makes provision for a publication ban and exclusion of the public from the courtroom. It enables a child witness under 14 to have a support person present and close by while testifying. In addition, Section 715.1 allows for a child witness to give evidence related to a sexual offence by way of videotape.

Related legislation

Other legislation related to the criminal justice system response to child abuse and neglect include the *Canada Evidence Act* (which, among other things, sets out the type of oath a child witness may take), and the *Young Offenders Act* and *Victims of Crime Act* (which are summarized in this appendix).

Handling Disclosures
(How Children Tell Us)

Adapted from material in Dealing with Child Abuse: A Handbook for School Personnel. Northwest Territories Department of Education, Culture and Employment, 1995. Used with permission.

HANDLING DISCLOSURES (How Children Tell Us)

1. Disclosure of Abuse

A "disclosure" occurs when a child tells you or lets you know in some other way that he or she has been, or is being abused. Sometimes children will tell you directly that they are being abused. Often they use indirect ways to let you know, for example, drawing pictures about hitting or inappropriate touching, writing about abuse in journal stories or play-acting frightening scenes. These indirect ways may be a child's way of hinting about abuse.

Children may disclose abuse which is ongoing, or abuse which happened weeks, months or years ago, abuse which took place in another location (community or province), or abuse that is happening to someone else. You need to report all disclosures of abuse, no matter where or when they happened.

2. Handling a Disclosure

Listen to disclosures in a caring and calm manner. Let the child tell their story in their own way - don't ask leading questions about the disclosure. Make sure the child knows that you believe them and that what happened to them was not their fault. Let them know that telling someone was the right thing to do and that now you are gong to contact the child protection social worker to try to get some help. The child may receive some comfort in hearing that they are not alone and that other children have gone through this. Do not judge the events, circumstances or individuals involved and, don't express to the child what you think they might be feeling, for example, "You must hate him for what he did to you".

When the child has finished what they have to say and has disclosed enough so that you have reason to believe they have been abused, tell the child that you and they need to share this information with a child protection social worker. It is very important that at the end of the disclosure, the child must continue to think that what they have to say is important, and they must feel safe enough so they can relate the complete disclosure to the child protection social worker.

Don't make promises to the child that you have no way of keeping. For example, telling a child that "everything is all right" or "now you will get the help you need" are promises that cannot be guaranteed.

It is the role of the child protection social worker and/or the police to question the child about the details of abuse. They are trained to do this type of interview. They will then be able to document this information first-hand and present it in court if needed. If you question the child for details, it could cause serious problems with the investigation.

Immediately after a disclosure, you should write down and date any comments or statements made by the child during the disclosure. Try to use their exact words. Keep notes about the child's behaviour and emotional state, as well as the circumstances at the time of the disclosure, e.g., "Child stayed at her desk with her face hidden after all the other children went home. She cried for 15 minutes".

Call and make a report of child abuse to a child protection social worker at the Ministry for Children and Families.

Maintain confidentiality. Don't discuss the disclosure with other staff members.

Recognize and respect the child's feelings in the days following the disclosure. These may include:

- feelings of guilt for having told;
- fear and anxiety about what will happen next;
- anger or withdrawal, including anger at, or withdrawal from you;
- uncertainty;
- feelings of being blamed;
- feelings of low self-esteem; and
- feelings of shame.

Be aware of your own feelings about the disclosure.

Practise using non-leading or open questions and comments, as discussed below.

3. Appropriate Questioning: Non-Leading or Open Questions and Comments

Use non-leading, open questions and comments when responding to a child who is disclosing or talking about abuse. This type of questioning doesn't make assumptions about what may have happened to the child. It doesn't put words in the child's mouth. Non-leading questions and comments describe the child's behaviour or condition in a factual way, and open up a chance for the child to respond and describe what has happened.

Examples of non-leading questions and comments:

"Please tell me about what you had to eat this week."

"You look as though things aren't going well."

"Tell me about your home." (In response to a child who says he doesn't want to go home after school because it's not nice there.)

"Tell me a bit more about that."

4. Avoid: Leading Questions and Comments (Inappropriate Questioning)

Leading questions can often be answered by a "yes" or "no". Avoid leading questions or comments -they direct the child and hint at how the child is to respond. Leading questions or comments often label the child's feelings, threaten their sense of privacy, or put words in the child's mouth. They often make assumptions about what may have happened and don't allow the child to describe what has taken place entirely in their own words. This type of questioning or commenting isn't helpful, as the court will consider the child's evidence to be tainted or spoiled.

Examples of inappropriate questioning (leading questions):

"Has your dad been beating you up at home? How does he hit you?" (In response to a child who says that someone is hurting him.)

"Is someone sexually abusing you?" (In response to a child who says that someone at home is bothering her or him.)

5. Types of Disclosures

Direct disclosures: verbal or written statements by the child.

Indirect disclosures: verbal, written or graphic hints, e.g. journal writing, drawings, art work that appear to be about abuse.

Disclosures with conditions: the child says they will tell you about something that is happening to them only if certain conditions are met.

Disguised disclosures: the child isn't ready to tell you that they are being abused, and so pretends that it is happening to someone else.

Third party disclosures: the child tells you about abuse which is happening to another child.

6. Sample responses to disclosures of child abuse

a. Direct Disclosure - "I am being abused".

Circumstances	Child's Direct Disclosure	Leading Response (wrong)	Non-Leading Response (right)
Teacher wants young child to remove his gloves in school.	"I don't want to. My hands hurt because someone burned me with cigarettes last night. He said I took some money from him."	"This is terrible. Did your dad do this? Has he done this before?"	"May I look at your hands to see if they need taking care of? After we do that, I'll call the social worker to let them know what happened to you. They'll want to talk to you about what happened so that they can try to help you."

b. Indirect Disclosure - "He bothers me."

	Child's Indirect Disclosure	Leading Response (wrong)	Non-Leading Response (right)
Example 1	"I don't like the way that ____ bugs me all the time."	"Is someone abusing you?"	"What do you mean by bugging you? Do you want to tell me more about that?"
Example 2	"_____ doesn't let me sleep at night."	"Does ____ come into your room and touch you or do things like that?"	"How does _____ disturb your sleep?"
Example 3	"I don't like it when _____ does those things to me."	"Are you talking about being sexually or physically abused?"	"What kinds of things don't you like?"

In the above examples, the child might or might not have been talking about abuse. They could have been talking about a brother who plays loud music or plays jokes on them. The leading responses above suggest that abuse has taken place and is not the correct way to respond.

Because there is a possibility that the child is hinting about abuse, the best responses should be open or non-leading. Then the child knows you are listening and has the chance to share more if they want to.

c. Disclosure with Conditions -
"You must promise not to tell anyone".

Children will sometimes want to talk abut something that is happening to them or to someone else only if certain promises or conditions are met. The child might want you to promise that no one will be told about the secret, that the police or the social worker will not be involved, that the family will not be broken up, and that no one will get into trouble. Don't make these promises. Try to convince the child that the problem cannot be taken care of unless people are allowed to help. If something is happening to the child that is harmful in any way, it's a secret that cannot be kept. You can reassure the child that the social worker and police will do their best to try to keep him or her safe and to prevent the abuse from happening again.

Child's Disclosure with Conditions

Child's Disclosure with Conditions	Leading Response (wrong)	Non-Leading Response (right)
"I want to tell you something, but you have to promise not to tell anyone else or I'll get into big trouble."	"Is someone in your family abusing you? If so, I'll have to tell the social worker."	"There are some secrets that shouldn't be kept. If I do have to tell someone else, it will be someone who will try to help you."

The child may not be ready to talk about the problem without conditions. For example, they may not want to tell you anything unless you promise not to call the child protection social worker. Let the child know that you are concerned for their safety and will be available if they would like to come back and talk another time. Make a written note of the comments that the child has made up to this point.

If older students have difficulty talking about the problem, suggest that they try writing it down first. Then you could talk together about ways to get help.

d. Disguised Disclosure - Child Pretending that the Abuse is Happening to Someone Else

"I'm not ready to tell you it's me."

Child's Disguised Disclosure	Leading Response (wrong)	Non-Leading Response (right)
"I have a friend who says that her grandfather hurts her all the time. He gets mad and hits her a lot. She doesn't know what to do."	"Are you trying to tell me that this is really happening to you? Does your grandfather beat you?"	"It's important for your friend to talk to someone who will try to help. Tell her that I'll be available if she wants to come and talk to me. It would be difficult for her to deal with these things by herself. There are other children who have gone through the same thing as your friend, and talking to someone is the first step in trying to get some help.

e. Third Party Disclosure - Child telling about abuse that is happening to someone else

"I know someone who is being abused".

Child's Third Party Disclosure	Leading Response (wrong)	Non-Leading Response (right)
"My friend and I were at a sleep-over, and we were telling secrets. He told me that his uncle has been abusing him since he was four. He says that it has stopped now."	"Is this your friend Jimmy who lives with his uncle Fred?"	"Do you want to tell me your friend's name and anything that he said about this? Your friend trusts you and so he has told you about this. I'm glad that you trust me as well".

If possible, get the name of the child involved and report to a child protection social worker immediately. Don't try to get more details about what happened or to talk to the child who was named.

11. Questions and Answers

I have recently received a couple of 'family picture' drawings from a child, in which one person is always scribbled over and has both hands missing. This is unusual for this child. What should I do?

If you have reason to believe the child is being abused, report your concerns to a child protection social worker. If you need a little more information, ask the child to tell you about the pictures.

A student disclosed that a neighbour had abused him. Since the abuser was not his parent, I called and told them what the child said. Was this wrong?

Your first responsibility is to report the matter to a child protection social worker. It's their role to inform the parents of the abused child. This prevents any interference with the investigation. In this case, the parents might become very angry and confront the abuser who could then destroy evidence or make up alibis.

A child in my class made a disclosure of abuse to me. Can I remain with her for support during her interview with the child protection social worker?

If a child asks you to go with them to the interview, you may. Children are encouraged to take a support person with them. The support person is there to help reduce the child's anxiety and to make sure they understand what is happening and what is being said. The support person may not take notes or participate in interviewing the child. (Anything written during the interview could be subpoenaed and provided to the lawyer defending the alleged abuser.)

If a child is in the care of the Ministry for Children and Families, the child protection social worker can veto the child's choice of support person when they feel it is not in the best interests of the child. A support person may be subpoenaed as a witness if the case goes to court.

Appendix F

Guidelines
for Hospitals

GUIDELINES FOR HOSPITALS

Preamble

The following guidelines are intended to provide a guide for hospitals and their personnel, but it is emphasized that responsibility for making a report rests with the person who has reason to believe a child has been or is likely to be abused or neglected or needs protection.

In a hospital environment, a coordinated system is needed for reporting, because of the number of individuals likely to be involved in the care and protection of the child. It is the legal responsibility of the individual having knowledge of possible child abuse or neglect or protection needs to ensure that it is reported to the appropriate child protection social worker. This legal responsibility over-rides professional obligations of confidentiality to the patient, family, employer or other third party.

Hospitals' Accountability:

- identification - the child may be an inpatient, emergency patient or ambulatory care patient;

- diagnosis and documentation;

- provision of a safe environment while medical investigation and assessment is taking place;

- development of a management plan in consultation with a child protection social worker from the Ministry for Children and Families; and,

- follow-up and review.

In addition the hospital, together with its medical staff or SCAN (suspected child abuse and neglect) team, can provide a comprehensive consultative service to the Ministry for Children and Families, particularly where medical and psychiatric issues are of importance in the management of the abused child.

Protocol

Each hospital must develop a protocol for the identification, assessment and management of abused children. It is recognized that not all hospitals will have the full range of resources necessary for complete management and assessment of child abuse cases and that, in some instances, referral to a larger and more comprehensive centre is advisable.

Hospital protocols should include:

- administrative and board responsibility;

- medical staff roles and responsibilities;

- patient care staff roles and responsibilities (e.g. nursing, social work, physio and occupational therapy, child life, psychology, nutrition, housekeeping);

- a hospital mechanism for reporting to the Ministry for Children and Families and ensuring compliance in reporting by hospital staff;

- procedures which support investigations by child protection social workers and law enforcement agencies.

It is emphasized that the statutory responsibility for the protection of children rests with the Ministry for Children and Families, and responsibility for legal investigation rests with the police. The hospital and medical staff have a responsibility for the medical care and management of the child, and to cooperate with the Ministry for Children and Families and the police, but it is not their role to perform legal investigations or to obtain disclosure statements, etc. A partial exception would occur in a case where it is mutually agreed by all concerned that it is in the best interests of the child to conduct a joint meeting rather than to subject the child to repeated interviews.

The protocol will include formal mechanisms for handling cases of actual and suspected child abuse or neglect through:

- the designation of an individual or group of individuals as the responsible agent for dealing with such cases;

- the development and implementation of procedures to be followed by hospital personnel; and,

- the development and maintenance of clear lines of communication and responsibility with the other agencies involved, both in the immediate community, and with referral institutions elsewhere.

The extent to which each hospital can meet the needs for diagnosis and treatment of the child will vary in accordance with resources, particularly human resources available to assist hospitals in determining the level in their individual circumstances. These guidelines are divided into four levels:

Level 1:   Small community hospitals with no social worker on staff.

Level 2:   Hospitals with at least one social worker.

Level 3:   Hospitals with social workers and two or more pediatricians (e.g. those hospitals with organized pediatric units and departments).

Level 4:   Large referral hospitals with an array of child health services, such as specialized child social workers and at least one pediatrician with a special interest in child abuse cases.

Some hospitals will not fit neatly into any of the above categories, and so should choose those elements which suit their circumstances.

Team Composition

Level 1:

- A responsible individual, preferably a health professional such as a nurse, who has some experience in child health care and a knowledge of the local community agencies, who would be involved in the investigation and management of (suspected) child abuse cases.

- A physician should be involved in the setting up of policies and procedures and in the handling of cases.

- The attending physician or family physician of the child should be a member of the team when an individual case is being dealt with.

- A representative of the local office of the Ministry for Children and Families should also be a member, wherever possible, and/or a police officer or an RCMP officer.

Level 2:

- A member of the social work department.

- A member of the medical staff.

- The head nurse of the pediatric unit or a nurse with equivalent authority and/or experience.

- The attending physician and/or the family physician of the child.

- A representative of the local office of the Ministry for Children and Families should also be a member wherever possible and/or a police officer or an RCMP officer.

Levels 3 and 4:

- A member of the social work department responsible for the pediatric unit.

- A member of the pediatric unit of the medical staff.

- The attending physician and/or family physician of the child.

- The head nurse of the pediatric unit.

- A representative of the local office of the Ministry for Children and Families and/or a police officer or RCMP officer.

Additional members may be added to the team as appropriate (e.g. the local community health nurse, or a member of the local police force/RCMP). Members of the team should, where possible, keep a colleague well informed of the work of the team in order that there may be a reasonable alternate available when the team member is not available.

Purpose of the Team

- To ensure the provision of appropriate services to children and families through clinical diagnosis and case management. In the case of Level 1 and 2 institutions, the provision of such care will often involve the referral or transfer of the child to a higher level facility with more specialized services. In the case of Level 3 and 4 facilities, this will include the acceptance of referrals from smaller institutions and the provision of advice on the management cases.

- To provide consultation/support to other professionals who are not specialized in handling cases of suspected child abuse and/or neglect. Again, in the case of Level 1 and 2 institutions, such advice and support is often likely to be by means of referral procedures rather than specialized clinical assistance and support.

- To provide assistance to Ministry for Children and Families staff who are responsible for actions taken under the *Child, Family and Community Service Act*.

- To identify gaps in services and to participate in long-term planning for child abuse services and cooperation with other community agencies. In cases where the physician of the abused child is also the physician of the (suspected) abuser, the doctor will have to consider where his/her primary duty lies. The abuser will also require support, and it may be appropriate for the doctor to stay with the child abuse team that is dealing with the case, passing the duties of attending physician over to a colleague, and acting solely as the physician of the abuser.

Functions of the Team

- To develop a plan for the hospital with policies and procedures for the handling of suspected or actual cases of child abuse and/or neglect, updating this as necessary.

- To develop and maintain, with local Ministry for Children and Families officials, a community-wide plan for the management of cases.

- To provide education and consultation to physicians, hospital staff and the community.

- To ensure that cases identified in the hospital are reported to the local Ministry for Children and Families office.

The following functions will be carried out to some degree by teams in all levels of institutions, but in full only by Levels 3 and 4:

- To gather and collate data needed to make a medical assessment.

- To meet regularly to discuss referred cases with appropriate hospital and community personnel.

- To formulate plans with other agencies for family treatment.

- To provide consultation and support for those preparing for court hearings.

- To help support the family through the diagnostic/assessment process.

In Level 1, 2 and 3, it is likely that the team or one of its members may be designated as spokesperson for the hospital when questions are raised by the public or the media concerning a specific case. In Level 4 facilities, there may well be a public relations office to handle this aspect.

Relationships With Other Organizations

It is emphasized that the purpose of the team is not to replace or duplicate the work of the RCMP or the Ministry for Children and Families. Its function in fulfilling the hospital's responsibilities in cases of child abuse can be greatly strengthened by a well coordinated and smooth working relationship between the various parties involved. Such a system is also likely to provide quicker and more effective treatment and care for the child and the family.

In cooperating with these agencies, questions often arise concerning confidentiality and liability. As clearly stated in the *Child, Family and Community Service Act*, the notification of known or suspected cases of child abuse is a legal requirement which over-rides the usual duty of confidentiality between a health professional and a patient. It follows that information known about the child and relevant to the case can also be released to the investigating agencies, and indeed, should be provided on request, without fear of liability. Such sharing of information is not only helpful in establishing the basis of evidence for a charge of child abuse, but can save the child the stress of multiple interviews. It may be noted that the flow of information in the hospital's child abuse team is not one-way, and that the non-hospital members, such as the police officer, social worker or community health nurse, may often be able to provide staff with facts which make interpretation of the clinical evidence more obvious, or may help in focusing the direction of diagnosis and treatment.

Roles and Responsibility of Team Members

Ministry for Children and Families

- To represent the ministry in broad terms, e.g. statutory regulations, services available, etc., and to liaise between the hospital and the local ministry office.

- To help in the development of plans for useful and realistic community services.

Nursing

- To foster awareness among the nursing staff, particularly in the emergency and pediatric departments, of the signs of possible child abuse in order that detection of cases is made as early as possible.

- To maintain close communication with the social worker and the physician in the handling of a case.

- To ensure that there is careful and complete recording of physical injuries and changes in such injuries (or their appearance) while a patient is in the hospital, whether as an inpatient or an outpatient.

- To ensure close observation and documentation of the child's behaviour with staff, parents and visitors, and the parents' attitude towards the child and each other.

Physicians

- To act as liaison between the team and other medical staff members, both in the development of protocols and in the handling of individual cases.

- To provide (if appropriately trained and experienced) a second opinion on particular cases.

Physicians who may be involved in the diagnosis, treatment and care of abused children must be fully familiar with *Indicators of Possible Abuse or Neglect: The Role of the Physician in Incidents of Child Abuse and Sexual Abuse of Children - Protocol for Communication between Staff of the Ministry for Children and Families and Physicians.*

Social Worker

In outlining these functions, the responsibilities that could reasonably be expected of hospital members of teams in Level 1 facilities are asterisked (*).

- To prepare psycho-social assessment of family functioning and home safety as soon as possible after the admission of a suspected or actual case to emergency or pediatrics.

- To gather relevant information from social and public health agencies regarding a child and family (*in conjunction with the MCF representative).

- To collate the information gathered with the observations of doctors and nurses (*).

- To notify the family doctor and, in conjunction with him/her, determine the need for further discussions with the team.

- To communicate and maintain contact with community resources (*).

- To maintain a registry on all identified/suspected cases of child abuse or neglect.

- To advise the local office of the Ministry for Children and Families (*).

- To coordinate the setting up of community case conferences (*).

- To maintain an "at risk" file on children under 16 who present in the emergency department or pediatrics (*).

All team members are expected to contribute their skills and knowledge in case management and in the education of other professionals and the public.

Specific Departments

Some departments are more likely to be involved in the investigation and/or treatment of child abuse cases than others. Apart from the pediatric unit, these include the emergency department, psychiatric and psychological services, and the laboratory. In all departments, **documentation** is of the utmost importance, since such evidence is often crucial in establishing proof of abuse in the courts.

Emergency Department

It is in the emergency department that many cases of child abuse are first seen. The signs and symptoms are covered in detail in the *Handbook - Part Two*. The staff of the emergency department are best placed to observe the reactions of the child and the accompanying adult in the acute situation, often when the abuse has been freshly committed. For example, it is important to interview the child alone and with the accompanying adult(s), and to observe the interactions and the variation in the versions of events.

While some parents are upset to the point of partial incoherence by an injury to their child, this is usually easily distinguished from the vagueness and/or aggression by the child abuser.

Aside from the opportunity to observe the adult and the child (and their interaction) first- hand, the staff are also well placed to notice a pattern of visits to the department which may indicate non-accidental causes of injury. Such patterns of repeat visits, while not diagnostic, should create a heightened index of suspicion, and hence, a more scrupulous search for specific signs and behaviour. In regions where there is only one emergency department, the outpatient/emergency record itself will show the pattern of visits. In places where more than one source of hospital care is available, the pattern of utilization will require specific inquiry, and possibly follow-up and investigation if the history is unclear or suspicious. Inter-hospital cooperation in selected cases is encouraged.

Documentation in the emergency department is of particular importance in clearly establishing the grounds upon which the suspicion of abuse was based, and the evidence gathered at a time when the abuse was 'fresh'. This is particularly important in cases of sexual abuse. Some hospitals will have their own kits to handle the collection of specimens, etc. Those that do not may be able to obtain a Sexual Assault Kit from the local detachment of the RCMP. This kit is intended for use only in cases of recent sexual assault, and is very comprehensive. Hospitals without their own kit and located in areas not served by a detachment of the RCMP should create their own kit. Assistance in this is obtainable from larger hospitals with their own sexual assault/rape kits.

The taking of (colour) photographs in these cases is of great assistance if the case goes to court. Lay judges and juries have difficulty understanding medical terminology, and the use of photographs is encouraged.

In a busy emergency room, a dedicated child abuse assessment team may be better able to fulfill the above functions.

Psychiatric and Psychological Services

Children who have been subjected to mild forms of physical abuse, or to non-physical abuse/neglect, are not likely to be detected through visits to the emergency department for physical examination. They are more likely to present with behavioural or psychological problems, and hence, first come to the attention of a hospital program through the above services. Staff in these departments should have a high index of suspicion of abuse as a possible cause of signs and symptoms. As in the case of the emergency department, great importance is attached to completing an accurate documentation in the child's health record.

Aside from this diagnostic function, staff will be involved in the care and therapy of children who have been abused. As psychological and psychiatric serves are only likely to be available in larger institutions, such centres must be prepared to accept referrals from smaller institutions and to provide help in the form of education and training, as well as consultation to staff from smaller centres.

Laboratory Services

In seeking to prove a charge of child abuse/neglect, the chain of evidence which uses laboratory results is vulnerable to allegations of mislabelled specimens and improper procedures being used. The laboratory services should draw up, in consultation with other relevant departments, strict protocols to be followed in the collection, labelling and handling of specimens collected from children in which the possibility of abuse is being considered. This is particularly important in the case of specimens which need to be sent to laboratories outside the hospital of analysis, e.g. forensic studies. Laboratory staff should develop with the referral laboratories a clear record of the specimens, and how they were transported. Help in developing such protocols should be available from the staff of the referral laboratories and the RCMP/police who are familiar with this type of case. Laboratory staff should be closely involved in the development of the hospital's Sexual Assault Kit (see the section on the emergency department).

Liability and Confidentiality

Liability

Cooperating with outside agencies, especially in situations where legal action is likely to be involved, often raises questions of the liability of hospital staff, and of the legal status of hospital information, i.e. confidentiality issues. The requirement to report suspected child abuse/neglect and/or protection needs is absolute (see page 1) and, in most circumstances, the identity of the reporter will not be revealed without consent unless the child protection social worker is required to give the reporter's name for the purposes of a court hearing.

Other areas where liability is often considered include the taking of blood and other specimens, either from the child or from the person suspected or known to have committed the abuse. In these situations, the normal requirements to obtain consent, either from the individual or, if a child, from the parent or guardian, apply. Under such circumstances, i.e. a valid consent has been obtained, the staff member is safe from charges of assault.

Confidentiality

The issue of the confidentiality of the hospital's health records is also sometimes raised as a reason for not cooperating to the fullest extent in sharing information with the RCMP/police. As discussed in the section on relationships with other organizations, information concerning the abused patient may safely be given to the agencies charged with investigating the case - Ministry for Children and Families and the RCMP/police - provided, of course, that it relates to the abuse. Indeed, release of such information on request is a requirement.

General

The attention of all team members is directed to the *B.C. Handbook for Action on Child Abuse and Neglect*, particularly the section on recognizing indicators of possible abuse and neglect. The handbook is of no value if cases are not recognized and reported.

Appendix G

Protocol for Communication Between Staff of Ministry for Children and Families and Physicians

PROTOCOL FOR COMMUNICATION BETWEEN STAFF OF MINISTRY FOR CHILDREN AND FAMILIES AND PHYSICIANS

The purpose of this protocol is to clearly establish guidelines for information sharing between the Ministry for Children and Families and private physicians in order to ensure the safety and well-being of children.

When a physician has reason to believe that a child needs protection

Obligation of Physicians

Physicians are required by law to report situations which indicate that a child may need protection to the Ministry for Children and Families (for more detail see College of Physicians and Surgeons Child Abuse and Neglect Guidelines). The duty to report overrides the confidential requirements of the physician-patient relationship to the extent required to provide the information necessary to fulfill the reporting obligation. This information is likely to include:

- the physician's name, address and telephone number;

- the full name, age, birth date, sex and address of the child;

- the full names and address of the parents, if known;

- if known, the full name and address of the alleged "offender" and any other information that may assist in locating or identifying that person; full details of the incident or situation precipitating the report;

- family history as it relates to the child's risk for abuse/neglect.

When a physician refers a patient to the Ministry for Children and Families for voluntary support services (e.g. homemaker, child care) the information required for a report, as outlined above, is not required.

Obligations of Ministry for Children and Families

On receiving a report from a physician, the Ministry for Children and Families assesses the information in the report and may:

- offer support services to the child and family;

- refer the child and family to a community agency;
- investigate the child's need for protection; or

- take the necessary action to ensure the child's protection.

(*Child, Family & Community Service Act*, Section 16)

The child protection social worker must not disclose information to others that will identify who made the initial report unless that person consents. After the investigation is complete, the Ministry for Children and Families will report the findings to the person who made the initial report.

Ongoing Sharing of Information

Responsibilities of Physicians

New incident indicators
Following an initial report to the Ministry for Children and Families, physicians must report any new incidents indicating abuse or neglect has occurred or that the original situation is not resolved or indicates the child is in need of protection.

Protocol for Communication - June 16, 1997

Information required by the Ministry for Children and Families for the purposes of a child protection investigation after a report has been received.
During the investigation, staff of the Ministry for Children and Families may request, from a physician, full details or a written report related to the report of a child in need of protection. Physicians may release that information:

(a) with the patient's written consent, or

(b) pursuant to a court order under Section 65 of the *Child, Family and Community Service Act*, or

(c) in situations in which "maintenance of confidentiality would result in a significant risk or substantial harm to others or to the patient if the patient is incompetent." (CMA Code of Ethics, Section 22).

Information required for the purposes of providing health services
For the purposes of providing ongoing health services in the course of developing or implementing a health treatment plan, the physician will provide any information necessary for the child's health and well-being

(e.g. required medication and treatment for a child with diabetes if that child is in a temporary care situation). This includes all children in care, children remanded with consent and children under supervision order if this is a condition of the order.

Responsibilities of the Ministry for Children and Families

Information required by the Ministry for Children and Families for the purposes of a child protection investigation
Ministry for Children and Families social workers may request full details or a written report from physicians related to the report of a child in need of protection. Physicians will only release that information with the patient's consent, by court order, or in circumstances which fall under Section 22 of the CMA Code of Ethics (see (c) above). Unlike hospitals, private physicians are not public bodies and, therefore, are not covered by the *Freedom of Information and Protection of Privacy Act*. Section 96 of the *Child, Family and Community Service Act* does not apply to records of private physicians.

If the physician refuses the request (i.e. the patients will not consent to the release of the information), the social worker may apply to the court to obtain the information under Section 65 of the *Child, Family and Community Service Act*.

Responsibilities of both Ministry for Children and Families Social Workers and Physicians

1) It is recognized that comprehensive, adequate records are kept by both Ministry for Children and Families staff and physicians.

2) If either social workers or physicians discover that information disclosed to or obtained from the other is inaccurate, they must inform the other about the inaccuracy.

This document has been reviewed and approved by:

_____   _____
Director   Executive Committee
Child, Family and   College of Physicians and
Community Services   Surgeons
Ministry for Children and Families

July 31, 1997

Appendix H

GLOSSARY

GLOSSARY

The following definitions will be of use to those who respond to child abuse and neglect.

aboriginal child
A child who:

- is registered under the *Indian Act* (federal);

- has a biological parent who is registered under the *Indian Act* (federal);

- is under 12 years of age and has a biological parent who is of aboriginal ancestry and considers himself or herself to be aboriginal;

- is 12 years of age or over, of aboriginal ancestry and considers himself of herself to be aboriginal.

accused
A person charged with a criminal offence.

advocacy
An action in support of others, to try to ensure that their needs are met and/or their rights respected. It includes assisting children and families, or acting on their behalf, to obtain information, communicate their view and be heard.

child
A person under 19 years of age.

child in care
A child who is in the custody, care or guardianship of the director under the *Child, Family and Community Service Act* or the director under the *Adoption Act*.

child neglect
Child neglect involves an act of omission on the part of the parent or guardian that results or is likely to result in physical harm to the child. It generally refers to situations in which a child has been, or is likely to be physically harmed through action or inaction by those responsible for care of the child. This may include failure to provide food, shelter, basic health care or supervision and, protection from risks, to the extent that the child's physical health, development or safety is harmed or likely to be harmed. This also includes failure to thrive. Not always intentional, neglect may be a result of insufficient resources or other factors beyond a person's control.

child protection

A specialized child welfare service legally responsible for investigating suspected cases of child abuse and neglect and for intervening to protect the child in substantiated cases. Child protection services are child-centred, focusing on health, safety and best interests of the child while providing or arranging for services which address the situations giving rise to a child's need for protection.

child protection social worker

A person who has been delegated with any or all of the relevant powers, duties or functions of a director under the *Child, Family and Community Service Act.*

child with capacity

Generally refers to a child who is able to understand information and make decisions about his or her requirements. Capacity is often assessed by considering:

- the child's age;

- the child's developmental level and maturity;

- the nature and complexity of the information and the decision required;

- the child's ability to understand and evaluate the consequences of the decisions.

These considerations are strongly linked with each other and must be considered together.

collaboration

Collaboration occurs when two or more individuals jointly develop and/or agree to a set of common goals to guide the actions. They share responsibility for using the expertise of each collaborator to address the child's needs and to promote the child's best interests.

community

A geographic place (a community of place), or a group of people who share a common interest (a community of interest). Both interpretations are used in the handbook.

criminal offence

An offence under the *Criminal Code of Canada* and includes an offence under the *Young Offender's Act.*

director

A person designated by the Minister for Children and Families under the *Child, Family and Community Service Act*. The director may delegate any or all of the director's powers, duties and responsibilities under the act.

emotional abuse

Emotional abuse is the most difficult type of abuse to define and recognize. It may range from habitual humiliation of the child to withholding life-sustaining nurturing. It can include acts or omissions by those responsible for the care of a child or others in contact with a child, which are likely to have serious, negative emotional impacts. Emotional abuse may occur separately from, or along with, other forms of abuse and neglect.

Emotional abuse can include a pattern of:

- scapegoating;

- rejection;

- verbal attacks on the child;

- threats;

- insults; or

- humiliation.

emotional harm

When emotional abuse is persistent and chronic, this can result in emotional damage to the child. A child is defined by the *Child, Family and Community Service Act* as emotionally harmed if they demonstrate severe:

- anxiety;

- depression;

- withdrawal; or

- self-destructive or aggressive behaviour.

failure to thrive

A serious medical condition most often seen in children under one year of age. A failure-to-thrive child's height, weight, and motor development fall significantly short of the average growth rates of normal children. In about 10% of failure-to-thrive children, there is an organic cause such as serious heart, kidney or intestinal disease, a genetic error of metabolism or brain damage. All other cases are a result of a disturbed parent-child relationship with severe physical and emotional neglect of the child.

maltreatment

Actions that are abusive, neglectful or otherwise threatening to a child's welfare. Frequently used as a general term for child abuse and neglect.

offender

A person who has been convicted of a criminal offence.

organized abuse

This generally refers to abuse of more than one person by one or more perpetrators. Examples include child pornography rings, organized sexual exploitation of children, and multi-victim abuse. Ritual abuse is a highly sophisticated form of organized abuse involving a combination of severe emotional, physical and sexual abuse where control may also be gained through the use of torture, forced perpetration, mind control techniques and religious symbolism. It is generally linked to criminal activities, including child pornography and drug dealing.

parent

The mother of a child, the father of a child, a person to whom custody of a child has been granted by a court of competent jurisdiction or by an agreement, or a person with whom a child resides and who stands in the place of the child's parent. This includes a child's guardian. It does not include the director under the *Child, Family and Community Service Act.*

physical abuse

Physical abuse is a deliberate, non-accidental physical assault or action by an adult or significantly older or more powerful child that results or is likely to result in physical harm to a child. It includes the use of unreasonable force to discipline a child or to prevent a child from harming him/herself or others The injuries sustained by the child may vary in severity and range from minor bruising, burns, welts or bite marks to major fractures of the bones or skull, and in its most extreme form, the death of a child.

probation officer

A person appointed under the *Corrections Act* who is responsible for carrying out the duties and responsibilities established under Section 5 of that act and under Section 721 of the *Criminal Code*, and includes a youth worker defined in the *Young Offender's Act* (federal).

public body

Under the *Freedom of Information and Protection of Privacy Act*, are defined to include:

- provincial government ministries;

- crown corporations;

- municipalities;

- educational bodies; and

- health care bodies.

removal

When a child is taken into the care of the director under the *Child, Family and Community Service Act*.

risk assessment

Involves using specialized instruments to evaluate the likelihood that a parent will harm a child in the near future. The product of a risk assessment is an educated prediction concerning the likelihood that a child will need protection. It is based on a careful examination of the factors identified through research as the most likely related to re-occurrence.

service provider

Any person who works directly with children and/or families. This includes:

- those who are directly employed by the government;

- those who volunteer their services;

- those who are employed by agencies that are funded under a contractual agreement with government;

- all professionals who may be publicly funded (e.g., police, educators, post secondary staff, physicians, nurses).

sexual abuse

Sexual abuse generally means any sexual use of a child by an adult or a significantly older or more powerful child. There are many criminal offences related to sexual activity involving children. The Criminal Code prohibits:

- any sexual activity between an adult and a child under the age of 14 – a child under 14 is incapable in law of consenting to sexual activity (s. 150.1 of the Criminal Code). The criminal law recognizes that consensual "peer sex" is not an offence in the following situation: if one child is between 12 and 14 years and the other is 12 years or more but under the age of 16, less than two years older, and not in a position of trust or authority to the other.

- any sexual activity between an adult in a position of trust or authority towards a child between the ages of 14 and 18 years

- any sexual activity without the consent of a child of any age. (Depending on the activity, non-consensual sexual activity may constitute the criminal offence of sexual assault.)

- use of children in prostitution and pornography.

The Ministry for Children and Families states that sexual abuse is any behaviour of a sexual nature toward a child, including one or more of the following:

- touching or invitation to touch for sexual purposes, or intercourse (vaginal or anal)

- menacing or threatening sexual acts, obscene gestures, obscene communications or stalking

- sexual references to the child's body or behaviour by words or gestures

- requests that the child expose their body for sexual purposes
- deliberate exposure of the child to sexual activity or material.

The Ministry for Children and Families states sexual exploitation includes permitting, encouraging or requiring a child to engage in:

- conduct of a sexual nature for the stimulation, gratification, profit or self-interest of another person who is in a position of trust or authority, or with whom the child is in a relationship of dependency

- prostitution

- production of material of a pornographic nature.

Sexual aspects of organized or ritual abuse should be considered a form of sexual exploitation.

suspect

A person suspected of having committed a criminal offence.

take charge

To take charge of a child means to take physical control of a child for a limited period of time. The *Child, Family and Community Service Act* authorizes a director or a police officer to take charge of a child under certain circumstances, such as when a child is in immediate danger.

The Slow, Tired and Easy Railroad

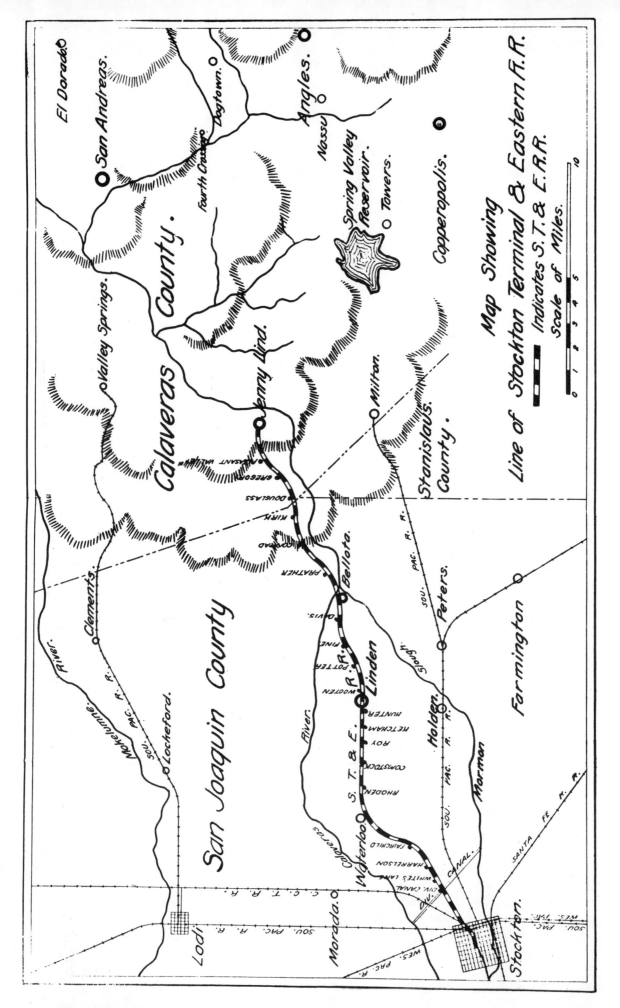

Map of the S.T. & E. route at a time when they still planned to extend the tracks from Bellota to Jenny Lind.

The
Slow, Tired and Easy Railroad

The Story of the
Stockton Terminal & Eastern Railroad
and Its Rough Roadbed to Success

by
OLIVE DAVIS

COMMISSIONED BY
THE STOCKTON TERMINAL AND EASTERN RAILROAD

Fresno   Valley Publishers   1976

International Standard Book No. 0-913548-36-7

Library of Congress Number 76-40632

Manufactured in the United States of America

DEDICATION
to
Warren L. Davis, without whom
I would not have written this book.

PREFACE

People of the San Joaquin Valley know of the Stockton Terminal and Eastern Railroad, but few are aware of the S.T. & E.'s distinctive contribution to the development of our great Central Valley.

In the year 1908, the S.T. & E. was founded. The year 1910 saw the beginning of what was to become popularly known as the "Slow, Tired and Easy Railroad." As in many of the Central Valley's success stories, the S.T. & E. has, over the years, incorporated the talents of many notable and prominent businessmen of Northern California, men who helped Stockton grow.

I have had the pleasure of knowing Thomas K. Beard, President of the Stockton Terminal and Eastern Railroad, for many years. Under his guidance, the railroad has developed a central distribution center and warehousing facility not to be matched on the West Coast. We congratulate Tom Beard and his fine company for their outstanding contribution to the community.

I warmly commend Mrs. Olive Davis for her effective efforts to provide a charming, yet factual chronicle of an organization that has played a meaningful part in the Central Valley's colorful past, and which is a proud account of our progressive present.

We will be forever grateful.

Robert M. Eberhardt, President
Bank of Stockton

INTRODUCTION

The Stockton Terminal & Eastern Railroad had brought great hope to the small farming community of Linden, California in 1910, but the town had grown slowly and in the 1950's had reached its peak with a population of less than 1,000. During the late 60's the town was in difficulty, as the business district was dying. There was much self examination by the residents; their concern and that of others focused attention on the town.

Although the S.T. & E. Railroad did not depend on the area any more the company officials were concerned about the town at the end of their line. At a town meeting Thomas K. Beard, president of the railroad, brought forth many constructive ideas for revitalizing the business district and offered the assistance of the railroad company.

Thinking of publishing a short history of the S.T. & E. Railroad to be sold to tourists, I approached Mr. Beard. He agreed it was a good idea but said, "If we are going to do it, let's do it all the way."

He was interested in a complete history of the road, and commissioned me to do it, for which I will be forever grateful. After I got into the project I found that a history of the road had never been compiled. I had to deal with basic materials—newspapers, documents, interviews and company records. It took every source to compile the story because most of the men involved with the early development of the road are dead. Even those who are left were too young at the time to know much of the company's business dealings. There were, however, many people who loaned pictures, letters and documents to help complete this history.

I must give full credit to Tom Beard who made this project possible. A special thanks to Gerald M. Best for his special assistance in helping me understand and fathom the mystery of railroad locomotives. A special thanks also to R. M. Eberhardt who was kind enough to write the Preface.

Thanks must also go to Mrs. Myrtle Seymour, Mr. and Mrs. Lloyd Potter, Mrs. Joseph Dietrich II, Miss Helene Dietrich, Joseph Dietrich III, Mr. and Mrs. Stanley Crawford, John Hewitt, Charles Widdows, Glen Kennedy, Horace Spencer, Tom Evans, Richard Cowan, Raymond Hillman, Miss Bethel Gurnsey, Miss Irene McCall, Don Watson, Leonard Covello, Mrs. Faye Cady, Guy Dunscomb, Mrs. Estella Staples, Mrs. Florence Grant, Mrs. Lois Darrah, Mrs. Muriel Saunby, Miss Lorinda Navone, Mrs. Bonnie Stockman, Leonard Hardaway, Mrs. Leah Bowen, Chet Packard, Dave Smith, Jack Melton, Dr. R. Coke Wood, and Don Smith and Dr. Ronald Limbaugh.

A special thanks is also due the staff members of: Stockton Library, University of Pacific Library, Pioneer Museum and Haggin Galleries, Los Angeles Parks and Recreation Department, Oregon Historical Society, California Department of State, California Public Utilities Commission, San Joaquin County Recorder's Office, San Joaquin County Law Library, San Joaquin County Clerk's Office, Stockton Chamber of Commerce, Linden Fire Department, Linden branch of the San Joaquin County Library and the Bank of Stockton.

TABLE OF CONTENTS

CHAPTER I

ORGANIZATION

"Like a story from the pages of fiction reads the history of the new Waterloo-Linden-Jenny Lind road. Most railroads are built by men of large capital, but working men are supplying, from their small earnings, the money with which to finance the project."

These words appeared on the front page of a Stockton, California newspaper on September 5, 1910. In spite of being caught up by the excitement of the official opening of the short line, Stockton Terminal and Eastern Railroad, the reporter had hit the key to the enterprise. Most of those involved were not men of money, but men who had dreams of sharing in the riches of the times, men of vision who believed in the area, and just plain dreamers.

The Stockton Terminal and Eastern Railroad, comprised of approximately 13 miles of mainline track, runs from Stockton, located in the rich agricultural interior of California, along the Calaveras River in an east north-easterly direction to the small farming community of Linden. Today this short line road is a modern thriving business with the major portion of its activity carried on within four miles of its western terminal in Stockton.

The history of the road is one of periods of feast and famine, reflected by the nicknames given it by local "wags." These names have been based on the initials, S.T.& E. The first was the Stop, Talk and Eat Railroad. This came from the grand celebration and barbecue held in Linden during the summer of 1910, when the tracks reached the town. The next name seems to have been the Stop Talking and Eat Railroad. This probably originated during the period when disillusion had set in and there was a need for less talking and more action. Then for a number of years it was known as the Slow, Tired and Easy Railroad. This was started in ridicule, but eventually was nurtured into a name of endearment. The present name, Strong, Tenacious and Energetic, is new and not yet widely used, but reflects the energy of

the company that in sixteen years, between 1958 and 1974, multiplied its business more than six times over. But let us return to the early dreams and even before.

Stockton was an old railroad town by the beginning of the twentieth century. The Stockton Copperopolis Railroad had been organized in 1865 and was followed by other short line roads and the Central Pacific or Southern Pacific and the Santa Fe transcontinental railroads.

The San Joaquin River had long offered convenient and comfortable, year around transportation to San Francisco from Stockton but the roads out of Stockton to the areas north, east and south were another story. In the summer great plumes of dust choked man and beast alike. In the winter wagons or the "newfangled" automobiles stuck fast in the mud, which was notorious enough to give the town the nickname of Mudville by early settlers. As late as 1907 the Stockton Chamber of Commerce president, D. A. Guernsey deplored road conditions and said the "wretched condition of the county roads which span the adobe district interferes materially with the work of the promotion and turns many investors and homeseekers to other fields."

It is understandable that many men believed another railroad would be the answer to their needs. It was in this climate that Thomas Stroup envisioned a railroad from Stockton eastward through a highly productive agricultural area and into the foothills. He could see this road providing passenger service to Stockton, hauling crops to market, and tapping rich gravel and mineral deposits further east.

Stroup endeavored to call the attention of investors to the area and many capitalists investigated the project, but none saw it as he did. Always fearful that publicity might ruin his plans, he swore newsmen to secrecy. If reporters sought him out he would stall them.

Consequently newsmen avoided him on the oc-

A hunting or fishing party photographed in 1908 just north of Fanning Hall, behind the barley mill in Linden. At the far right is W. H. Newell, the engineer who secured most of the rights of way for the S.T. & E. R.R. Shown from left to right are Walter Guernsey, Alva Cady, Leon Delmas, Albert Davis, Ed Davis, Charlie Harrison, Charles Klinger, Joe Ross, Henry Grimsley and Newell. (Faye Cady collection)

casions when word leaked that investors were in town. If they printed a story, Stroup would admonish them. "Where in the dickens did you get that story? Didn't I tell you to see me before printing anything about that railroad?"

Stroup had apparently conceived the idea for the railroad up the Calaveras River around 1904. At about the same time, J. Egbert Adams was working at Cooperstown, a jack rabbit station on the Sierra Railway. Bert, as he was known to his friends, was earning $75 a month for the varied jobs of station operator, agent, and general roustabout, but still found time to think, dream and scheme. Now in his mid-thirties, he had come west as a boy of 17 to seek his fortune, arriving in Stockton in 1888. For several years he had earned a living driving a bakery wagon for Ezra Butters' Family Bakery. Studying telegraphy in his spare time, Adams finally landed a job with the Sierra Railway, a short line road to the southeast in Stanislaus and Tuolumne Counties.

Sometime around 1905 Adams approached W. H. Newell, the civil engineer for the Sierra Railroad. Newell had acquired an outstanding reputation for the work he had done on a Mexican road even before he designed the famous switch backs on the Angels Camp branch of the Sierra Railway. Adams enticed him with his dream.

"Let's build a railroad ourselves," said Adams.

"Where?" asked Newell.

"Oh, anywhere. Wherever there is a good field."

"Where will we get the money?"

"We'll organize a stock company and sell stock at a dollar a share."

Obviously Adams had been studying finances as well as telegraphy. Together he and Newell looked over several possibilities and did some figuring on a number of them. Finally Stroup heard of their interest and urged them to examine the territory along the Calaveras River, east of Stockton. The pair agreed this was the place they would work and dropped all other plans. No doubt Adams was intrigued at the idea of returning to Stockton as a railroad man, but Newell might not have been so easily persuaded if he had not had a change of plans after the San Francisco earthquake and fire in 1906. He had been supervising the construction of the Yosemite branch line of the Sierra Railway when the catastrophe struck. He was in San Francisco the day of the earthquake and had received approval for more extensive work on the road, but the quake caused financial losses that made it necessary to stop the project immediately. Because of the financial squeeze on the Sierra Railway, Newell stayed on only long enough to complete the mainline into Tuolumne City. He then turned to the San Joaquin Valley where he did some engineering for the town of Oakdale before proceeding to Stockton to lay out the route for the new railroad along the Calaveras River.

In the meantime Adams had gone to the San Francisco Bay Area and interested others in organizing an investment company. The United Investment Company was formed as an Arizona cor-

Myrtle and Ruth Davis in the family's only means of transportation, with Dexter the horse. This picture was taken in 1907 just before the S.T. & E. R.R. acquired a right of way through the ranch. (Mrs. Myrtle Seymour)

poration under Arizona Territorial law. The papers were signed in Alameda County, California and filed in Arizona, August 17, 1907. The following signatures appear on the incorporation papers: J. E. Adams, R. N. Griffith, P. A. Ayhens, J. A. Nesbitt, C. C. Bacon, A. M. Webster and R. M. Brown. All of the men except Nesbitt and Webster were named directors. Nesbitt was to be a major factor in the railroad in future years but at that time seemed to be taking a back seat. R. N. Griffith must have been named president for he signed papers the next spring increasing the capital stock from $500,000 to $750,000. The investment company immediately opened an office in the Monadnock Building on Market Street in San Francisco.

By the spring of 1908 Newell had determined the route and was securing rights of way, in his own name, from farmers east of Stockton. He convinced most that the railroad would be good for them, but he took a line of least resistance and if a farmer did not want to give, he went to his neighbor to acquire the necessary property.

Papers designating Adams as an agent for the U. I. Co. in California were filed in Arizona on May 18, 1908. His first action under this authority appeared to be securing an option to buy ten acres of land on the Stockton waterfront from the Weber Home Company. The original option was for seven months, given for only one dollar and including a sale price of $60,000 for "properties known as Wood Island." The paper was signed by C. M. Weber, the son of the city's founding father, and Wolf, the company secretary. Adams must have gotten much mileage out of the papers for they gave him additional prestige and would set the trend for most of his future dealings. He had the knack of attracting people of influence and using that influence to his advantage. The document is in the S.T. & E. company files today. It clearly states that the Weber Company wished to extend all the help possible towards the proposed electric road by giving an exclusive option on waterfrontage owned by them.

Adams contacted an attorney, Robert F. Burns of San Francisco, to do the legal work of organizing the railroad, while he set out to sell stock in the U. I. Co. It was not an easy task and did not go well until the day he went aboard a ship at the Mare Island Navy yard near Vallejo. Having strong fraternal connections, he won the confidence of Navy men who were his lodge brothers. He told them of his railroad and they willingly

J.E.Adams, Secretary S.T.& E. R.R.Co.

For and in consideration of the sum of $1.00 receipt of which is hereby acknowledged, The Weber Home Company hereby extends the time limit on option held by you on Wood Island, a property of ours bordering on Stockton Channel, said option bearing date of June 12th 1908, from that date up to and including *Dec 12th* 1909.

Stockton, Cal., *June 2d* 1909

Weber Home Company,

C M Weber President

_____ Secretary.

Weber Home Company,

Incorporated

Agents C. M. Weber Properties

Insurance

25 E. Channel Street

Phone 791 Main

Stockton, Cal. May 19, 1909.

Stockton Terminal & Eastern Railroad Co.
Mr. J.E. Adams, Secretary,
#920 Phelan Bldg.
San Francisco, Cal.

Dear Sir:--

Yours of the 18th, enclosing a $5.00 bill at hand. Mr. Weber is satisfied to extend the option on Wood Island to December 1st, 1909.

I do not know what shape you wish the endorsement to be in . This letter will probably be enough, if you will attach same to the original document. Trusting that you will be successful in the near future, I remain,

Respectfully yours,

Davd Wolf

Sec. Weber Home Company.

An extension on an option on Wood Island, located on the north bank of Stockton Channel. C. M. Weber, who signed the paper, was the son of the founder of Stockton. The option was apparently used to interest influential Stockton people in the project to build the railroad. (S.T. & E. collection)

bought stock. "Pay as you go" was Adams' policy. He was selling the stock at a dollar a share and was willing to take one dollar or a hundred, and the money began to accumulate.

It was after dark on a Saturday evening, October 24, 1908 when a group of men gathered in the office of Dr. M. J. Cogdon in Berkeley. Besides Adams, Newell, Burns and Cogdon, E. F. Davis of Linden, A. A. Grant of Sonora, R. V. Dixon and S. L. Steidley of Oakdale were present.

Burns had been diligently preparing incorporation papers for the Stockton Terminal and Eastern Railroad Company, for it had already been determined that the capital stock would be valued at $600,000. This was to be divided into 6,000 shares at a par value of $100 each. Burns called the meeting to order and passed a subscription paper among the men. Each signed up for one share or $100, except Adams, to whom would go 292 shares at $29,200. It was agreed that the nine men present would constitute the Board of Directors.

Four days later, on October 28, 1908, papers for the Stockton Terminal and Eastern Railroad Company were filed in the San Francisco County Clerk's office. By 10:30 the next morning most of the directors of the new railroad corporation were on hand in the San Francisco office for a meeting. Newell was elected president, Burns first vice president and Shane second vice president. Adams was named secretary and Cogdon was given the job of treasurer.

The group set aside 500 shares of S.T. & E. capital stock to be used for promotion. It was agreed that in return for the payment of one dollar, the United Investment Company would be given the exclusive right to buy all of these shares.

In other business the directors agreed that none of the officers was to receive a salary except for the secretary, Adams. He apparently took $50.00 a month in cash and the remainder in U. I. Co. stock, which meant that every month he worked he received more voting strength in the holding company, if he did not already control it. Eighty thousand shares of U. I. Co. stock would go or had already gone to Newell for the work he was doing and "as an incentive for him to secure financial backing from influential people of his acquaintance." This would also account for Newell's election as president of the railroad board. Each S.T. & E. director received some free U.I. Co. stock, according to information brought out at a public hearing in Stockton some years later. Court records show that Davis received 2,500 shares of this

J. E. "Bert Adams was one of the original promoters of the railroad. He was with the company from 1907-1916, holding many jobs including president. (Stanley Crawford)

stock the following year and it is not unreasonable to assume that the others also did.

Adams made many more trips aboard ships in the bay to sell U.I. Co. stock to the sailors. Learning from his success, he decided to try other service men and visited the S. F. Presidio to sell stock to soldiers. As he traveled the San Francisco Bay, he took money from ferry boat captains and railroad men. Only a few so-called capitalists invested any money in the project and those only token amounts. Adams later told a Stockton news reporter about the problems he had encountered:

We met with many discouragements and were disheartened many time. Our little vessel came near sinking. The ever present knockers were busy.

"Who are W. H. Newell and J. E. Adams?" the

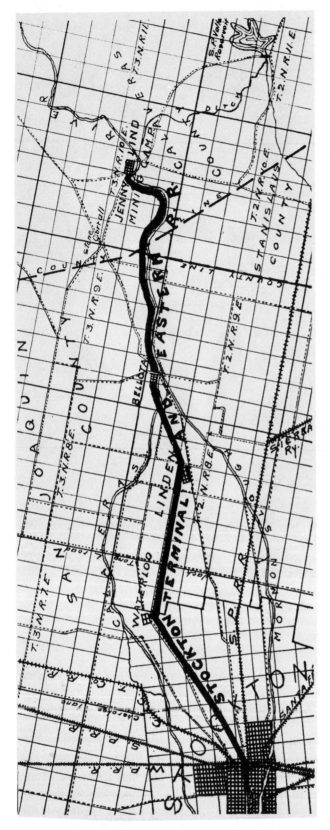

The planned route of the S.T.&.E. Railroad. (Mrs. Myrtle Seymour)

knockers would ask. "Where did they ever get any money? How can they build a railroad? How can they make it pay?"

A general ledger, a cash book and a minutes book were set up after the initial S.T. & E. stockholders' meeting. Original entries in both the cash book and general ledger indicate confusion over the money that Adams had taken in from the United Investment Co. stockholders. It finally took an auditor to settle the matter by issuing to the U. I. Co. stock certificates for money they used to pay the railroad company's bills. Adams' account was finally credited with only one share of railroad stock, the same as that of every other director, and every time a stock certificate was issued to the investment company his subscription account was credited, until the $29,000 he had collected was used.

Problems would eventually besiege the railroad because the two companies were so intertwined, but the real problems would boil down to the men involved. There were basically two types of men interested in the railroad—those who wanted the road for the benefits it would bring to the area through which it was to run, and those who were interested in making money and benefiting themselves. But the story has only just begun.

As the option on the Stockton waterfront was about to run out, Adams got his first renewal, giving the company until June to come up with the purchase money.

Newell had been too busy to hold any more meetings until February of 1909, when the men once again got together at the San Francisco office. He reported that he was satisfied with the progress of securing rights of way and presented a signed statement that he was acquiring them in his name for the company.

Before long the U. I. Co. sent out a notice of a change of place of business to a suite of rooms in the Phelan Building in San Francisco. The new offices were rented to provide space for E. Brox Randall, who was charged with the responsibility of stock sales. The company men had decided to hire a large force of agents to sell all of the U. I. Co. stock as soon as possible.

On May 19, 1909 Adams once again asked for another extension on the option, this time paying $5.00. He wrote to Newell, "This must be attended to quickly so we will have the waterfrontage argument to assist Randall."

As the project began to accelerate in the summer of 1909, attracting more attention daily, the Stockton Chamber of Commerce appointed a committee to investigate the United Investment Company. The committee was headed by an ex-mayor of Stockton, George F. Hudson, and ex-chamber

A view of the busy Stockton Channel which was to be the western terminus of the S.T. & E. R.R. Stockton Hotel, in the center background was the location of the second set of offices of the railroad. The company laid tracks on Commodore Levee on the left but never put a train on them. (Pioneer Museum & Haggin Galleries)

president, D. A. Guernsey. They presented their report on August 9, 1909. Excerpts follow:

We have made a careful inspection of the right of way from Stockton to Jenny Lind and find that for the first 22 miles from Stockton the proposed road will run through a territory whose fertility is not surpassed anywhere in the state and whose development had been greatly retarded by lack of proper transportation facilities.

This section includes the famed Calaveras River sediment lands which have made record yields of fruits, nuts and alfalfa without irrigation and are destined to become densely populated with the advent of a railroad.

The immense deposits of commercial rock and gravel at Jenny Lind and the mines now in operation and the industries that will undoubtedly be developed through cheap transportation will insure a large freight traffic from that section.

Stock subscriptions amounting to over $60,000 have been secured outside of Stockton and vicinity and would indicate that others are aware of the opportunities and possibilities of our county and have evidenced their faith in a substantial manner.

The personnel of the officers and directors guarantee a safe, conservative management and we recommend the project as very worthy of the endorsements of this Chamber and the support of the public.

The Chamber board of directors accepted the report and instructed the secretary to furnish copies of it to the press and to anyone who inquired about their judgment of the proposed project.

One of the Chamber directors who went to look over the project was Meyer Gardner. Either Newell or Adams persuaded him to become president of the United Investment Company. As an inducement, he received 34,000 shares of the company stock. At a par value of one dollar, they were of considerable value, but this information was not made public until some years later. Gardner was an ex-mayor of Stockton, a tall thin polished gentleman. He was a man in whom others had confidence and he brought much prestige to the company. He also convinced F. J. Dietrich, a Stockton real estate man, to join the company with him. Dietrich came in without a stock gift; what promotional stock he did get did not come to him until 1911, after he had worked for the company for more than two years. Getting Gardner into the company had been a shrewd manuever, indeed.

Railroad fever was at a high pitch in 1909; railroads in general were thriving in the river city of Stockton. The Southern Pacific Railroad was spending a million and a half dollars for improvements and doubletracking in town. The Western Pacific Railroad was about to complete its new transcontinental line; Santa Fe was spending forty thousand dollars on a new depot and yards. The Modesto Interurban Railroad, estimated to cost $500,000, was being organized, and the Central California Traction Company was building an electric line to Sacramento. New buildings were going up all over town and the taxpayers had voted money for county roads and an irrigation district. Walton Tilly, a local boy who had become a famous New York playwright, was amazed at what he saw on a visit to his hometown:

"Stockton must have secured new blood. It looks as if the knockers and the mossbacks have died."

It was in this atmosphere of optimism, enthusiasm and general confidence in the future of their county that the Chamber of Commerce endorsed the project and Stockton leaders joined the effort to build the Stockton Terminal and Eastern Railroad.

Immediately following the Chamber's endorsement a special meeting of the S.T. & E. board of directors was called in San Francisco. Newell was absent but sent a request for $1,500 to "help close up certain rights of way and prepare plans necessary for franchise for the railroad in Stockton." He also requested a monthly salary of $200 because he had been forced to give up his "other business to work full time on the project." The board readily granted his requests.

CHAPTER II
LOCAL SUPPORT GAINED

The day the news broke in Stockton that M. J. Gardner would take the reins of the United Investment Company, August 18, 1909, he was already in the San Francisco office, presumably to consult with Adams, Burns and Randall. He had made a public statement that the company offices would be moved to Stockton but did not get his way entirely on that matter. Offices were soon opened locally in the new Elk's building, but the official place of business remained in San Francisco, indicating that Gardner did not have complete control.

Newell was completing his engineering work. Before the end of October he had secured most of the rights of way and decided to take another job in South America. His last act before he left was to turn over to the company all of the rights of way he had secured. G. W. "Fuller" Broadhurst, also from the Sierra Railway, was hired as a replacement at a salary of $175.00 a month. Waldo A. Harscom, a former Western Pacific eomployee, was hired as an assistant to boss the survey crew.

Harscom was the brain of the outfit and a real railroad man in the mind of one survey crewman,

18-year-old Charles Widdows. Young Widdows had been forced to quit school and go to work when the family farming operation had been flooded out in the Delta in 1907. Undaunted, he took his books along on various jobs and studied at night. Harscom could see that Widdows was determined to be a surveyor so he took a special interest in the young man and taught him to run the instruments.

At first the crew of five to seven men stayed in Stockton and traveled by mule team to work the proposed route. Later they moved to the Linden Hotel, but all the crew members agreed that the best place to stay was at the Cody farm near Bellota. Mrs. Cody was reported to be a fantastic cook and was much appreciated by the working men. The crew stayed in Bellota as long as possible and longer than profitable—the company directors would later complain of the expense of boarding the crews there.

On October 24, 1909 the annual S.T. & E. stockholders meeting was held in San Francisco. Adams, who had dropped from the limelight, apparently had been working full time as company

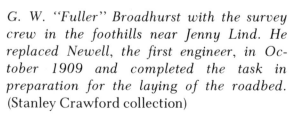

G. W. "Fuller" Broadhurst with the survey crew in the foothills near Jenny Lind. He replaced Newell, the first engineer, in October 1909 and completed the task in preparation for the laying of the roadbed. (Stanley Crawford collection)

The north side of the California Navigation Shed on Stockton Channel where the S.T. & E. R.R. built tracks but never used them. (Pioneer Museum & Haggin Galleries)

secretary and stock salesman. He presented proof of voting shares to the board, which included only 35 shares present with 30 of them being held in proxy by Gardner for the United Investment Company. The other five votes belonged to Burns, Adams, Davis, Steidly and Cogdon, who were all that were left from the original railroad company board of directors; already the United Investment Company had the upper hand.

The group proceeded to elect new directors. Newell, Grant, Burns, Adams, Davis and Cogdon were retained, and Gardner, Dietrich and James Barr were added. Grant, Dietrich and Barr were not present at the meeting but had agreed to serve. Barr was Dietrich's brother-in-law and Stockton Superintendent of Schools, and added more prestige to the company. Newell was named president, Gardner became vice-president but would act as president since Newell was in or on his way to South America. Burns was named second vice-president and Adams and Cogdon continued as secretary and treasurer respectively.

The next move was probably the most forboding made so far in the financial manuevers which had been taking place, one that would have repercussions for the next forty years of the railroad. It expanded the agreement between the railroad and the investment company, giving exclusive rights to purchase all of the railroad stock to the investment

company. However, no provisions were made to guarantee that the investment company would provide enough money to complete the railroad. The die was cast and from this point both companies would be plagued by struggles for control by the directors.

On November 2, 1909, Gardner, with the assistance of the law firm of Clary and Loutitt, filed an application with the San Joaquin County Board of Supervisors for a right of way on Front Street in the town of Linden, this being the only place the railroad was to run along a public road outside of Stockton. The supervisors were assured that the route was practically complete.

The same day Gardner and a group of men made a trip to Jenny Lind by automobile to inspect a rock quarry. It had been determined that the rock would be ideal for highway construction and the company planned to complete the railroad in time to haul the material and to collect a share of the tax money being spent on the current road project. The men met in Gardner's office before leaving in the new Mitchell automobile which had been purchased by the company for $1,500.

After the grading had started in December of 1909, the *Stockton Independent* editorialized on the subject of the railroad. No public relations man could have done a better job:

THEY'RE BUILDING THE ROAD—The businessmen who are backing the proposed electric railroad to be built from Stockton to the foothills at Jenny Lind, a distance of 28 miles from this railroad center are throwing up the grade from the roadbed and dirt is flying in both directions east and west. That is a new way of building railroads but it is the way the wide awake hustlers are proceeding with this promising enterprise and they mean to continue their work until they have the tracks laid early next summer and the road equipped for handling the large traffic of the rich Linden and Bellota sections. That is their announced determination and they are men who mean what they say. Actual construction of railroads is usually begun when the world has been apprised of the company's plans and capitalists have been inlisted to supply the funds for the project but the Stockton and Jenny Lind road has been started with the money of its shareholders and it is proposed to carry on the work with the same backing.

"There can be found no intelligent resident of the county who will say that the Stockton and Jenny Lind road cannot be made to pay, for it is a self evident proposition that a railroad which taps such a rich country must be a money maker. Every mile from the city limits of Stockton to the present terminus at Jenny Lind is a freight producer. The lines of the road will traverse the rich valley of the Calaveras for its entire distance of 25 miles. At Jenny Lind, a depot will be made for the shipment of the products of the foothills and mountains with their timber, fruit crops, minerals, gold and copper ores, marble and building stone, not to count the great macadam material which lies there in countless millions of tons. The farseeing men who planned the road counted on this big business now in sight and they have the undeveloped territory to add to the profits.

Maybe it was the publicity being received by the S.T. & E. or just the physical evidence of seeing the long-discussed railroad construction that stirred the Linden Farmers League into action. Whatever the reason, they called a meeting to be held on December 22, 1909 for their own members, but found interest so widespread that they opened it to the general public.

Two big Mitchell automobiles loaded with supporters and reporters arrived from Stockton. The men found standing room only in the newly completed hall of the Women's Home Missionary Society of the South Methodist Church.

"Men, women and children had come to hear of the benefits to be derived from the new enterprise that was going to open their community to the outside world," was the way a "big town" Stockton newspaper put it.

S.T. & E. director Ed Davis was a member of the farmer's organization; so he acted as chairman for the meeting. He had been raised on the family ranch east of Linden and owned property in the Linden area with his brothers Edgar and Albert. It was apparently Newell who had interested him in the railroad. A picture still in existence shows several Linden men, including Ed and Albert Davis, with Newell sometime during 1908 on the proposed railroad right of way in Linden. But back to the meeting in Linden on that fateful night.

Davis explained the purpose of the meeting before introducing J. M. Eddy, Stockton Chamber of Commerce secretary, who admitted that he owned no stock in the company but intended to buy a few shares. He started out by telling the local farmers what they wanted to hear about the richness of their lands. He told them it was the richest, deepest, most choice single area of farming land in the state and predicted that it would continue to produce heavily for a century. He stated that land assessed in 1908 at $56.22 per acre was now valued at $64.65. He concluded by warning that no matter where the money came from, the railroad would be built and its earnings distributed out of the produce of the area. He went on to discuss the traffic potential of the road. Citing vehicle traffic figures established earlier for Linden, Waterloo and upper Sacramento roads, with a daily average of 625 vehicles, he figured with two persons in a vehicle at 25 cents each, the railroad would get $93,750 a year. He did say that it probably would not come immediately but that it was reasonable to suppose that it would soon reach that amount. One newspaper used his figures at 10 cents per person making it $37,500.

Senator John T. Lewis, a true politician and a native of Linden, strode to the speaker's stand and said, "A city that isn't on the railroad isn't on the map." He predicted a great population increase for the area and concluded with, "I've sparked, plowed, hunted or threshed over every section of San Joaquin County and the Linden soil is the richest of all, for I know it."

The next speaker was Rev. W. F. Coffin of Linden. "It would really be criminal for the people of Linden to get in the way of this road. You would get run over, for sure. We want the road so that we can get our chickens, eggs, butter and milk to market. Our time in traveling is worth something to us."

F. J. Dietrich, the new director and the man who was destined to stay with the road longer than any other, was introduced as a partner in the Stockton real estate firm of Grunsky, Dietrich and Leistner. He stated that real estate men of Stockton had less Linden land for sale than any other in the county.

11

Linden's Main Street around 1910. The S.T. & E. R.R. surveyors boarded at the two-story hotel at far right. (Stockton Chamber of Commerce)

He declared that it was the richest soil in the county and few owners wished to sell. If they did, their neighbors bought the land before the real estate men heard about it. He said that transportation was more important to the farmer than water since every man could develop irrigation to some extent but would be helpless without transportation.

"In the end, the cost of the road will be paid by those who live tributary to the road and the wise investor should subscribe for the stock and pay the money from one hand to the other," Dietrich concluded.

Rev. W. G. Lopeman followed with what one of the reporters called a most inspiring speech. He predicted that the Pacific coast from Washington to Southern California was destined to become the most thickly populated region on the earth, and that Stockton would have 100,000 and Linden 10,000 people in the "not too distant future."

Frank Wooten, a local landowner, admonished the crowd: "It looks as if Stocktonians are the boosters and the Lindenites the boostees. We ought to be the boosters. We will reap ten times the benefit from this road that Stockton will. Stockton has more transcontinental railroads than any other interior city in the state, including Fresno, Sacramento, San Jose or San Diego. This new railroad will place our cars within a half hour of the transcontinental roads."

Finally Gardner explained the organization of the road and answered questions from the audience. J. A. Drace introduced a resolution to the members of the Farmer's League which was immediately passed with no dissenting votes. The resolution approved the project and pledged $25,000 from the residents of the area. Six men immediately pledged $1,000 each. These were James A. Drace, Andrew McCormick, Harrison Brothers, Board Brothers and D. W. Miller, all landowners in the area.

A Stockton newspaper summed it up:

Linden farmers are not only rallying to the first call for stock subscriptions; but they have donated rights of way. They realize that the road will make their country a golden empire, increasing the value of their lands many fold, besides opening the way to social and educational advantages previously denied because of being shut off from Stockton, the center of population.

Having proved their ability to get things accomplished, Gardner, Davis and Dietrich were appointed as an executive committee the following week by the S.T. & E. Board of Directors. They were given full power to act in constructing and equipping the railroad. The financial control was still in San Francisco but the physical action was now in Stockton.

The New Year of 1910 arrived with great expectations for the investors, but Gardner was not

The railroad survey crew working on the right of way through Linden, winter 1909–10. The newly-constructed Mission Hall is in the background. From left to right are: Waldo Harscom, supervisor of the survey crew, 17-year-old Charles Widdows on one of his first survey jobs, Doug Sparks, an unidentified assistant, and F. W. "Fuller" Broadhurst, head engineer. (Stanley Crawford collection)

resting on his laurels. He appeared before the San Joaquin County Real Estate Agents Association on January 4, seeking and getting an endorsement of the project. He declared that nearly $100,000 had been invested in outside money and the company now had $125,000 subscribed, including the recent pledges from Linden. He announced the stock would be on sale the following week in the Stockton company office and added that as soon as one-third of the stock was sold the balance of the money would be available. Guarded statements had been made in the past about possible eastern investors.

Gardner was now spending most of his time supervising the road building. Grading and fencing were continuing as fast as the weather permitted. The survey crew, having completed the preliminary work, joined the construction men. They drove stakes to make sure the road bed was properly located and aligned. Boss of the construction crew was a big Irishman known as Micky the Liner, who was quick to point out a survey stake a quarter of an inch off. Railroad gangs were

rough, hardworking men, but Micky easily established his authority with this crew, which was composed mostly of Mexicans. Early in the job a crew member had displeased Micky, who quietly took the underling by both shoulders, lifted him off the ground and scratched his back on a nearby barbed wire fence. Widdows recalled that thereafter Micky had no more problems with the men.

The road gang used horses, mules and Fresno scrapers to work the road bed. However in some places there was little done because only a minimum strip of land had been donated. Other places, where the farmers were more generous and 50 feet had been set aside, dirt could be pulled in to raise the roadbed. The job went slowly because of winter rains which at times made the ground impossible to work. Area farmers and businessmen, however, were already getting a taste of prosperity, for many were receiving checks for labor, rent of horses and equipment, and other expenses being charged to the road grading project.

Early in April Gardner appeared before the Stockton City Council to apply for a franchise down Miner Avenue through Stockton to the waterfront. The city councilmen called a meeting so protestors could be heard, and there were those who objected strongly. The general complaint was that there were too many railroads on the east side of town, that it was becoming a checkerboard of tracks. They protested that Miner Avenue was the only wide thoroughfare left and that the passing of trains would disturb the church congregations. Several voiced disapproval and an officer, Dutschke, told the councilmen that in the event the franchise was granted his house would float away in the first high water. Councilman Heimann suggested that he could chain his house to the new railroad tracks.

Following the protests, Gardner was asked if he had anything more to add. He accused the protestors of having selfish motives and said they did not give the city's welfare a moment's thought.

"Now you who have been so ardently protesting," Gardner said, "take up among you some good honest proposition and let the people see that you are as good boosters individually and collectively as you are backward about granting of this franchise."

It was not until May 9, several meetings later, that final approval came. At this time Gardner said that the company had sold $220,000 worth of stock and had expended $20,000 of the money in Stockton already. He announced that grading was completed to within one mile of Bellota and added that the managers hoped to have the road built by July and that the ties were on hand and rails on the way.

The final route of the Stockton franchise was from Roosevelt Avenue at its entrance into the city, along Fremont and Miner Channels to Miner Avenue, down Miner Avenue to McLeod Lake, crossing the lake inlet to the south by a combination trestle-drawbridge, to Commodore Levee and on to the north bank of the Stockton Channel. The franchise also included a clause that all freight hauled in the city between 6:00 A.M. and midnight had to be transported in cars having the same general appearance and color as the passenger cars. Regular freight cars could be used in trains of no more than four cars each at other hours. Also

included was a restriction to electric motor coaches only and a requirement that dust be kept down along the dirt streets by regular watering. The final clause stipulated that work on the road in the city must be started within four months and be completed within three years.

The franchise had obvious faults including some of the complicated requirements in traffic control but the route itself was the major problem. Tracks over the entire distance from the intersection of Union and Fremont streets, west along Fremont to Grant and then curving along Miner Channel to American Street, where Miner Avenue began, would have to be constructed on trestles. Fremont Street was not actually a street but a waterway, emptying into Miner Channel. Officer Dutschke had believed, probably rightly, that the resulting trestles would obstruct the flow of flood waters, endangering his home. Stockton was only eight feet above tide level, and constantly plagued by floods. A major problem would be the crossing of three other railroad tracks in the vicinity of Fremont and Grant Streets. All of these were already on trestles and S.T. & E. would be required to maintain the crossings indefinitely in the future. These problems, however, apparently did not seem insurmountable to Gardner.

Six years later Adams lamented the disadvantages of this franchise and filed a formal letter to be entered into the minutes book of the railroad Board of Directors:

This whole franchise question was mishandled from the start, not so much the fault of Gardner as of the poor engineering employed by him. Gardner first figured with the California Traction Company for an entrance over their rails and our franchise is a direct result of a quarrel between Gardner and McLunnigan, then president of the Traction company, the former saying, "Well then we will get our independent line into town."

At the time Adams made this statement major differences had developed between him and Broadhurst, the engineer. So although he had the advantage of hindsight, his viewpoint was clouded with other motives. Regardless, at the time, the granting of the Stockton City franchise removed another major obstacle in the path of the Stockton Terminal and Eastern Railroad.

CHAPTER III

BUILDING AND CELEBRATION

In May, 1910 the S.T. & E. Railroad management leased a triangle of ground from the Western Pacific Railroad at Poplar and Union Streets in Stockton for five dollars a month, to be utilized as railroad yards. Material was being accumulated there in preparation for the big push to come, with 70 carloads of redwood ties stacked and ready to be delivered where needed. On May 21, a front page story announced the much awaited news that the rails were on the way; a shipment of 60 pound rails had left Denver. As soon as they arrived in Stockton several gangs went to work on the road.

The company had acquired a steam locomotive and other cars from the Norman B. Livermore Company. The locomotive carried the number 2 when it arrived and the company never bothered to change it.* The construction train usually consisted of the locomotive, a box car and two flat cars. The box car carried the men and tools, and the flat cars were used for the ties, rails and a wooden water tank with a supply of water. The men were prohibited from riding on the flat cars

*See addenda note #1

but frequently rode on top of the box car to take advantage of any cooling breeze on a hot day.

When the "gandy dancers" went to work Micky "the Liner" lived up to his name. He eyeballed the rails and quickly informed the crew, in no uncertain terms, if they were not right. No tie plates were used in the original construction even though the redwood ties were brittle and most of the roadbed was the natural soil of the area with no rock or gravel added. Ballast, usually sand or soil, was then dumped on top of the ties and worked down by hand, although early pictures prove this was not always done immediately. These haphazard methods would eventually add to the problems of the new road. Locomotive #2 followed the track and moved up as the rails were laid, to keep the materials close at hand.

From the railroad yard the road grew across East Street (now Wilson Way) and plunged through the vineyards, ranches and small acreage truck gardens. Work came to a momentary halt as it reached the west bank of the Diverting Canal, recently constructed to divert flood waters around Stockton. Here hoppers were built in a manner to allow the dirt to be scraped into them from the new

A United Investment Company post card shows ties being unloaded from Western Pacific tracks in preparation for construction, 1909. George Broadhurst is standing on top of the ties facing the camera. (S.T. & E. collection)

70 CARLOADS OF RAILROAD TIES UNLOADING AT STOCKTON FOR THE S.T. and E.R.R.

RST TRAIN FROM OROVILLE TO SALT LAKE ON W.P. RY" HOGAN PH...

JUNE 9TH. 1910. LAYING THE TRACK OF THE STOCKTON TERMINAL & EASTERN RAILROAD

Top: S.T. & E. Locomotive #2 before it came to the road. Here it is shown in front of the uncompleted Oroville station on the W.P.R.R. The picture is labeled "first train from Oroville to Salt Lake." (Gerald M. Best collection) Center: Locomotive #2 in the Stockton yards on Union Street, 1910. (U.O.P. Library) Left: Another U.I. Co. post card was used for stock promotion. Kegs of railroad spikes are stacked on the right. (S.T. & E. collection)

16

Above: The construction train powered by Locomotive #2 on the Potter Ranch east of Linden, 1910. (Lloyd Potter Sr.) Right: A note written by Laura Davis. "Papa" in the note refers to her husband, Edgar. "The S.T. and E. Railroad laid their track through the town of Linden, and the first Engine that ever went through the town went through to-day, Aug. 17th 1910. Papa and I went out and sat on a wood pile and took a picture of the train as it passed." (Mrs. Myrtle Seymour)

canal embankment. A switch and spur were added so gondolas could be filled from the hoppers. It is strange that no one objected to the removal of dirt from the Stockton side of the levee of the flood control canal. The material was used for ballast on the roadbed and the company men were quick to point out how little it would cost. Apparently they were right, because later the company auditor reported to the Railroad Commission that only $263.59 had been spent on ballasting for the first fifteen miles. After the bridge piles and timbers arrived, the trestle was built across the canal without the necessary permit from the U.S. War Department, which had jurisdiction over the waterway.

From the canal eastward the road crossed ranches, vineyards, vegetable gardens, orchards and grain fields. On each the farmers watched the progress and were duly impressed to see a train in their fields. The road was laid to the Lagomarsino ranch where a siding was installed near Alpine Road. This station name was abbreviated to Largo. The road continued to the Drais place, the nearest point to the community of Waterloo. Here another switch and siding were installed to accommodate bunkers being built by the

Moreing Contracting firm, the company which was working on the county road project and intended to have road-rock delivered by rail cars. This became Waterloo Station and a county road was laid into the community a half mile north, so people could "come out and catch the train to Stockton."

From Waterloo Station, the rails turned east again to Jack Tone Road where Comstock station was located. The laying of tracks continued eastward to Roy Station which was built near Tully road. Next were grain fields where more than 6,000 sacks of grain were already piled awaiting shipment.

By August 10, 1910 the next ranch, owned by the Davis Brothers (no relation to the author), was the scene of the rail laying project. The property was the former Archer Ranch which had been recently acquired by Edward, Edgar and Albert Davis. The Archer place was probably one of the reasons that Edward Davis had originally been persuaded to serve on the Board of Directors of the railroad. He believed that it would make the brothers some money if they subdivided the property. Edgar had established his home here and he was not nearly as interested in breaking up the property as were his two brothers.

Fortunately for us Edgar's wife Laura was one who recorded many events of the day. She kept

17

This was described as the first train to Linden, which would have been on August 17, 1910. This is locomotive #2 but the picture was enscribed as "Old 93." Fanning's Hall is the two-story building in the background. The family lived on the second floor. (S.T. & E. collection)

close track of the progress of the railroad through the ranch and on to Linden. It was August 10 when the track laying commenced on the ranch and three days later when the tracks were in Linden and the first train rolled into the small town. The next day was Sunday and a group of people rode the flat cars out from Stockton. The Davis family left a chicken dinner on the table and went out to wave at the people as the train went back to town. On August 17 the first train hauled freight into Linden and several people took pictures of it.

The railroad builders continued at a rapid pace as the road proceeded past the large two story home of E. Fine, where Fine station would be located. The tracks were laid through the Hunt Brothers' peach orchard, where on the east end of the ranch the station of Plora, named for the famous peach grown there, was to be established. By September the rails reached the Davis Brothers' home place, a large grain ranch west of Bellota on the Calaveras River. The track laying came to a halt as the railroad men concentrated on hauling the numerous crops from the area to market.

Linden had long been a farming community established around a stage stop, Fourteen Mile House, which had been built by W. D. Treblecock on the Stockton Mokelumne Hill Road in 1849. Miners traveling to the gold fields over the road recognized the richness of the soil and took up the land. The location soon became Forman's Ranch

but in 1862 it was given the name of Linden when Samuel Forman sold the property to C. C. Rynerson. At first there had been only livestock ranches but these were followed by grain fields when California became the bread basket of the world. Grain was the major product of the area for a long time but finally orchards became common. Walnuts, peaches, pears, cherries, plums, almonds and other orchard crops were well established by 1910. The coming of a railroad to the area meant that for the first time fruits could be placed on a train without a bruising six mile wagon trip to the S.P. tracks in Peters.

In 1910 there was a small business district in Linden with two blocks of business houses located on the north side of Main Street. The first street north of Main was Front Street along which the tracks ran. A railroad station and water tank were installed on Front Street where it intersected with Mill Street. There were homes on Front and also on Back Street which was located a block north. The entire population of the town was around one hundred. There was a two story elementary school, but students had to go to high school in Stockton. Before the railroad was built many of the young people boarded there. Linden was a small town, but then as now people from miles around claimed to be from there, for many got their mail through the Linden Post Office and went to school or church there. It is little wonder that the people of

SPRINKLING WAGON LAYING THE DUST
ON LINDEN ROAD. ABOUT 1895

A Ralph Yardley cartoon from Laura Davis's scrapbook depicts the road in Linden before the building of the S.T. & E. R.R. The county hired water wagons to help keep the dust down in summer. This windmill and tank provided water for both travelers and dust-settling. (Mr. Myrtle Seymour)

19

Right: The Linden School as it looked in 1910 when the S.T. & E. R.R. was built to Linden. The bell at the top was rung as the first passenger train arrived in town. (Mrs. Myrtle Seymour) Below: Picture post card invitations were sent out by the United Investment company. This one went to B. Crickmer, a sailor on the U.S.S. Albany *stationed in the Pacific. Pictured is the three wheeled scooter used by the surveyor's assistant, Charles Widdows, and others. The man in the picture is probably M. J. Gardner, the company's president in 1910. (S.T. & E. collection)*

At the front - Ten miles out.
Road now completed into Linden, 13 miles S.T. and E. R.R
Big barbecue at Linden, Setp 1st.
All our subscribers invited.

Linden were excited about the arrival of a railroad, believing that it would bring prosperity to their community and provide them with good transportation for their abundant crops.

On the evening of August 11, 1910 a meeting was held in the town to make arrangements for a grand celebration to welcome the S.T. & E. Railroad. Dave Board was named general chairman and others were appointed to assist him. Ed Davis, in charge of publicity, told a Stockton newsman, "We desire to invite the citizens of San Joaquin County to come to Linden and rejoice with us on the completion of an enterprise which means so much to the eastern end of the county." The plans called for the event to be held on Labor Day, September 5. A program was printed and the

United Investment Company sent post card invitations to its stockholders. These cards were, no doubt, used to reassure the stockholders and to interest new people in investing in the company. The post card showed a section of completed track near Linden.

A finance committee had raised $1,500 for the celebration; so it was decided that besides a free meal everyone would receive a free basket of famous Linden fruit. A Stockton jeweler prepared a silver spike which he displayed in his store window before he presented it to the Linden group, with a letter of congratulations.

Even though the railroad was receiving much public acclaim, the behind-the-scene company control and finances were rather vague. We do

Top: This picture was used in a promotional brochure. The company never owned such a car so the lettering must have been put on a picture. J. E. Adams named the car the Jenny Lind Queen for his wife whom he called "Queenie." (Mrs. Myrtle Seymour) Above: F. J. Dietrich and E. Grunsky opened a real estate and insurance office on San Joaquin Street. It was located in the narrow building in Stockton—5 feet wide and 45 feet deep. Dietrich is shown sitting at his desk, 1903. (F. J. Dietrich III collection)

HO! FOR LINDEN

On Jenny Lind Railroad---Free Amusement
For All

Including Barbecue

Monday, September 5th

Trains for Linden Leave W. P. Depot | Returning Leave Linden

10 a. m.; 12:20 p. m.; 7 p. m. | 11 a. m.; 5 p. m.; 11:50 p. m.

ROUND TRIP FARE, 50c

The Stockton Independent *of September 4, 1910 invited one and all to the big celebration to be held in Linden to welcome the S.T. & E. Railroad.* (San Joaquin County Library)

know that Adams had not been active in building the road, for although he was secretary of the S.T. & E. Board of Directors, he attended no meetings from January through June of 1910. He had apparently been selling stock and concerning himself with finances and he took company-financed trips to Hawaii and New York to "sell Uncle Sam's sailors." We know that thirty percent of all money finally raised came from these servicemen. We also know that he was involved in preparing the promotional booklet. The car on the cover, labeled the Jenny Lind Queen, was named for his wife, whom he affectionately called "Queenie."

The United Investment Company had been paying the railroad's fast rising costs, as agreed.

Late in June the board of directors met and went over the company books which showed $68,463.51 paid out. The investment company money must have been running out, however, for late in July when the voucher book showed another $43,762 in expenses the board met again. This time Gardner was given permission to negotiate a loan in the amount of $30,000, this in spite of the fact that at the Stockton City Council meeting in May Gardner had stated that 220,000 shares of stock had been sold. It is likely that he had included in this total the promotion stock held by himself and others. We know that stock selling costs had been extremely high. Some salesmen had received 33% commission and there was an overall

22

Top: A view of Jenny Lind from the west in 1909. The planned eastern terminus of the S.T. & E. R.R. (Mrs. Myrtle Seymour) Above: A certificate for 100 shares of United Investment Company stock, owned by 12-year-old Stanley Crawford who purchased the stock with his hard-earned paper route money. (Stanley Crawford collection)

average of 20% only because stock being sold in the company's office had no charges against it.

We do not know who was controlling the company at this point, August of 1910. We do know that Davis had been elected to the United Investment Co. board of directors in May, a move probably engineered by Gardner, with his 34,000 shares of the voting stock. Burns was making regular trips to Stockton, for he attended all of the board of directors' meetings and he and Gardner seemed to be working closely. Dietrich was actively involved in his real estate business, developing The Oaks, a new residential area in Stockton, through which the railroad ran. Davis was making preparations to subdivide the Archer place in Linden and was president of the board of directors of the Farmers and Merchants Bank in Stockton, besides doing some farming at home. Adams finally showed up at the July S.T. & E. board meeting and was named superintendent of the railroad. No matter what was going on behind the scenes, we do know that Gardner was getting all the credit and being praised from every quarter.

Late on Sunday afternoon, September 4, the Linden people were making final preparations for the big celebration. In this atmosphere charged with excitement, the annual stockholders' meeting of the United Investment Company was held at the railroad office in Stockton. Although many stockholders from the Bay Area and as far south as Los Angeles were in town for the celebration, those present at the meeting were far from a majority.

Gardner reported on the railroad's progress and promised to push the road to Jenny Lind by winter. During the course of the meeting, Adams left importantly to take telephone calls from shippers. He announced that he had received orders for 20 cars to ship grain and fruit from along the railroad. Gardner predicted 700 to 800 carloads of freight would be moved within the following 60 days and the directors decided to use the construction steam engine until more equipment arrived. Gardner discussed passenger service and said that the current prevailing opinion among the company men seemed to favor an electric trolley line.

It was announced that $300,000 worth of stock shares had been sold to 15,000 stockholders. Because of this it was decided to discontinue the sale of stock through solicitation and to offer it only at the company office.

The total stock sold had to include the approximately 128,500 shares of promotional stock we were able to determine had been issued in exchange for influence and work, although there could have been even more. We were able to find only sketchy accounts through court records and public hearings as to who owned the promotional stock and how they got it.

The final business of the meeting was to elect "directors to serve both the United Investment Company and the S.T. & E. R.R. for the coming year," even though the latter could not be officially confirmed until the annual meeting in October. These included M. J. Gardner, Jas. A. Barr, F. J. Dietrich, J. E. Adams, Edward F. Davis, Andrew McCormick, C. L. Newmiller, A. D. Rothenbush and Robert Burns. The new directors then elected officers for the coming year. Gardner was named president and Dietrich vice president. James Barr was elected secretary and Davis became treasurer.

People from every walk of life had purchased stock in the U. I. Co. Thousands of servicemen had put up money, including sailors from eight U.S. Navy ships. One of the youngest stockholders was probably twelve-year-old Stanley Crawford. He was a nephew of J. E. Adams and invested $100 of his hard-earned paper route money. The Linden Cemetery Association had become a stockholder when the board of directors decided to invest their reserve funds in the company. A Stockton housewife, Avah Kennedy, held 50 shares that she received as a birthday present from her husband, E. "Walter" Kennedy. These were the stockholders and many looked forward to the grand celebration for their railroad.

Linden was "dressed in gay attire" on the dawn of the big day. The picnic grounds, located on the Wasley place in the heart of town, was decked with flags, streamers, and greenery, plus yards and yards of red, white and blue bunting. Piles of fruit were in place near the Wasley house, and a welcome sign was stretched across the Main Street entrance near the barbecue pits that had been manned for hours. Many a Linden child waited impatiently for parents to get ready, others hurried through chores, but all were excited in anticipation of the big day. Those working on the celebration arrived first but before long local farmers began to arrive in buggies and a few of the richer and luckier ones in automobiles.

A Stockton news story reported on the Linden scene: "Her people were joyful. The spirit of optimism was everywhere. The people had first doubted, then waited and at last were convinced their fortunes were made."

In Stockton the plans had not developed as smoothly. A California Traction Company engine

The full front page of the Stockton Record *was devoted to the S.T. & E. R.R. on the day of the big celebration in Linden, September 5, 1910. (U.O.P. Library)*

Unloading of the first passenger train at the flag-bedecked celebration grounds in Linden, September 5, 1910. (Mrs. Myrtle Seymour)

was to pick up two Santa Fe passenger coaches and deliver them to the Western Pacific depot. Because the engine was involved in a collision on the company's Lodi line, it did not get back to Stockton on time. So instead of the planned five cars there were only three Western Pacific coaches available to couple to S.T. & E.'s Locomotive #2 at the Western Pacific depot. People milled about, each one hoping for a good seat on the first train to Linden. There was not room for all so it was a scene of mass confusion, but finally as many as possible got aboard. A Stockton newspaper reported: "Promptly at 10 o'clock the first excursion train carrying hundreds of enthusiastic visitors, left the Western Pacific depot for the maiden trip to the metropolis of Eastern San Joaquin County. In every possible space in which the great crowd of merrymakers could find standing room, including the pilot and tender, tops of the coaches and hanging onto the step railings and within the aisles, rode the surplus capacity passengers."

The train moved slowly in town, with its bell and whistle telling all of its passing, but gained speeds of up to forty miles an hour in the open

country. Those hanging on the outside clung tightly as the train rocked along. People along the way stopped to wave to the happy crowd aboard, while those on the train waved back and admired the rich farm land. In some areas orchard trees almost brushed against the sides of the cars. All along the route were stacks of grain waiting to be transported to Stockton. Real estate signs were posted on some of the property beside the road and many of the passengers expressed an interest in buying land.

Long, loud and shrill whistling of the locomotive informed the thousand or more Lindenites and visitors of the approach of the train. As the excursion pulled into town, the explosion of bombs, the ringing of the school house bell and "Apalochicolaola" by the 16-piece Linden band, added to the tumultuous cheering of the gay throng assembled.

As soon as the passengers unloaded, the train started back to Stockton to get another load. The crowd gathered in front of the speaker's stand which stood just south of the tracks. Benches for more than a thousand people had been placed un-

26

Locomotive #2 with passenger coaches at the Linden Celebration, September 5, 1910. The sailor in front of the engine was very likely one of the many servicemen who owned stock in the investment company that owned the railroad. (Lloyd Potter collection)

der the huge oaks but there was standing room only long before the program began.

Frank S. Israel, chairman of the day, started the ceremonies by welcoming one and all to Linden. Speaker after speaker strode to the platform and delivered flowery oratory to the happy throng.

"The mission of the Stockton Terminal and Eastern Railroad will be told by the historians not by the prophet," proclaimed Dr. Bane. He added, "The Linden land is so fertile that the farmer but has to tickle it with a plow and it smiles a golden harvest."

U. I. Co. directors Newmiller and Burns reassured the stockholders and praised Gardner.

The program was interspersed with recitations by children and music by the Stockton band that had arrived on the train. Some of the Linden band boys were slightly miffed because the "Linden Dads" had not considered them good enough to play after the arrival of the Stockton groups. One 14-year-old Bellota girl recited the poem "Asleep at the Switch" which described a terrible train wreck. Tears flowed down the cheeks of a woman in the front row, leaving a profound impression on the girl. Today a grandmother, it is her only

memory of the Big Celebration.

Finally Israel presented "The President of the Railroad, M. J. Gardner." The crowd broke into cheers and prolonged applause. Gardner told the audience that the S.T. & E. Railroad was not built by millionaires but by the "common man." He said that within a fortnight he hoped to initiate passenger service between Linden and Stockton, and promised every effort would be made to give the best in transportation in both freight and passenger service.

Israel, calling Gardner the man who built the railroad, presented the silver spike to Gardner who accepted it on behalf of the company, then left the speakers' platform, stepped to the tracks, placed the shining spike in place and dramatically raised a sledge hammer overhead. He held the pose for photographers before proclaiming, "Ladies and gentlemen, the only man in Linden today with a hammer." The hammer dropped to signal the completion of the road. Caught up in the moment, the crowd cheered long and loud for "The man who built the road! The man who built the road!"

The ceremony over, people scattered to various activities on the grounds. Some sat and enjoyed a concert by the Stockton Union Band while others went to the barbecue pits where Joe Stenner, a famous barbecue chef, watched over "three heads of beef, six bulls heads and a half dozen sheep." It was tantilizing odors from these that greeted the second train which arrived with all five coaches filled with more visitors.

Children were admonished by their mothers not to get their good clothes dirty, as they scurried off to join their friends. Some lingered long enough to beg money to buy canes, flags, buttons and other souvenirs from the vendors who hawked their wares through the crowd. Others flocked to the table where forty gallons of ice cream were waiting to be enjoyed. Nearby some adults gathered around the 250 gallon coffee pot. Others sampled the delicious fruits of the district.

Swept up in the excitement of the day, many persons inquired as to where they could buy stock in this most promising enterprise. They were directed to Adams or E. M. Hadley, one of the company's stock salesmen. Individual sales during the day ranged from $20 to $2,000. Everyone wanted to get the stock while it was still $1.00 a share, for rumors were flying that the next day it would be going to $1.25. It did go as high as $1.50 per share, but we do not know how soon.

Some of the young people headed toward Fanning's Hall for the dance. A baseball game drew a good crowd while others gathered to watch a basketball game and still others went to cheer the bronco busters. All of this activity was interspersed with friends greeting each other and kissing cousins catching up on the family news. Some visitors took the opportunity to visit the famous Hunt Brothers orchard and pick a ripe peach off a tree.

Not all of the military men who held stock had come, but at least one sailor was captured on film by a member of the Potter family as he was crossing the track in front of Locomotive #2. There were those who returned to Stockton on the train that was scheduled to leave the W. P. depot at 7:00 P.M. On its return it was filled with those who were coming out only for the dance, which by now was in full swing. No doubt a fight or two occurred; fights were frequent at the Linden dances.

Dave Board summed up the day when in his characteristic slow accent he said, "Folks said Linden couldn't get up a celebration so we just thought we would show 'em." And they did it so well that the railroad got a new name—The Stop Talk and Eat Railroad.

CHAPTER IV
GOLD BONDS ISSUED

The stockholders had had their day and now it was time to get back to running the railroad and hauling the abundant crops of the area to market.

The company acquired a yellow, secondhand combination passenger and baggage coach to be pulled by the steam locomotive. There was room for 24 passengers and any express and mail going to Linden. Gardner had already signed a contract with Wells Fargo. Passenger service was initiated as promised and the Linden youths going to high school or business college in Stockton flocked aboard. The passenger train logged 38-plus hours during the month of September and jumped to 134 hours in October. Laura Davis and her husband took their first ride on the train on September 21, 1910. Not everyone rode the train, however, for there were those who thought it too "rocky and dangerous."

The road earned $100 a day for some time, clearing the backlog of freight. An extra locomotive was leased from the Yosemite Valley Railroad to help haul freight and ballast for the roadbed. The company had a picture post card made of Stockton yards showing train number four being fulled by Y.V.R.R. Locomotive #20.

Up to this time all expenses including labor went into the company's construction account. This included rent of the extra engine and crew, freight and passenger cars and even Gardner's salary. All money was channeled through this account, a way to charge as many costs as possible to the construction rather than to the operation of the road. The yet-to-be-organized California Railroad Commission would later question this practice.

Fencing of the railroad right of way had been continuing as cattle guards were constructed and gates hung. Passenger sheds, a one stall engine house and stations were built. The Stockton station had a tiny ticket office at one end, a shelter area for waiting passengers and an open shed for freight storage.

The Mitchell automobile that Gardner had purchased the year before was converted to run on the rails. The rubber tires were removed and flanged rims substituted to keep the wheels on the rails. A Stockton news reporter marveled that these cars could travel a mile a minute. The brakes were not good, however, so the speeds had to be kept down. Later the vehicle was reported to be making six round trips a day on the railroad. A small trailer was added behind, to haul a few cans of milk or baggage, leaving the autocar for passengers.

Before the annual S.T. & E. Railroad stockholders meeting in late October, the company directors finally took action to make the Stockton office the official place of business and confirmed Adams' transfer of railroad stock to the U. I. Co. At the annual meeting Gardner held the proxy for

This is Yosemite Valley Railroad's locomotive #20 leased to the S.T. & E. during Y.V.R.'s slack season. The ballasting material was from the S.T. & E.'s sand spur at the Diverting Canal. (S.T. & E. collection)

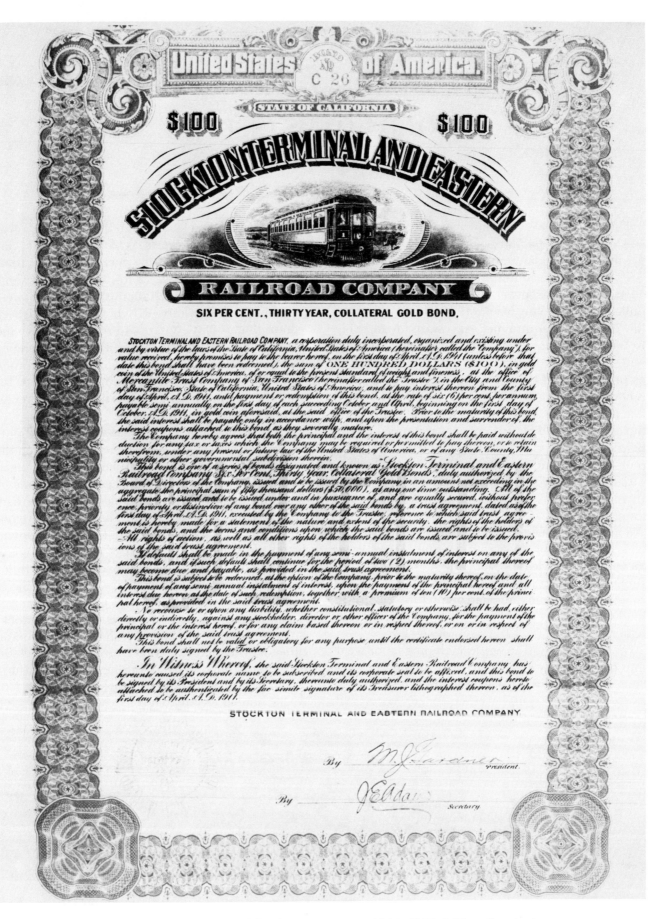

A $100 gold bond issued by the company in 1911. (S.T. & E. collection)

the U. I. Co. and picked a new board of directors, the same as elected by the parent company back in September except that Robert Burns was replaced by Dr. M. J. Congdon. Gardner was president, Dietrich vice president, and McCormick second vice president. Adams was returned as secretary and Rothenbush was named treasurer.

In spite of the heavy traffic during the fall, all of the optimism voiced the year before and all of the efforts put forth by the promoters, only $150,000 worth of the S.T. & E.R.R. stock had been picked up by the U. I. Co. by January of 1911. The operating road from Stockton to the Hunt Brothers orchard had cost $180,000; so it was obvious that more capital must be generated. It appeared that the United Investment Company was out of money, but why?

We know that Adams had given up selling stock the summer before when he became superintendent of the railroad, and Gardner had been busy building the road for even longer. Apparently when Adams quit selling stock, the whole sales force was discontinued. At a "Blue Sky" Commission hearing several years later, it was revealed that some of the promotional stock was sold off at half price or less when the owners were short of money. If this was happening it certainly would account for the depression in the sale of shares at par value.

In March, as a new approach to the problem the directors voted a bonded indebtedness of $500,000. They agreed to give the Mercantile Trust Company a mortgage on the real property for the initial $200,000 worth of bonds to be offered for sale. The bonds were identified as "The Stockton Terminal and Eastern Railroad Company First Mortgage, six percent sinking fund, 30 year Gold Bonds." They were to be issued in $100, $500, and $1,000 denominations. The coupons were to be redeemable in gold semi-annually at the company office on the first of April and the first of October. An elaborate offering circular was printed to distribute to prospective investors. One of the original circulars is in the Califronia Room of the Stockton Public Library. It describes the territory and traffic of the road, the property and planned expansion. It indicates that optimism still ruled the thinking of the men in control. An estimate of net earnings for the road after completion was placed at $67,300 a year. The word "estimated" on the copy in the library is underlined heavily, indicating someone's personal judgment of the matter or perhaps a reminder that it was only that—an estimate.

The company books show that $1,080 was spent on the bond issue alone. The board of directors set the official selling price at 90% of par value. Gardner and Adams were authorized to accept subscriptions, which Adams did immediately, taking as little as one dollar as a down payment for some. Notes were issued to the United Investment Company for money used to pay the railroad bills until the bonds could produce some cash. In addition Gardner and Adams were directed to negotiate loans up to $60,000.

Passenger service from Linden stopped entirely for awhile during the winter of 1911 when the Diverting Canal bridge underpinning washed away. The ties and tracks hung suspended across the raging current until the flood waters receded. The piers had to be replaced and concrete reinforcement added. This would allow debris to pile up and meant that from then on company men would be required to be on flood watch during heavy storms. Company officials did attempt to get the proper permission to construct the bridge this time, even though it was after the fact. The Army sent an engineer out to look over the project and he discovered that the bridge had already been built. A letter from Washington noted that because of this it would not be appropriate for the Secretary of War to approve the plans but the bridge did not seem to be an unreasonable obstruction to navigation.

By now some school children had already quit riding the train. There were those who convinced their parents to let them drive an automobile over the newly constructed Linden road to Stockton High School. Frequent train breakddowns and delays were the excuses used by many students for not riding the train, because every time the train was late they were forced to sit in the school office until classes changed, and that soon became "old stuff." Some parents also worried about the practice of the youths who cut across the Asylum ground between Union Street, where they left the train, and the high school. One of the former students, using the slang of the day, said, "The crazies scared us." Other than these few complaints the S.T. & E. appeared on the surface to be doing well.

During February, 1911 the California State Legislature passed a far reaching railroad regulatory measure. It was the act providing for the organization of the California Railroad Commission. To the railroad operators in the state it was to mean the public would be looking over their collective shoulders. Railroads had long used abusive practices in dealing with shippers,

Andrew McCormick was president of the railroad from October 1911 until October 1912. (Pioneer Museum & Haggin Galleries)

receivers and competition. At one time the big railroads were in complete control of the state government but when Hiram Johnson became governor he set out to make changes. The new act defined the duties of the railroads and other transportation companies and the duties of officials, agents and employees. It also gave the commission the right "to define the rights, duties and remedies of the shippers and offenses by both shippers and transportation companies, their officers, agents, employees and others." It also gave the commission the power to provide penalties for failures to comply with the commission rules.

Perhaps it was the new regulations that caused the S.T. & E. board of directors to ask for a legal opinion from Judge Jones before the gold bonds were actually sold. It was May before the reply came. He ruled that the sale of the bonds was legal but only for clearly defined proposed purposes in specific amounts of money. The directors ordered the Mercantile Trust Company to deliver bonds to be sold, the money to be used for construction and equipment costs only. Bonds were in turn issued to the construction material companies, and to banks for money owed.

The bonds were not generating cash immediately but being issued in a way that would begin running up interest charges. The company was in real trouble when the June 30, 1911 report showed a total of a little over $3,000 in passenger revenue. Even with the freight revenue at double this amount there was only about $10,000 in income for almost a full year's business. This information was not generally known, and on the surface all seemed to be going well.

During the summer the S.T. & E. had an impressive daily passenger schedule. Trains departed from Stockton at 9:30 A.M. and 1:00 and 5:30 P.M., with an additional 6:20 A.M. departure on Mondays. The train left Fine Station at 7:07 and 10:15 A.M. and 2:00 P.M. with a special departure at 6:14 P.M. on Saturday and Sunday.

August 1911 proved to be a busy month for the road. Fruit was shipped out daily. Two growers, W. H. Anderson and D. W. Miller, together shipped 9,000 crates of plums to eastern markets. For a time Hunt Brothers shipped a carload of peaches a day to their Hayward cannery.

On September 10, 1911 a Stockton news story reported on the Railroad's progress, "About 20 stockholders in the S.T. & E. went over the route this week and were delighted with the company freight receipts for the month." It is not surprising that in the minds of most people, including many of the directors, the Stop, Talk and Eat Railroad was doing well on the first anniversary of its completion to Linden.

About the same time another news story must have set tongues wagging. The item announced that M. J. Gardner was the principal stockholder of the San Jose Terminal Railway Company. This was to be another short line railroad running from San Jose to Alveso, with shipping rights on the bay to San Francisco.

At the next S.T. & E. board of directors' meeting, official action was taken to change some of the $1,000 bonds to $100 denomination ones, apparently to make them easier to sell. Gardner also revealed that he had contacted the U. I. Co. and asked for its assistance in selling the gold bonds. A proposition was presented and after some discussion was accepted. The investment company, which had recently been reorganized, agreed to allow the purchasers of bonds to exchange them for U. I. Co. stock. They would do this in return for 800 more shares of the S.T. & E. capital stock or for a cash payment of $60,000. The resolution was ambiguous and some of the directors may have been in the dark as to the real meaning. It stands to reason that no one would want to exchange gold bonds, secured by real property, for the unsecured U. I. Co. stock. These minutes were signed by Robert Burns, as secretary pro tem. He was no longer a director of the S.T. & E. but he seemed to be working closely with Gardner. A hearing held later in Stockton revealed that Gardner had transferred to Burns 10,000 of his shares of U. I. Co. stock, but we do not know when this occurred.

As soon as the bond selling agreement was approved the company books show payment of commissions to bond salesmen, more than $2,000 for September alone. Fifteen or more salesmen's names appear on the company books. Had the bonds been pledged or sold already, and only waiting for an agreement between the U. I. Co. and the S.T. & E. Railroad?

The first wreck on the S.T. & E. Railroad occurred on the evening of October 17, 1911. It was 5:15 P.M. as the Mitchell autocar, towing a trailer, was approaching the Cherokee Lane crossing from the east. It was preparing to stop to pick up a passenger at Graco Station, located just west of the crossing. A California Traction Company city passenger car had just crossed the S.T. & E. tracks so the Mitchell driver assumed the tracks were clear. However, closely behind was a Traction Company water car which had just started to roll. The brakes were applied on both vehicles. The light Mitchell could not stop in time and rolled in front of the heavier water car which had managed to slow almost to a stop. Just before the collision, Christobonlos Kalwokis, one of the train crewmen riding in the trailer, jumped in an effort to avoid being hit. In the process he broke his left leg. As it turned out the Mitchell was not even knocked from the tracks nor the trailer derailed. The California Traction Company was involved in a fatal accident just a few days later when Eugene Grunsky, Dietrich's real estate partner, was killed at the Linden road crossing. After investigation the Railroad Commission ordered the companies to clear trees in both areas to make the crossings less hazardous.

On October 24, 1911 the Railroad Commission ordered the S.T. & E. officials to furnish maps and profiles of the railroad and an inventory of its property, together with its original cost. It also requested that the company, if it so desired, submit an estimate of the reproductive value and the current value. This action was taken by the Commission under section 20 of the act ratified by the legislature the previous February. This section gave them the power to ascertain the actual value of the railroad property, and to investigate the salaries of officers, wages of employees and all expenses of operation. It could also investigate the bonded indebtedness and the quantity and market value of its capital stock.

That same day the Commissioners issued a public statement on the action:

This is the first, so called, valuation brought upon the Commission's own initiative for the purpose of ascertaining the fact entering into the value of the property of the various steam railroad corporations in California.

These valuations were to be used in determining railroad rates so that the companies would not make excessive profits. Why was the S.T. & E. selected to be the first investigated? It was probably no worse than most of the other roads operating in the state. Perhaps it was chosen because it was small and easier for the inexperienced Commission to handle than a big one would be, or had there been some behind-the-scenes complaints against the road? Very likely the S.T. & E. was selected because it had much less political influence than a larger road.

Only four days later the annual S.T. & E. stockholders meeting was held with Gardner holding the 1,500 U. I. Co. proxies. He proceeded to reelect all of the directors but Burns was not put back on the board. As soon as he accomplished that, Gardner announced that his business interests in San Jose required his full time.

The directors promptly elected McCormick, the only board member absent, as president. Dietrich was named vice president, Burns was selected secretary, even though he was not on the board, and Davis was made treasurer. The four men were also named as an executive committee.

Gardner stated he had a month's salary due, but Neumiller presented a resolution to clear Gardner's overdraft account by crediting to it all money due him plus the remainder, for past and future services rendered.

By December Gardner had resigned as director and was replaced by Burns, who was voted a salary with the understanding that he would devote his full time to the company. He was given the responsibility for the sale of the bonds and the U. I. Co. stock. Probably the exchange of stock

A view at the corner of Miner Avenue and El Dorado Streets in Stockton, looking north. The S.T. & E. R.R. officials installed double tracks down the center of this block in December of 1911 so the city could continue with their street paving project. The tracks in this block became rusty stripes as they were never used. (Pioneer Museum & Haggin Galleries)

"Linden road starts work on its Miner Avenue extension for the purpose of running cars to the waterfront"—Stockton newspaper headline December 5, 1911. Looking west on Miner Avenue. (Leonard Covello collection)

from Gardner to Burns occurred at this point, which would account for Burns' strength in the company again.

Andrew McCormick, the new S.T. & E. president, was a well known Stockton businessman and president of the family-owned meat company, mining and ranching operations. He immediately put a gang of men to work laying track in downtown Stockton. The town buzzed the night of December 15, 1911 when a Stockton paper headlined the news:

McCORMICK IS PRESIDENT—Headed for the waterfront, the Stockton Terminal and Eastern Railroad has just completed one big block of double track railroad on Miner Avenue, in front of the Episcopal Church. The construction is first class and built to stay.

Would the Stop Talk and Eat Railroad finally be completed as planned? Only time would tell.

CHAPTER V

POWER STRUGGLE

The new Stockton-controlled S.T. & E. Board of Directors had already made changes but in the new year of 1912 apparently resolved to make more. They moved the company offices to a suite of three rooms in the new Stockton Hotel annex. McCormick later told of the problems encountered:

I was elected President of the Stockton Terminal and Eastern Railroad Company and upon investigation found we were running behind in our operation. Taking the three months of November, December and January, we found a loss of $3,367.79.

We were convinced from these figures that something was lacking in management; therefore we employed a man who was very highly recommended and made him general manager.

As near as we could tell no one had been managing the company since Gardner had acquired other interests and Adams had left to sell bonds in September.

George S. Cameron was hired as superintendent of the railroad and went to work as of January 15, for a starting salary of $175 a month. He had 20 years' experience in the operation departments of C.R.I. & E., the B. & Q. and the S.P. railroads. He was a dynamic man who made steadfast friends or bitter enemies while he handled the road.

Cameron wasted no time in deciding the motive power was unsuitable for operation; seven days later he signed a contract with the Hall Scott Motor Car Company of Berkeley for a 60 passenger car. It was to have a wooden body on a steel frame, powered by a four-cycle 110 horsepower engine, and was to have those "fantastic electric lights." There was a required down payment of $1,500 which was provided by a loan from McCormick, who took a promissory note in return.

Cameron was not the answer to all the company's problems, however, for there were bills that had not been paid, bonds that had not been sold

and stock subscriptions which had not been honored, plus the added burden of meeting the interest payments becoming due on bonds and outstanding notes. Last, but far from least, the Railroad Commission was sending men to examine the books and physical properties of the railroad.

In order to sell more bonds the board of directors agreed to sell them in any way that would net the company 80%, and gave Burns a free hand in the arrangements to be made with bond salesmen. The same resolution allowed bonds to be given as security for borrowed money at the ratio of not more than two to one. The resolution was in wording typical of Burns, but strangely enough the minutes do not show who presented it. This was unusual because in the past when Burns acted as secretary he always recorded the fact.

A request was sent to the Mercantile Trust Company of San Francisco for money paid by an insurance company for damages caused by a fire to Locomotive #2.* Cameron did not use the money to repair the engine immediately but had it inspected and declared beyond repair. He found it expedient to rent an engine from the Southern Pacific Railroad.

What happened next is complicated and not entirely clear. Burns sent out a meeting notice over McCormick's name on March 14, 1912 calling for a special meeting to be held on the 19th. McCormick was not present at the meeting but Burns came armed with three resolutions. One gave the U. I. Co. 330 more shares of S.T. & E. stock for promissory notes which had been issued by the last board of directors. The next two were ambiguous ones, with legal language that transferred 800 shares of stock to the investment company "as directed by the board the previous September in exchange for their assistance in selling the bonds."

Immediately a dispute arose among the board members. Four more meetings were held in March with no formal resolutions passed. There must have been some lively discussions, for the meetings

*See addenda note #2

35

May 21 1912. The first gasoline car was run from Stockton to Linden, 41 ft. long and seated for thirty nine passengers. Ruth rode home from Stockton on it and the next day Elsie + Ruth rode on it.

This note written by Laura Davis refers to the Hall Scott Motor Coach ordered by the company in January of 1912. (Mrs. Myrtle Seymour)

were held in a five-day period, with most of the directors present. The dispute was apparently settled at a sixth meeting, when in Burns' absence, he was "railroaded out of office," as the position of secretary was declared vacant and his salary discontinued. Those voting for the action were Dietrich, Rothenbush, Congdon, Adams and Davis. Davis was elected secretary to replace Burns.

On May 3, 1912 Burns sent a complicated proposition in a letter to each of the board members. It contained his plan to solve the company's financial problems:

I am in communication with a man of prominence and high attainments in electric railroad management. I expect to receive a definite proposition from him for financing this enterprise by purchase of sufficient bonds to construct the road. If I succeed in my arrangements, and the proposition is accepted, it means that I shall sacrifice all my stock to accomplish this purpose, but all the rest of the stockholders will receive the benefits of my sacrifice; if, however I am unable to successfully complete my negotiations and I will know in a short time, then I will agree as follows:...

This led to a rambling offer of "great personal sacrifice" of his 15,569 shares of U. I. Co. stock. He offered to sell 15,000 of these shares to net him twenty cents a share provided the stock was then sold to someone else for $1.25 per share, the extra money going into the railroad company treasury. In addition he would buy, from other stockholders, 8,000 shares at 30 cents a share to be used in the same way. If all of this was done he promised to then donate $1,000 to the railroad company. The letter concluded:

In short, the plan to sell the stock, as indicated will bring a donation of $19,750 to be used as a payment on the $25,000 proposed to be borrowed. I may be able to do more, if I can, I shall do so. I want the railroad built for the benefit of the stockholders who have invested their money in good faith. I have always intended to use a part of my stock for their benefit, keeping only a comparatively small amount for myself, when the proper time came, but now I am going to prove that for the benefit of the stockholders who have invested their hard-earned dollars in this enterprise, I stand ready to sacrifice every share of stock I own."

For all of the sacrifice being made, it is rather obvious that his terms would not be met. How did he expect anyone to pay $1.25 a share for stock he was willing to sell for twenty cents a share? The 15,569 shares he was offering must have included not only his promotional stock but also the 10,000 shares of Gardner's promotional stock.

A real rift had developed, for at the next six meetings, called on May 7, 10, 15, 25, 27 and June 1, no quorum of directors was present to take any action whatsoever. In spite of this, all was fine in outward appearances—on May 20 Cameron accepted the delivery of the Hall Scott Motor car. It caused excitement along the line for it was modern and up-to-date, powered by a gasoline engine which in turn generated electricity to power the wheels and light the car. The Linden people flocked aboard for a luxurious ride.

On May 30 the Railroad Commission issued an order giving the railroad permission to sell $65,000 worth of additional bonds. It was stipulated in the order that the company must net 80% of said bonds and that the money could be

This Hall Scott Motor Coach was powered by a 4 cylinder, 110 horsepower gasoline engine. The railroad purchased it new and began to operate it over the road on May 21, 1912. As near as can be determined, this is the only large piece of rolling stock ever purchased new by the S.T. & E. Railroad. (Mrs. Myrtle Seymour)

used only to pay old bills and acquire the necessary property and materials to construct the line to Bellota. It also directed that the company keep accurate and separate accounts of the bonds sold under the order. In approving the request filed by the company, the Commission gave as reasons for its approval, "Find value of property is considerably in excess of sum of issuance. Trust deed contains adequate provisions for a sinking fund."

This finally stirred McCormick, Dietrich, Neumiller, Rothenbush, and Davis, the Stockton group, to take additional action against Burns. On June 6 they met and ordered the auditor to "make up a statement of all company expenses incurred by the recent campaign for the sale of bonds managed by Robert F. Burns."

The secretary was directed to make a demand on Burns for the return to the company of all the monies advanced by him to salesmen. The group agreed to notify all salesmen that no one was authorized to sell the bonds. They rescinded the authority of all previous officers to borrow money. McCormick and Davis were given new powers along with a limited authority to issue bonds as collateral. They were also instructed to execute a promissory note to the Hall Scott Company for the balance due on the motor car.

On June 28, 1912 another spirited meeting was held. Cameron was directed to see that the railroad company was credited and the investment company charged with recent bond expenses handled by Burns. Congdon, Rothenbush, Davis and Dietrich voted yes but Adams voted no. The secretary was directed to collect from Burns any commission paid out in excess of 10% for the sale of bonds. Adams again objected and submitted a written statement to this effect:

I vote no for the reason that sales made by different members of the company, including myself, on which no commission is paid, act as an offset to the commission paid to Herring and Stone and that the commission said to be authorized by the Board was not exceeded in the aggregate.

Loose financial practices were finally surfacing and the board of directors was in no mood to bargain with anyone. Newell had sent along a request for unpaid expense money and the group refused to pay it on the grounds that they understood he owed the company money from previous advances.

The road was under construction once again, financed with borrowed money. Dietrich, Davis and McCormick signed a note for $5,500, presumably in hopes the bond sales would soon generate cash. They desperately continued trying to borrow money but found no one would make loans to the railroad without their endorsements, which made each of them personally responsible for the debts. The banks were saying in essence, "Stop talking and produce." The three men did just that; they cosigned notes to four more Stockton banks for a grand total of $27,000. The banks were given $54,000 worth of the railroad Gold Bonds as security on the notes.

The road building continued toward Bellota and the harvest freight once again kept the line busy. Any evening farmers with their wagons could be seen unloading empty lug boxes and loading full ones onto box cars at every siding along the line. When the tracks were completed to Bellota late in August, a picnic train took a large crowd to the end of the line for a day of relaxation.

The board of directors finally paid for the right of way through the Rothenbush property. They also agreed on a price of $1,600 for the four lots in the Oaks on which the Stockton Station stood. Cameron asked for and got a contract for $200 a month to continue until December 1913.

About the same time, tucked in the financial section of the Stockton newspapers was the notice of the annual stockholders' meeting of the U. I. Co. It is obvious that this proposed meeting would determine who would be controlling the railroad after the annual meeting due to be held in October.

On September 9, 1912, the story appeared in the *Stockton Record:*

J. E. ADAMS RESUMES HIS POSITION AS MANAGER—J. E. Adams, the original promoter of this road to the foothills, at the head of a committee, selected the directors who were elected Saturday. Mr. Adams will again be manager of the road, the position which he has held almost continuously for the past five years.

The directors chosen are: Jacob Eppler of San Francisco, president; Theo. C. Bee of Oakland, vice president; H. N. Clark, treasurer; John Svenson, G. Herring and Robert Burns of Oakland and Irving Martin, William Nicholls Jr. and J. E. Adams of Stockton.

J. A. Nesbitt the present auditor of the S.T. & E. was elected secretary.

No wonder the *Record* story was so glowing in praise of Adams; one of the new directors, Irving Martin, was the newspaper's publisher. Apparently Adams was again using influential people to his advantage! Did Irving Martin also get some free stock in the investment company?

Adams had gained control of the U. I. Co. and eliminated Dietrich, Davis and McCormick, which now meant sure death for the present S.T. & E. board of directors. William Nicholls Jr. had purchased 20,000 shares of Gardner's promotional stock for $6,000. He later testified, with sarcasm, that his good friend Burns had convinced him to buy the stock.

Two days later Martin's paper carried a front page item out of Sacramento:

STATE RAILROAD COMMISSION PHYSICAL VALUATION OF RAILROADS IN CALIFORNIA—War on the "bloated" profits of California railroads is promised here today by the state railroad commission which has appointed a corps of engineers to make a physical valuation of railroad property.

J. F. Esheiman, president of the Commission insists that prevailing rates are way out of proportion with the amount of money invested and if his suspicions are true the Commissioner intends to order sweeping reductions in freight and passenger rates.

Was this the result of feedback from the S.T. & E. railroad valuation investigation underway?

A traffic count taken in San Joaquin County at this time revealed why some of the great expectations for the railroad had failed to materialize. Of the 50,000 vehicles counted, more than half were motorized vehicles, which greatly reduced railroad passenger service. There was still hope for the freight service, though, because only 1.4% of the vehicles counted were trucks and almost half of those were still horse drawn.

On a Sunday evening in late September the bubble burst on the high hopes that the motor car would solve the breakdown problems of the S.T. & E. passenger service. The coach was approaching Largo Station when the motorman, Otto Effenbeck, suddenly realized that they had left the main line track and were speeding down a siding with box cars parked ahead, He yelled at E. G. Tuttle, the brakeman, who quickly applied the brakes, but the car skidded into a box car loaded with crates of grapes. Otto was cut by flying glass but Tuttle and the conductor, W. H. Ruggles, the only other person on board, were uninjured. The car was damaged enough to make it inoperable and had to be transported to the Hall Scott factory for repairs. Cameron leased S. P. Engine #1416 to pull the combination passenger and baggage coach in the interim. Adams would later use this accident as one of the reasons to get rid of Cameron as general manager.

The California Railroad Commission had ordered the company to send monthly accounts of the disposition of the last gold bonds that they had been allowed to issue. When the July 1912 report was received, the Commission immediately notified the S.T. & E. company that the order had not covered the right to use the bonds as collateral on notes. A hearing was called to clear up the matter. The results were released as a Commission order on October 7, 1912, after the company had

The back platform of the combination passenger/baggage coach owned by the S.T. & E. Railroad, fall of 1910. The woman is Mrs. Minnie Crawford, with her son Stanley, age 12, in front of her. On the right is G. W. Broadhurst who met Mrs. Crawford in the S.T. & E. office where she worked. He married her in 1912. (Stanley Crawford collection)

39

filed a formal application to pledge the entire amount of bonds issued on the previous order. The Commissioner in charge, Max Thelen, presented a statement with the order:

I am convinced that none of the applicant's directors intended to violate this Commission's orders. They adopted the expedient which seemed to them nearest at hand to secure the necessary funds, without reading carefully this Commission's order. While there has been a violation of this Commission's order it has not been such a violation as to call for further steps than those which the Commission promptly took. I am satisfied that it would be advisable to modify the Commission's original order as to give the applicant the alternative right to pledge the bonds therein authorized, with the right to sell the bonds which may be outstanding as collateral, there will be a wide margin between face value of the bonds and the value of the property. ORDERED—right to pledge under former regulations.

Well aware that they would be removed from office at the upcoming annual stockholders meeting, the directors voted to transfer to McCormick, Dietrich and Davis the $54,000 worth of gold bonds held by the Stockton banks to secure the five promissory notes cosigned by them. All other matters were referred to the new board soon to be elected.

McCormick opened the annual meeting and gave a report concluding with praise of Cameron. He thanked the men for their cooperation during his year as president of the Railroad. Having secured their hold on the company in the best way they knew, the Stockton business men and community leaders withdrew from the S.T. & E. Railroad.

With the U. I. Co. votes held in proxy by Jacob Eppler and William Nicholls Jr., it was only a matter of routine to elect their hand picked board of directors, J. E. Adams, George Broadhurst, Theodore C. Bee, John Svensen, Grover Herring, H. N. Clark, J. Nesbitt, Eppler and Nicholls.

Eppler and Bee were named president and first vice president, the same positions they held on the U. I. Co. board. Broadhurst became second vice president and Nicholls was elected treasurer. Adams was named secretary and traffic manager. Nesbitt was appointed auditor, to be shared by both companies.

Broadhurst had recently become Adams' brother-in-law. Minnie Crawford and her young son, Stanley, had come to live with her sister and brother-in-law, Bert Adams. She had gone to work in the railroad office, where she met George, or Fuller as he was known to his family and close friends. Both Minnie and Fuller had been born in the Bellota area but had not known each other as children as he was quite a bit older than she, and she had moved away while still a small child.

"When I first laid eyes on her, I said, 'That's the girl for me' " he later recalled. He started bringing candy to the office but it took Minnie and the other two ladies working there more than a month to decide which of them he was interested in courting.

Broadhurst was a very practical man, unlike Adams, and this would lead to differences between the two, but as of the time of the 1912 board meetings, their relationship was still tolerable to both.

The first action of the new board was to increase salaries, probably the ones previously reduced by Cameron. Once again the majority of the power was in the hands of the men from the San Francisco area. Were they wise in eliminating the local businessmen? Time would tell, but it should have been obvious that the constant seesawing of power was beginning to deprive the railroad of the continuity desirable in carrying out any reasonable plans to complete the road.

CHAPTER VI

CALIFORNIA RAILROAD COMMISSION ISSUES ORDERS

Early in December of 1912 the new S.T. & E. board of directors made plans to occupy the franchise over the city streets of Stockton. They filed another request with the Railroad Commission to sell bonds to finance the rest of the construction.

Broadhurst was told to proceed in securing rights of way east of Bellota but was ordered not to agree to pay cash for anything without consulting the president, Jacob Eppler.

The board decided to apply for a change in the route over the city streets. Adams had objected to the cost of trying to construct the line over the original franchise as secured by Gardner, but he also objected to this new change. The company now applied for a route over Miner Avenue from Union Street to American but ran up against strong opposition at a city council meeting. After considerable negotiations the application was withdrawn when it appeared the council would end up in a tie vote.

Because six of the new railroad directors lived in the San Francisco Bay area, they voted to hold meetings in the Hearst Building in that city. With the physical property and business being conducted in Stockton, it seemed expedient to name a new executive committee to run the business. Adams, Broadhurst and Nesbitt were given the job with limited powers, particularly in the matter of spending money.

Almost immediately the friction between these three men and Cameron surfaced. They opposed him in almost every decision he made. Adams later complained that Cameron was operating the road at a loss, citing December and January with a deficit of more than $900, a small amount compared with past winters. He blamed Cameron for the wreck at Largo the previous fall, and accused him of using vile language to shippers and creating enemies for the road. He claimed that I.C.C. reports were not properly filed and that vegetable growers were lost as shippers because Cameron had collected for empty box shipments, when com-

mission houses had already deducted these costs, but connecting railroads had not delivered the boxes freight prepaid. The two also had a dispute over the moving of a spur at Roy Station and Adams accused Cameron of causing antagonism in the W.P. office.

Obviously, Cameron could see the handwriting on the wall, for he told a subordinate about his contract and said, "When the S.T. & E. gets ready to release me, they will have to come with a silver platter."

Money was once again scarce and the payroll was held up during January and February of 1913. It was reported as being due to a lack of funds, but we suspect it was Nesbitt's and Adams' way of getting at Cameron. The Hall Scott car was finally redeemed by a cash payment and a note issued for the balance due. Orders were given over Cameron's protest to reduce trips to Linden to once a day. This would completely eliminate any possibility of the Linden youths' using the train to attend Stockton High School. Office space in the Stockton office was sublet to save money and Cameron was instructed to repair the Mitchell autocar so it could be used for light loads.

In San Francisco the board of directors ordered the Executive Committee to cut back on Stockton expenses even if it meant releasing Cameron. At the same meeting, however, Nesbitt got a raise of $50 a month and Broadhurst was again hired for $100 a month. Nicholls objected, but the two men overcame the objection by intimating a willingness to purchase some company gold bonds as a show of good faith.

Next Nicholls tried to get expense money for the directors and failed. He seemed to be the one director whom no one supported. After all he had purchased Gardner's stock shares at far less than par value!

During February 1913 the hearings were finally held in San Francisco by the California Railroad Commission to determine the official valuation of

Locomotive #1 is shown here as Central Pacific's second #31; it was already ex-Western Pacific "G"-Mariposa. This picture was taken at Upper Soda Springs, California in 1884. (Gerald M. Best collection)

the S.T. & E. Railroad. The commissioner in charge, Max Thelen, reported that after receipt of the S.T. & E. valuation statements, the commission's engineering department, represented by Richard Sachse, had an investigation of its own, including a physical examination of the real property. The greatest areas of discrepancies in the two sets of figures occurred in the cost of selling bonds. The Commission determined that the agreement with the U. I. Co. to sell S.T. & E. Railroad bonds, in exchange for 800 shares of capital stock and exchange rights for U. I. Co. stock, was of little or no value to the railroad company. They ruled the value of this stock was not allowable as a cost in establishing construction costs.

There was also a disagreement over the date on which the railroad had begun operation. Hart, representing the company, tried to prove the road was still under construction , but the commission ruled that the road was operated as of April 1, 1911, since at that time a deed of trust was executed on the property to the Mercantile Trust as security for the gold bonds. Actually the road was in operation by September 1910 when it began to haul freight and passengers over the line. Alterations made in the company's books at that time were obviously an attempt to make construction costs appear high. The company claimed an average cost of approximately $17,000 per mile, but the commission engineers determined it

should have been around $13,000. The commission finally ruled that the S.T. & E. Railroad had an original cost of $213,059.13, approximately $46,000 less than the company figured.

The Commission allowed the value of the right of way although noting that it was a questionable matter since most of it had been donated. The total valuation set by the Commission as June 30, 1912 was $199,717.83.

Between the time the first hearings were held and the final decision was made, the company did receive permission to issue bonds to finance the completion of the road to the waterfront in Stockton. Commissioner Thelen included a statement of explanation.:

I was at first disinclined to recommend the issue of any additional bonds, unless they were all sold, so as to guarantee the completion of the railroad. Otherwise a portion of the bonds might be sold and proceeds invested in the property, and then, because of the impossibility of disposing of the remaining bonds, the entire enterprise might go into the hands of the receiver. In view of the urgent need, however, of building to the waterfront to save applicant's franchise, as well as increase traffic, and also of the further immediate need for a steam locomotive and a motor car, and further fact that applicant can not improve its condition unless it secures funds, I have decided to recommend under special conditions...

The special conditions were the restriction on

S.T. & E. Locomotive #1 was renumbered to Central Pacific #1193 in 1891. This picture was taken at Biggs, California in 1893 after the engine had come from the Sacramento shops where it had received a new boiler and overhaul. (Gerald M. Best collection)

how the bonds were to be sold and specifics for the use of the money.

The S.T. & E. board once again discussed means of selling bonds. Robert Burns and Irving Martin represented the U. I. Co. at one of these meetings, but it was only history repeating itself. Once again the investment company came through with a small amount of money and the rest was raised by using the bonds as security on loans.

The three-man executive board fired Cameron. He refused to accept the dismissal and continued to work. On April 24, 1913 he took the Mitchell to Linden and left it sitting on the main line near the station. The motor coach, pushing two carloads of sheep ahead of it, slammed into the autocar. There were passengers aboard the motor coach but fortunately no one was injured. This incident gave the executive committee one more reason to demand Cameron's removal and the railroad board finally complied.

Broadhurst was immediately rehired on a full time basis at $200 a month and took great delight in scratching Cameron's name off the glass door of the office. He started the road construction again at once.

Late in May the State Legislature passed the "Blue Sky Law" or the Investment Companies Act. The act created the office of the Commissioner of Corporations and defined investment companies and investment brokers and agents plus providing penalties for violation of the law. It was designed to prevent investment companies from capitalizing by selling only "blue sky." The U. I. Co. was only

*See addenda note #3

one of many corporations this law had been designed to supervise, but it was guilty, for it had used many of the legal but bad practices common to the times. The Blue Sky Commission or the Commission of Corporations was to regulate investment companies, just as the Railroad Commission regulated the railroad. It was the state's way of protecting stock investors in California. Approved on May 28, the law was put in effect on November 1, 1913.

At the June board of directors meeting Clark resigned from the board and was replaced by J. F. Treat, a conductor on the railroad. After considerable objection by Adams, the directors agreed to honor the decision of the former directors and buy the five lots in the Oaks, from the real estate firm of Grunsky, Leistner and Dietrich. Engine #2 was once again declared unfit for service and beyond repair, and was put up for sale as junk.*

Early in September of 1913, at the annual stockholders meeting of the U. I. Co., George Hudson was named president. Certificate #3529 for 2,500 shares of U. I. Co. stock was transferred to him by Burns. Hudson was an ex-mayor of Stockton and a co-chairman of the original committee appointed by the Stockton Chamber of Commerce to investigate the U. I. Co. back in 1909. He was a partner in Hudson and King's Shoe Store on Main Street and was well known in Stockton.

Broadhurst met with Hudson and the new directors of the investment company immediately, because he realized that they would soon control the railroad. He asked them to outline their plans, which they did. Both Adams and Nesbitt were at

S.T. & E. #1 received a new number in 1901 when it was given Southern Pacific's second #1215. It was converted to an oil burner and received a new silhouette. The driver fenders were removed and the engine received a new steel cab, an extended smoke box on the boiler, a straight smoke stack, a new headlight and pony truck wheels. The tender got a new frame and trucks. (Gerald M. Best collection)

the meeting and raised no objections.

Broadhurst was tired of all the "dilly-dallying around" and decided to follow the desires of the new board. He went to work laying double track between Hunter and San Joaquin Streets on Miner Avenue. After Adams tried unsuccessfully to stop Broadhurst he requested by telegram that S.T. & E. president Jacob Eppler do so. Broadhurst went to see Eppler and agreed he would pay the extra money spent in doubletracking the block, if the company got enough money to complete the franchise and did not interfere with his work.

A special meeting to air the grievances of the executive committee was called in San Francisco and Adams made a lengthy statement of his version of what had happened. Then a letter was read from his brother-in-law Broadhurst.

Broadhurst said he could not attend the meeting because he had to supervise the men he had working. He reiterated that according to both Adams and Nesbitt there was $2,850 available for the development of the Stockton franchise. He told of the meeting with the new U. I. Co. board and lack of objection at that time by Adams, Nesbitt and Bee. He continued:

The future success of the enterprise lies largely with the new board. To my way of thinking nothing should be done at this or any other time to embarrass or deter their progress. To this end I have executed the work on Miner Avenue and would ask that you pass a resolution ratifying that action, also giving instructions to proceed

under advice and counsel of President Hudson and Board of Directors of the U. I. Co. This would be courtesy, would stimulate good feeling and harmony.

Adams objected again, saying a large portion of the money being used had been gathered through a special franchise fund and that he had promised those contributing that the fifty-year franchise would be protected from American Street to the Waterfront, even if only single track were used where double track privilege existed. The group agreed that Broadhurst had exceeded his authority but declined to censure him. They did, however, issue an order that no more double tracking be done after the completion of the tracks under construction without further permission by the board.

G. Herring, one of the stock and bond salesmen, resigned from the S.T. & E. board and was replaced by Hudson. Fortified by Hudson's support, Broadhurst now had the upper hand. He called special meetings to deal with the franchise and got authority to complete the road as much as possible, west of San Joaquin Street, since not enough funds for the whole franchise were available. Tracks were laid along Union Street south of Poplar. Fremont channel had to be filled to accommodate these tracks and extra expense was incurred when the crew ran into an abandoned fire cistern at Union and Channel Streets. The tracks were completed to Weber Avenue where a bulletin board was erected as passenger trains began to use this point as the Stockton down-

S.T. & E. #1 had been renumbered to S.P. #1488 in 1907. In 1908 it was being used on an East Bay commute run when it was derailed near the Oakland Estuary bridge in Alameda. This is the only evidence found of the locomotive ever being on its side. (Gerald M. Best collection)

town terminus. All tracking was completed along the Stockton City Franchise route west of San Joaquin Street except for the drawbridge, yet none of the trackage would be of any use until it was connected with the Union Street line.

About this time a sailor aboard the *U.S.S. Utah* sent a letter of complaint to the S.T. & E. officials. He claimed that he had sent $45 in currency in a printed envelope addressed to Robert Burns in care of the United Investment Company. Burns denied he had received it. Nesbitt voiced an opinion that stock should be issued to the serviceman, and the matter was referred to the investment company.

At the annual S.T. & E. stockholders meeting in 1913 a lengthy statement was issued showing an operating loss of more than $10,000 with most of the blame laid on Cameron by Adams. No one was willing to admit that the revenue from the road was insufficient. Every year the passenger service was taking in less and less as automobiles became more popular and the railroad service less dependable. The freight from the farming area was definitely seasonal and would continue to be so. It was a common occurrence for a company official who wanted to make someone else look bad to cite lack of profit during the winter months; however, if he wanted to make himself look good he would use the summer revenue figures.

Bee, Nicholls and Nesbitt tried to elect the new directors at the stockholders meeting but were blocked by Hudson with the U. I. Co. proxies. Broadhurst and Adams were smart enough to back him up. A week later the directors were elected at a meeting attended by Hudson, Broadhurst, Nesbitt and Treat only. Hudson had hand picked an almost completely new board including G. Mc-Millian Ross, Amos Jones, E. H. McGowan, John Humphreys, Theodore Bee, Warren Clark, John Strohm, J. E. Luddy and himself. The first four men were prominent Stockton business and professional men—Gilbert McMillian Ross was a consulting mining engineer, Amos Jones and Elmer McGowan were real estate and insurance men, and John Humphreys was president of the Western Normal School. Only Clark had served a full year on the preceding board of directors of the S.T. & E. Railroad.

Adams was again persona non grata and was immediately fired as traffic manager and replaced by Nesbitt. Perhaps 1914 would be a better year with the new board and a new man in control!

The California Railroad Commission assisted by granting permission to issue enough bonds to raise $2,000 to be used as a deposit with the city of Stockton for a change in the franchise. Economics in general were not good in the state, and the S.T. & E. was in worse shape because it was unable to make the annual interest payments on the gold bonds. Late in March 1914 Broadhurst must have had high hopes for getting the railroad out of trouble by way of a government contract. Major General Arthur Murray was in Stockton looking for a possible site for Western Army maneuvers. Broadhurst made a trip to Bellota with Murray's party. A Stockton newspaper quoted Broadhurst as saying the S.T. & E. Railroad could carry a division of soldiers to Bellota. The speculation had been that the area near Bellota was much like Mexico where political trouble had been brewing for some time. The bubble soon burst, however, when an announcement came from San Francisco stating that any maneuvers would be held along the coast.

Early in April, 1914 Luddy, Strohm, Humphreys and Jones resigned. Three weeks later, after Adams and Nesbitt had been reelected to the board, Hudson and McGowan gave up too. Broadhurst also resigned and Adams became general manager again. He immediately moved the company office to the newly remodeled Yosemite building in Stockton. He was elected vice president and picked Charles M. Prater as secretary-treasurer. Prater was a Stockton East Main Street grocer and Adams' landlord and neighbor.

Adams immediately went to work selling bonds. He took installment sales with as little as $15 as a down payment and used some of the first money to make some of the past due interest payments.

During May rail traffic again increased. 14 carloads of sheep were loaded out of the Bellota corrals and cherry shipments moved out of Linden regularly. With the traffic picking up and Adams out generating cash again, the company men decided to solve the motive power problem. Palmer McBride and Quayle Co. had a steam locomotive for sale. It received an official inspection in Santa Fe's Richmond yards on May 28, 1914. An entry was made in the S.T. & E. construction ledger for $29.76, the transportation cost of moving the engine to Stockton.

The new locomotive carried the #1 and, as with the previous engine, the number was retained. S.T. & E. Locomotive #1 was the second locomotive and its Locomotive #2 was the first owned by the road. There would be much confusion in identifying the two engines in later years when new

Here S.T. & E. #1 was still S.P. #1488. It had been repaired following derailment and its modern headlight replaced by an old type light. It was sold shortly after this picture was taken in 1908. (Gerald M. Best collection)

men managed the company.*

Hudson had gained control of the U. I. Co. when Burns had transferred stock, and now Hudson wanted to be protected in a dispute between the railroad and Burns. The S.T. & E. board of directors agreed to transfer the stock into Nesbitt's name to be held in trust for the railroad in return for protecting Hudson from any demand made by Burns or anyone else in the future.

Sometimes the big troubles remain hidden and the smaller ones get the glaring light of publicity. This was especially true now, for the *San Francisco Call Post* ran a front page story with bold headlines on July 19, 1914:

LOOTED, CRY RAILROAD BACKERS—R. M. Cornell, representing 450 stockholders of the United Investment company, holding concern, and the Stockton Terminal and Eastern railway, has filed a complaint with the state railroad commission, in which he accuses the officers of the company of misuse of funds of the corporation, mismanagement and other gross abuses. He says $161,090.76 has disappeared from the treasury.

He charged that the company was loaded with debts, earnings were inadequately accounted for,

*See addenda note #4

and stock donations had been made to 28 favorite stockholders.

Adams reply was also included in the story. He denied all charges and said the road would be built to Jenny Lind. Then he attacked Cornell:

Why that man only owns 15 shares of stock! He has been making his demands from us for the last four or five weeks. He wants money. He is a blackmailer!

The article told of court orders issued to open the company books to representatives of the stockholders group. It concluded with Cornell's attack on Adams:

Behind the charges of Cornell and his 450 associates are intimations of high finance that would make some of the directors of the New Haven road green with envy, says Cornell. He also says the man at the wheel, on whom rests chiefly the responsibility for getting the company into its present predicament, is J. E. Adams, the vice president and general manager.

Martin's *Stockton Record* played the story down the next day, making a point that Cornell was only a switchman and had made the charges by letter. The article quoted Adams extensively and concluded with his comment that the charges were being treated as a joke:

In regard to his statement that 220,000 shares were

donated to favored stockholders it is of course false. Cornell's estimated earnings of $592,000 for our road would surely indicate the ravings of an imbecile. Everyone knows that the road has not any more than paid operating expenses and been lucky to do that on twenty miles of track.

Adams was now walking a fine line in his absolute denial of the charges. He could say that the stock had not been donated but given for services rendered, but it was true that stock had been given and within less than a year a public hearing would reveal that 200,000 shares were handled in this manner. Cornell might have had more success if he had taken his complaint to the new Blue Sky Commission, for the Railroad Commission had no jurisdiction over the investment company.

The working men on the railroad read the stories but they were not bothered by all the board meetings, the commission hearings and court actions, for they had other things to keep them busy. It was the everyday problems of running a railroad that consumed their time.

CHAPTER VII

THE BLUE SKY COMMISSION STRIKES

Although Nicholls had objected strongly to the nomination of a woman on the board of directors, a Mrs. Mary Turner of Mare Island was elected along with Horace J. Kennedy of Stockton in the summer of 1914. Kennedy was a millman for Holt Brothers company and one of the working men who had invested in the railroad. The office of president had been vacant for some time and Bee was named to fill it.

On September 12, 1914 the Stockton Courts granted judgments to Davis, Dietrich, McCormick, the Farmers & Merchants Bank, Stockton Savings & Loan Society and the Commercial and Savings Bank on notes held by all of them and secured by the S.T. & E. gold bonds. Most had received no interest payments and desired to take possession of the bonds.

Adams sent a letter to each S.T. & E. board member on October 1, stating his opinion of the franchise situation in Stockton. He gave his recommendations fortifying them with those of other railroad officials. He wanted the company to apply for a change in the city franchise and advised they abandon the bridge across McLeod Lake and get an extension instead to Lindsey Point. Adams was again in control, for his recommendations were approved by all but two directors. In his next move he applied to the railroad commission for permission to extend the line eastward from Bellota to the county road between the Cady and Conrad ranches.

The annual stockholders meeting proved why Adams was entrenched; he held the proxies for the U. I. Co. stock. Directors for the coming year besides Adams were Bee, Nesbitt, Francis George, H. J. Kennedy, D. F. Owens, C. M. Prater, M. L. Scott and Mary Turner. Scott was from Sonora and Owens was a Lodi vineyardist. Adams was elected president and Bee vice president. Prater was re-elected to secretary-treasurer and Nesbitt was renamed auditor and traffic manager. The new executive committee was made up of Kennedy, Nesbitt and Prater, all residents of Stockton. Most

of the men who now accepted a directorship on the railroad board had watched others over the years and decided that they could do a better job of running a railroad.

Late in November 1914 a stock transfer was made that gave the S.T. & E. Railroad 50,000 shares of U. I. Co. capital stock, which according to board minutes was to be used for a stock donation to anyone who would purchase enough of the company's bonds to complete the line to Jenny Lind.

On January 15, 1915 all the Stockton railroad companies joined together in an attempt to amend the city charter so that they could make extensions within the city. Adams represented the S.T. & E. at a hearing on the subject. He advocated that it was necessary to have more than a 25-year franchise in order to receive a return on the original investments. There was some indication at the meeting that the city might ask for up to 5% of a railroad's gross income.

Adams also testified at a Railroad Commission hearing on the California Traction Company's request to abandon its Stockton tracks. He objected strongly and suggested the S.T. & E. could use the tracks jointly to get to the waterfront.

The cash flow was again off to almost nothing for the railroad and it was time to renew outstanding notes. This was done by issuing new ones and putting up gold bonds as collateral. Demand letters were coming in regularly so the company borrowed $600 apiece from A. Grant, Mary Turner and J. J. Dorman, since it was getting next to impossible to borrow from a bank. The money was used to pay interest, not old bills.

Early in March 1915 the secret financial dealings of the companies involved in the railroad were finally laid out in the open for all to see. The cynic must have been joyful, the pessimist satisfied and the optimist crushed by a news release put out by the California Commissioner of Corporations, H.L.Carnahan.

Here is part of the story as it appeared under a

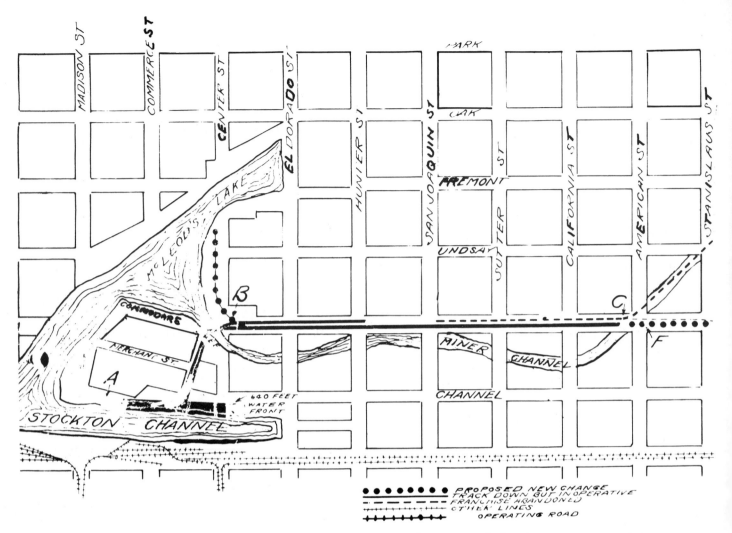

Legend:
● ● ● ● ● ● PROPOSED NEW CHANGE
━ ━ ━ ━ ━ TRACK DOWN BUT INOPERATIVE
━ ━ ━ ━ FRANCHISE ABANDONED
OTHER LINES
╋╋╋╋╋╋ OPERATING ROAD

The S.T. & E. Stockton Franchise map and proposed changes made by the company in the fall of 1914. (City of Stockton)

Sacramento dateline on March 13, 1915:

Following an investigation and audit of the books of the United Investment Company of Stockton, H. L. Carnahan, Commissioner of Corporations will hold a public hearing Wednesday, March 17, at Stockton on the application of the company for permission to sell its stock to the public.

Stock in the investment company was sold throughout northern and central California and elsewhere and altogether 578,610 shares at the par value of $1 were issued before the blue sky law became effective.

For this stock $234,000 cash went to the company's treasury and some $60,000 cash commissions were paid to stock salesmen. The railroad company raised additional money by selling bonds in the sum of $83,700 and by borrowing $40,000 on notes secured by $100,000 of its own bonds.

The United Investment Company applied to the commissioner of corporations for permission to continue the sale of its capital stock. Upon the demand of the commissioner that it submit to an investigation of its books and accounts the company filed a supplementary application asking permission to issue only 47,567 shares of its capital stock, which it claimed had been subscribed previous to the blue sky law taking effect and on which it represented that the subscribers, about 400 in number, still owed the company $34,487.93.

It appeared from the statements made by officers of the company and from the investigation of its books that some 200,000 of the outstanding shares had been issued to various individuals, some of them present officers of the company, as promotional stock, for which the return to the company was of questionable value. Some of the holders of this promotion stock were offering their shares for sale as low as 15 cents per share while the company was endeavoring to continue operations by selling its stock at $1 per share. Of the stock which the company sold for cash some went for as low as 50 cents per share and some as high as $1.50. The company's stock is said to be held by approximately 2,000 stockholders scattered widely about the northern part of the state and the bay cities.

The officers of the United Investment Company, then on the 19th day of February, organized a new company under the laws of California, to be known as the Ter-

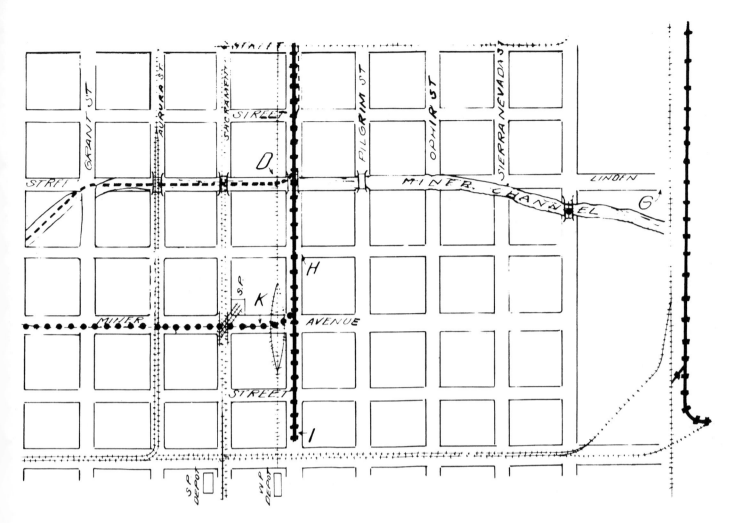

minal Development Company with an authorized capital of $750,000 and the company made application to the commissioner of corporations for permission to sell its capital stock to the public.

The alleged purpose of this new company is to take up the work of financing the Stockton Terminal and Eastern Railroad Company at the point where the United Investment Company left off.

The application of both companies will be considered at the hearing next Wednesday. As these companies are closely related to the Stockton Terminal and Eastern Railroad Company which is a public utility corporation and the State Railroad Commission will also be represented at the hearing.

We are sure the directors of the S.T. & E. did not need to be warned "to beware the Ides of March," after this news item appeared. Adams departed for New York to visit a sister who was reported to be seriously ill, leaving Nesbitt to testify at the upcoming hearing. We do not know how ill Adams' sister was at the time, but she did eventually die from tuberculosis.

At 10:00 a.m. on March 18, 1915, in Stockton, Commissioner H. L. Carnahan opened his first public hearing conducted by the so-called Blue Sky Commission in the state of California. Strangely enough the S.T. & E. Railroad, through the U. I. Co., was to be the subject of this hearing just as it had been the first under the California Railroad Commission's valuation hearing.

Carnahan explained the purpose of the hearing:

It is within the power of the commission to grant or refuse the application to issue and sell stock. If it should grant permission to sell stock it may fix the terms and conditions under which the stock may be sold. Any proposed plan must be fair, honest and just. This inquiry into the conduct of the affairs of the company is to determine these things. This commission wants to know the financial situation, the character of the people who are conducting the business and the character of the business they are conducting.

J. A. Nesbitt took the stand and remained under questioning until after 5 P.M. that evening and most of the next day. The questioning was led by Deputy Commissioner Horace Brown with additional questions from Auditor Roy W. Blair, who had inspected the company books, and Carnahan. The state Railroad Commission was represented by its auditor, T. G. Hughes and Attorney Douglas Brookman. A. H. Carpenter appeared as an attorney for the S.T. & E. Railroad.

Nesbitt related the early history of the railroad and revealed facts about the promotional stock that had been given to various people including Newell. He went on to say that Newell had failed to interest certain financial men in the project and that subsequently directors of the company threatened suit against him. The suit was dropped when the company secured an option on this stock which was finally returned. This must have been the 50,000 shares handed over to Nesbitt as trustee for the S.T. & E. in November. Nesbitt revealed that each of the present directors got 1,800 and the attorney 3,000 additional shares of U. I. Co. stock for their assistance in getting the stock back.

Commissioner Carnahan declared that the transaction was a remarkable one and that he wanted to hear all details. Deputy Commissioner Brown asked, "Did stock salesmen explain to prospective purchasers that holders of the promotion stock were offering their stock on the market at 15 cents per share?"

"It wouldn't be natural for them to explain that to a new prospect," replied Nesbitt.

Of course there was general laughter in the courtroom but to some it was not long a laughing matter, for they soon learned what the Terminal Development Co. had in mind to do with their stock. The new company wanted to issue $400,000 worth of stock immediately, of which 282,930 shares would be set aside for exchange with holders of the United Investment Company treasury stock, excluding the promotion stock, leaving promotional stockholders high and dry. Robert Burns asked Nesbitt if he was going to let the United Investment company die.

Nesbitt replied, "It is little better than dead now. We are no longer able to sell stock because of the large amount of promotion stock on its books."

"Is it true that stock salesmen represented that the United Investment Company had the exclusive option on all of the railroad's stock?" Burns asked.

"Yes, they did."

"If this stock is now sold to the Terminal Development Company, would this not be a violation of that understanding?"

"Something has to be violated to build the road," was Nesbitt's reply.

Carnahan asked, "How can the new company be expected to be more attractive than the present one?"

"It would have no promotion stock. All would be paid for and the new company would not be confronted with the embarrassing situation of trying to sell stock at $1 a share when its own stockholders, owning promotion stock which cost them nothing, are selling for prices as low as 15 cents."

Wm. Nicholls Jr., the former board member who had purchased some of Gardner's promotional stock, objected, saying that his shares would be worthless. He gave his version of the purchase of the Gardner shares. He said he had purchased 20,000 shares for $6,000 believing that he was getting all of the Gardner stock except 4,000 shares that were going to Andrew McCormick who would assume the presidency of the company.

"Business is business and friendship is friendship. My good friend Robert F. Burns induced me to purchase the Gardner stock and I afterwards learned that Burns fooled me. I have lost faith in my fellow man. It is now apparent that Gardner held 34,000 shares and that 10,000 shares went to Burns."

A discussion then occurred between the two with Nesbitt questioning Nicholls' innocence. Nicholls asked, "Did I ever offer any of the stock for less than it cost me?"

"You offered it for 20 cents."

"Is that so? Well, I would sell for that but I never offered any at that."

Nicholls then asked, "Did it cost the company about $10,000 to collect $12,000 due it?"

"It did."

"Could any set of officers pile up debts faster than you?"

"Yes, sir," was Nesbitt's reply.

Dr. Congdon, one of the original members of the board of directors of the S.T. & E., stated that stock salesmen had sold $100 bonds of the railraod for $80 and had given a bonus of 40 shares of U. I. Co. stock. He wanted to know what would become of the bonus shares in the event the plans went through as proposed. Nesbitt said they would be lost.

John Kenyon, a stock salesman, testified that he knew more about sailors than high finance: "I guess people who told me I had been used as a tool knew what they were talking about. I lied to stockholders repeating statements made by Adams who I considered honest." He added that Stockton bankers had told him they would not loan the railroad money because it was poorly managed and he had found much opposition to Adams among eastern stockholders.

BLUE SKY COMMISSION'S FIRST CASE

STOCKTON TERMINAL AND EASTERN RAILROAD ASKS FOR PERMISSION TO RAISE FUNDS TO COMPLETE ITS PROJECT

State Corporation Commissioner Carnahan, Who Is in Stockton Today Holding His First Public Hearing, Inquires Into Gift of Stock to Original Promoters of the Railroad—New Holding Corporation Has Been Formed for the Purpose of Taking Over the Paid Stock of the United Investment Company—Unraveling Financial Tangles.

The first public hearing conducted by the so-called "blue sky commission" in the state of California was opened in Stockton this morning by Commissioner of Corporations H. L. Carnahan, who, following the application of the United Investment Company for permission to sell its stock to the public, is endeavoring to unravel the tangle of transactions entered into by the company in its efforts to finance the construction of a thirty-mile railroad.

The United Investment Company was organized several years ago for the purpose of financing the construction of the Stockton Terminal ... placed, neglected from

Island, N. B. Long of Stockton, Bertha Helm, J. H. Dorman and Francis George of Crockett, D. F. Owens of Lodi, M. L. Scott and A. A. Grant of Sonora, J. W. Churchill of Cotati, Theodore C. Bee and F. Crawford of Oakland, J. E. Adams, J. A. Nesbitt, H. J. Kennedy and C. M. Prater of Stockton.

The application of the Terminal Development Company seeks permission to sell its 750,000 shares of stock at par. No stock has been issued, and it has no debts. Directors will be elected from among the organizers named, providing the "blue sky commission" o. k.'s the scheme.

What the Terminal Wants

The Terminal Development Company seeks permission immediately to issue $400,000 worth of stock, of ...ill be set

the project. Nesbitt said that Newell failed to use the $88,000 worth of promotion stock for the purposes for which it had been issued and that soon thereafter he departed for South America, where he became interested in another railroad. Subsequently directors of the company threatened suit against Newell and finally did commence suit to secure a return of the stock. The suit was halted when the company secured an option on 50,000 shares of the Newell stock, which was later returned to the company. Each of the directors was presented with 1800 shares of stock for securing the return of the Newell stock and the attorney who instituted the suit was presented with 2000 shares.

Commissioner Carnahan declared that the transaction was a remarkable one and that he wanted to hear all

In addition to the story in a Sacramento newspaper, the Stockton Record ran front page headlines on March 17, 1915. (San Joaquin County Library)

53

Kenyon concluded, "I believe the United Investment Company can still get money to complete the road if properly managed."

A Stockton blacksmith also appeared at the hearings and voiced concern for his hard earned investment, according to a local newspaper:

An element of pathos was introduced at the hearings by J. H. Kennedy, a white-haired, horny-handed son of toil, who declared that he had invested $150 in the United Investment Company, for which he had been issued 150 shares of stock. He declared that he was amazed at what he had heard during the day and wanted to know whether the commissioner of corporations proposed to permit such actions on the part of the directors to continue. He wanted to be assured that if the new holding corporation is sanctioned that he would be issued 150 shares of stock in the new concern.

Commissioner Carnahan had difficulty in convincing Kennedy, who had become skeptical regarding all things, that the very purpose of the blue sky law and the commissioner of corporations is to protect innocent investors and that the rights of Kennedy would be fully conserved.

Carnahan then asked U. I. Co. director Owens what he considered would be the solution to the company's problems.

Owens answered, "I wish I knew. I own stock in the project and I want to see the railroad line completed because I know it will prove a good thing. I went on the board of directors in order to get on the inside and make an honest endeavor to accomplish something. If we could only adopt some scheme of placing all stockholders on an equal footing dollar for dollar paid in, I think it would solve the difficulty. If we could call in 20,000 shares of stock for which a man paid $6,000 and issue him 6,000 shares in exchange, it would place him on an equal footing with the man who paid $1 per share."

At the conclusion of the hearings Commissioner Carnahan announced that the decision of the commission would be forthcoming in the near future.

Within two weeks a news item out of Sacramento directed the public not to purchase stock in any investment company without asking to see its Blue Sky permit. This was followed with regular releases of names of companies being approved by the Commissioner of Corporations.

Shortly after this the change in the city charter as proposed by the railroads was soundly defeated by a three-to-one margin. It makes one wonder if the blue sky hearing in Stockton had not after all influenced the voters. Immediately the S.T. & E. board gave orders to remove all track which

had been laid west of American Street as soon as permission to remove it was received from the railroad commission and the Mercantile Trust Company. They also ordered the 50,000 shares of U. I. Co. stock which had been transferred to Nesbitt, as trustee, returned, as ordered by the commissioner of corporations. The board minutes stated that the commissioner felt that the transfer was made to avoid dealing with his office but another resolution declared this was never intended.

On April 7, 1915 Adams and Nesbitt appeared before the Railroad Commission In San Francisco. A report on the hearing was contained in Dennis Donohue's column on the financial page of the *San Francisco Examiner:*

WOES OF AMATEUR RAILROADS—Although Commissioner Devlin could not restrain a pervasive smile at times, yet, all in all he was sympathetic in his treatment of the warring directors of the Stockton Terminal and Eastern Railroad, who had journeyed from Stockton to pour their accumulated grievances into his receptive ear.

Nominally, the proceedings took the form of an application for the approval of a contract entered into between the railroad and a concern calling itself the De Mayo Engineering Company of New York; but since J. E. Adams, president of the road, backed by a substantial minority of the directorate, disapproved of this contract, absolutely and unequivocally, the hearing bade fair once or twice to degenerate into that form of argument in which Jess Willard has just established his superiority over Jack Johnson. Devlin's suavity, however, saved the day.

The Stockton Terminal boasts the ownership of 18½ miles of track from Stockton to Bellota and as President Adams plaintively remarked, "No big money has ever come into the road."

It is owned practically entirely by the small stockholders-ranchers, country merchants and the like—four of these draw $150 apiece out of its slender earnings for "running" the enterprise.

The Stockton Terminal, as a concrete entity has always possessed a hankering for discovering some indurated optimist to put up the "big money" necessary to extend the road to Jenny Lind, which is almost 11 miles beyond Bellota—wherever on earth that may be!

So last year, the company dispatched its auditor, J. A. Nesbitt, to New York, with general instructions to dig up a capitalist with abundant and abiding faith.

Somewhere in the purlieus of Wall Street Nesbitt connected with the De Mayo Company with the result a contract was signed by which the engineering company agreed to build the road on the following terms: Cash in the amount of $750, as soon as the contract was approved by the commission; $750 more when the

The front of a picture post card used to advertise the railroad. This card contained J. E. Adams' request for company balance sheets from Nesbitt. (S.T. & E. collection)

engineers arrived; $360,000 first mortgage, 6 percent bonds of the road at 80% to be turned over at the rate of $14,000 for each mile completed; $50,000 stock of the United Investment Company as a bonus to be turned over at the rate of 5,000 shares per mile.

Corporation Commissioner Carnahan sat down hard on the bonus stock and as a result the $50,000 stock was turned back into the treasury and cancelled.

On cross-examination by Devlin, Nesbitt admitted that he had not verified the De Mayo reference before signing the contract.

President Adams, backed by director Adolf Michel, contended that the contract should not be approved and Nesbitt and his backers were equally bent on securing official sanction.

"We have chased five or six similar shadows," declared Adams, "and nothing save worry and loss ever came of our pursuit of these financial phantoms. At the same time I should like to get enough bonds authorized to justify us in building two miles out to the quarry, where we can get the hauling of as much as six or seven carloads of rock a day."

"I may say right here," remarked the commissioner, "that as far as the De Mayo contract is concerned, I do not look favorably upon it. I doubt much whether the commission would approve such a contract."

This belittling by the city folks was only a mosquito bite to the S.T. & E. Railroad compared to the venomous attack by Commissioner of Cor-

porations Carnahan the next week. He summarized the condition of the U. I. Co. and the S.T. & E. Railroad:

From the evidence taken at the public hearing and records of this case it would appear that this whole railroad scheme was conceived in ignorance, was reared in poverty and under incompetent management has now arrived at a state of premature decrepitude from which it seems almost impossible to rejuvenate it.

The commission did grant permission for the U. I. Co. to sell the stock subscribed before the Blue Sky law was enacted but also gave the subscribers the right to decline.

The Terminal Development Company was given permission to issue 60,000 shares of its stock with the money to be used only to purchase and develop the gravel beds and build two miles of additional railroad to reach them. Other conditions in selling the stock were laid out. All stock money would be held in the Union Safe Deposit Bank of Stockton unless $2,500 was raised by May 10, 1915 to meet a payment on the gravel property. Also included was a stipulation that $30,000 must be raised by April 1, 1916 or all but 7½%, which would go to stock salesmen, would be returned to the stock buyers. The Commissioner cited examples of abuses used by the company in past dealings:

55

The results of more than seven years expenditure of time and $309,270 in money paid in by the stockholders of the United Investment Company, is a present stock liability of 578,610 par shares outstanding and about 18 miles of railroad, which is operating at a loss and which is subject to bond and note obligations to the amount of approximately $130,000.

Of the 578,610 shares issued 297,296 shares were sold and 281,314 were given away. Of the $309,370 received from stock sales, less than $200,000 went into railroad construction.

Over $100,000 has been expended for commissions, salaries and office expense.

The charges went on and on but it suffices to say all the damage to the reputation of the S.T. & E. Railroad had been done. The stocks could not be sold. The directors did let a contract to Haney to do the necessary grading on the Marquardt ranch near Bellota and more loans were negotiated to add rails above Bellota.

Late in June a colored picture postcard arrived in the Stockton office. It showed a pastoral scene with the words, "378 cows in a pasture in San Joaquin Valley, California." There was also an overprint of words: "The Stockton Terminal & Eastern Railroad trains now operate through such level country as this. The owning company wants more shareholders."

The card had been mailed from Oakland on June 28. The message on the back was in definite contrast to the peaceful scene on the front, however; it was a curt appeal from Adams to Nesbitt: "Kindly mail me immediately copy of the last balance sheets each compnay. Kenyon has things in a deuce of a fix but I believe we will live through it."

More requests came in for money due. J. F. Dietrich sent a letter about the Stockton Savings and Loan bank note he had signed back in 1912, which apparently had never been paid, and several more lawsuits were filed against the company.

It was time for the railroad to become the Stop Talking and Eat Railroad, time for action instead of words, but the men in charge continued to plod along doing only what seemed to be expedient at the moment.

CHAPTER VIII

FRUSTRATION REIGNS

The section gang was working on the track almost constantly now. The poor track construction, over the unstable roadbed, was causing constant problems. The rails would literally creep ahead of the train and separate. In other places the original light steel rails would bow out of shape.

In the summer of 1915 a 17-year-old redhead, John Hewitt, left his home town of Bakersfield and traveled to Stockton to visit his sister. After a time he ran out of money, so he went job hunting and was hired as a section hand by the S.T. & E. in early September.

Hewitt recalls that around 20 people rode the motor coach to town daily after school started that fall. The coach left Bellota at 7:00 A.M. and Stockton's Western Pacific Station at 4:30 P.M., which made a long day for the high school youths.

Adams reported an unsafe condition of the track between Bellota and Fine Road late in September. He recommended the discontinuance of passenger service, but no action was taken. Apparently an attempt was made to repair the track instead.

Conditions in general were bad for the farmers who lived along the S.T. & E. railroad. Late in May a storm hit the area and caused as much as 30% loss of some cherry varieties. Peaches were late ripening, causing them to come into competition with eastern fruit and making it unprofitable to ship them. This only added to S.T. & E. problems for it cut into the usual summer revenue.

The gloom spreaders in general must have been busy. Mt. Lassen was erupting in northern California and earthquakes were being reported in all the western states and along the Pacific Coast. There was a minor earthquake in the company, too, on September 15, 1915 when Adams and Nesbitt were ordered to appear before the Stockton City Council, on summons from Mayor Ollahan. Adams asserted that the company did not have money to remove the tracks from Miner Avenue. The council declared if the company did not remove the tracks

the city would do it and charge it against the value of the rails.

Four days later one more blow was delivered by Commissioner Carnahan. He formally revoked the permit of the Terminal Development Company to sell stock shares. Investors were informed they had until October 1, 1915 to write to the Union Safe Deposit Bank in Stockton to get their money back.

The end of the long summer had come when in October Davis, Dietrich and McCormick, through the law firm of Clary and Louttit, requested payment of the notes issued in 1912, but still no action was taken. Finances were again a problem; Nesbitt's salary was reduced to $100 a month. A new tactic was attempted as an assessment of $10 was levied on all of the S.T. & E. capital stock. The deadline for payment was set for November 27. Since the United Investment Company owned all but the few single shares held by directors and past directors, this too was apparently another legal maneuver. The United Investment Company was in no position to pay such an assessment since it could no longer sell its stock and had never received any dividends on its S.T. & E. stock.

The home owners association of the Oaks subdivision put constant pressure on the S.T. & E. to improve the street around the tracks in their area. The group had assessed themselves to pave the streets and wanted the railroad to comply with the city franchise rules. Street Commissioner O'Keefe had ordered the company "to get busy and get the job done." Adams appeared before a home owners meeting to smooth things over. He promised that he would start the work soon. Yet within two weeks the city council initiated proceedings against the S.T. & E. for failure to do so.

In October 1915 the time for the annual stockholders meeting came again, with Adams still holding the proxies for U. I. Co. This time Adams, Bee, Owens, Prater, Scott, Nesbitt, Turner and George were all reelected directors and J. W. Churchill was added. The officers were all reelected two weeks later, with Adams still president and general manager and Nesbitt auditor and traffic manager.

The Yosemite Valley Railroad requested a note for money owed by the company but secretary Prater was told to advise them that "the company did not desire to comply."

Late in November the board met and declared the U. I. Co.-owned railroad stock was delinquent for nonpayment of the $10 assessment and levied another $10 assessment on the same stock. The whole thing was an exercise in futility.

New Year's Day 1916 dawned in Stockton with a four inch blanket of snow covering the landscape. It was a rarity that gave the town a fresh, clean, peaceful look for the new year. The mood did not last long for the faltering railroad, however, for when the men arrived at work the gasoline motor car would not start. A quick examination revealed that the carburetor was gone. During the night a thief had been at work. So the S.T. & E. Railroad started out the new year by failing to make its first scheduled trip to Linden and Bellota.

Each January had meant more financial problems and this one was worse than ever. The company gave a promissory note to a Stockton attorney for fees on service rendered three years before and another to the S.P. Railroad for more than $1,500. Wm. Nicholls went to court to prevent a judgment on the stock assessment and the Bellota school trustees claimed fire damage to the school building caused by "the carelessness of the section men."

During February 1916 the S.T. & E. Railroad Company office was moved from Stockton to San Francisco. Although the board of directors refused to take legal action against Davis, Dietrich and McCormick, as requested by the company secretary Prater, they did approve his action in doing so. The board passed a resolution stating that they considered the three men paid with the bonds they were holding as security. Prater's suit charged fraud and conspiracy and accused the former directors of illegally issuing the gold bonds.

Paper maneuvers had been continuing since the first assessment made against the S.T. & E. stock the previous October. Because the U. I. Co. could not pay the assessments, the railroad went to court to get judgment against the investment company. In turn the liability was prorated against each of the U. I. Co. shares. In order to avoid this liability, most of the large stockholders agreed to give their U. I. Co. stock away to other stockholders who

would accept their responsibility. Nesbitt accepted stock on these terms from Wm. Nicholls Jr., L. M. Nicholls, W. C. Nicholls (trustee), James Regan, J. L. Tisdale, G. Herring, Harry Lande, Adolf Michel, M. C. Voorhies and Samuel Gummett. Nesbitt then gave the S.T. & E. Company a promissory note for $4,372.84, using the stock as collateral and turning it over to the company as trustee.

The stock of E. F. Davis, F. J. Dietrich, Andrew McCormick, M. McCormick Co., Geo. F. Hudson, Irene Burns, Minnie Purington, Edward Pearne Congdon, and M. J. Congdon went to Churchill, W. C. Wuerth and Adams, under the same conditions. Nesbitt gained more in these transactions than anyone else, but as had happened so often in the company's history the whole thing was a paper action that produced no money to help the floundering railroad.

During the spring of 1916 Commissioner of Corporations Carnahan issued orders that promotion stock could not be sold or offered for sale except with permission from his office. A Stockton news story quoted him:

It was found that one of the worst evils in the promotion of companies was the practice of promoters to take stock for their services or in exchange for patents, mining claims, etc. and then to unload it upon the public under the representation that the proceeds were to finance the enterprise. Instead the money went into the pocket of promoters.

The Railroad Commission was also reacting much less kindly to the S.T. & E. Railroad. At a public hearing held in Stockton early in June the company once again tried to get permission to issue more bonds but was denied. The order was accomplished with a statement which read in part, "It further appears that applicants earnings as well as its general finances are in a most unsatisfactory condition: the commission would decline to grant permission for any purpose other than renewing notes."

In August of that year there was a threat of a nationwide strike. President Wilson finally intervened and sent a special message to Congress. On September 2 the "Eight-Hour Bill" was passed, which made it mandatory for interstate railroads to work men only eight hours a day for the same pay they had been receiving for ten hours. The new law would be in effect as of January 1, 1917. Although pessimists predicted that the bill would soon bring government ownership of all railroads, this did not occur. The strike threat did, however, have a detrimental effect on the price of local produce along the S.T. & E. track and cut into the revenue again.

In July Adams requested and received the S.T. & E. Company proxy of U. I. Co. stock for a meeting of the latter company to be held in Phoenix, Arizona on August 12, 1916. This was the normal time for the annual stockholders meeting but we found no record that the meeting was ever held, or what happened if not, or of it was held why it was once again moved out of California. An effort to avoid the troublesome Commissioner of Corporations would probably account for an out-of-state meeting.

Nesbitt was instructed to contact the S. P. Railroad Company and offer then the company franchise rights on the north side of the Stockton waterfront, but no response came from the S. P.

Late in August the directors decided to pay no more bond interest until it could all be paid, but to set aside in a separate fund any money available. Worse yet, they also agreed to take bonds or bond coupons in payment for the assessment on the company capital stock, another paper transaction which did not pay the bills.

The Stockton City Council was once again asking the company to lower the tracks in the Oaks and Adams appeared at a council meeting to ask for more time. He and Commissioner O'Keefe engaged in a "wordy battle" according to a Stockton news story: "O'Keefe said he was not willing to stand for a minute more delay. 'The Roosevelt tracks are dangerous.' "

Adams' version of this animosity was entered in the company board minutes two months later:

Early in 1913 our engineer reported that the street Commissioner O'Keefe had instructed him to raise our tracks in the Oaks. He promptly did this entailing an expense of $1,800. Later on this same O'Keefe ordered the whole grade in the Oaks dropped down again some eight or ten inches lower than any other part of town. Asphalt streets now make fine basins in the winter time and the cars of the S.T. & E. plow through water knee deep after dropping down into the Oaks coming into town. This lowering of the grade put everything under water and guilty officials try to shift the blame onto the little road.

During the work of lowering our tracks some of the city Dads came out to the Oaks in an automobile and attempted to cross our tracks while street work was in progress—tracks being up in the air about 18 inches. The automobile hung there unable to move either back or forward. In the meantime our motor car rounded the curve into their machine. Damages for $300 were asked of us, which we promptly refused to pay. Perhaps we should have paid it.

It is little wonder that the company found so little support in Stockton at that time. The managers had alienated city officials, state commissioners, local businessmen, bankers and most of the stock and bond holders.

An abortive attempt was made by the company to run a stage line from the end of the railroad to Jenny Lind in September 1915, but this lasted only a week. On the first day the stage driver got drunk and did not show up for work so young Red Hewitt was given the job. He had a carload of passengers and delivered them to Jenny Lind after dark. Fortunately some of the passengers knew where they were going for young Hewitt did not. He stayed overnight and started back to Bellota to meet the train the next morning. This time he had only one passenger, also a stranger to the area and they ended up getting lost and missing the train back to Stockton. The next day the regular driver showed up but the company abandoned the whole idea within a week.

In another desperate move, the board ordered Nesbitt to apply to the California Railroad Commission for permission to reduce the S.T. & E. stock from $100 to $1 per share. He did this by applying for permission to issue 263,900 shares of common capital stock at a par value of $1.00 each in exchange for 2,639 shares of its capital stock, $100 par value, outstanding. Nesbitt testified that the U. I. Co. would receive railroad stock on a basis of one share of railroad stock to two shares of investment stock. Not surprisingly, the Commissioner denied the application.

On September 6, 1916 Adams handed in his resignation as president of the S.T. & E. Railroad, as follows, "Being no longer in perfect accord with the politics which seem to be governing, I am herewith tendering my resignation as President and General Manager of this company."

The board relieved him of his job as general manager but did not accept his resignation as president. He was directed to spend time collecting the pro-rata charges of the payments due the company on the stock. Superintendent M. I. Dohmer was given full charge of the railroad operations. However, just two weeks later, Adams informed the directors that Dohmer had hired him to work for the company in Stockton. He again asked that his resignation as president be accepted but the directors again took no action.

About this time another mishap occurred at Largo station. The crew was switching cars around and attempting a fly-by, a means of

Stockton's busy Main Street looking west near California Street. S. T. & E. president J. E. Adams blamed the growing use of automobiles as shown here for the financial downfall of the railroad. (Stockton Chamber of Commerce)

propelling a car down the track and out of the way. In this case Engine #1 went up the main line pushing a box car ahead of it at high speed. It slowed down and as the two pulled apart a switch was thrown, opening the siding to the locomotive. The siding was too short and the locomotive with its brakes locked skidded off the end of the track and sank up to its axles in the mud.

Engine #1 was off the track for more than a week and then had to be sent to the S. P. shops in Sacramento for repairs. Adams signed a contract with the S. P. Railroad for the use of Locomotive 1416 at $15.00 per day, doing exactly what he had condemned Cameron for doing three years earlier.

Nesbitt filed a formal letter with the board of directors dated September 30, 1916:

I don't want to run things and I don't want you to take my word for anything, but I do want you to investigate for yourselves and see if this railroad property is being managed as if it were all your own individual property.

He complained of the expense of operation, the poor service offered by the road, poor operation of the company telephone, the excessive pay to the section crews, and a long list of grievances against Adams. Most of the charges were not new, just the old ones dredged up again.

Adams' resignation was finally accepted, but Bee refused to take on the presidency so the office was left vacant. The section gang quit work because they had received no pay checks, and took their problems to the State Labor Commission.

Adams sent a letter in reply to Nesbitt's accusations, on October 9. His communication was twice as long as Nesbitt's, going over the whole history of the railroad, and containing many accusations he had voiced before. He completely reviewed the franchise and concluded:

The automobile has completely changed the value of the franchise to any company and the much berated jitney is not the railroad's worst enemy either; the privately owned car is the culprit. When our franchises were obtained several farmers in the Linden section owned their automobiles. Now there are several of the said farmers who don't own one. Our passenger business used to be worth about six hundred dollars per month, now three hundred is good.

Coming back to the franchise matters. Stockton has a new Mayor and a new City Attorney. These two with Dennis O'Keefe are the City of Stockton and these three men are for driving the S.T. & E. from the city.

He concluded by recommending that all the tracks in Stockton be taken up and put on the eastern end of the line above Bellota. Nesbitt was laid off and the secretary was ordered to ask his

bonding company to audit the books. Adams, Prater, Turner and Churchill voted for the action; Nesbitt, George and Bee voted against it. Adams was left in charge again.

There was $500 due on wages in Stockton which the company had been ordered to pay by December 12, 1916. The directors decided to sell 8,000 shares of U. I. Co. stock for 10 cents a share, the proceeds to be used to meet the payroll. They also agreed that the bonds had little value so they decided to sell them wherever they could for 50% of the face value, even though the California Railroad Commission had ordered that they could not be sold for less than 80%.

On November 29, the Pacific Car Demurrage Bureau issued a draft for $5.00 on the S.T. & E. bank account and was notified that there were no funds.

Everyone was talking about the poor little railroad. A conversation between Frank Meier and some male friends in Linden occurred about this time. He turned and pointed to Muriel Stroup and said, "Her father was the one who started it all. It was his idea."

Let us read what followed in Muriel Stroup Saunby's own words:

I sought Mrs. Meier and asked, "Did my father do wrong starting this railroad?"

"No indeed. It was a very good idea and was started to help the farmers transport their produce and service the gold mining towns. At one time there was a corral, where farmers could leave horses with hay and water for the day, while they hopped a train to do business in Stockton. It gave good service for a long time. Be proud of your father."

I was with Papa soon and asked him if he started the S.T. & E. He looked wry.

"Why?"

I told him what Mrs. Meier had said.

"Yes, I did, it was my idea. After we got it going, they wanted more important people on their first board. I was squeezed out."

I am sure I looked crestfallen. He said, "Don't feel badly. This is the Motor Age and there will be trucks to haul freight."

Judge J. A. Plummer denied Prater's legal petition against Davis, Dietrich and McCormick. He included a lengthy statement which concluded with his learned opinion of what was wrong with the S.T. & E. Railroad:

The allegations of fraud and conspiracy contained in the complaint were unsupported by any evidence worthy of consideration, and seem to have been based entirely upon the disappointment experienced by the promoters of the enterprise which failed to take tangible form. It is only one more instance of where lack of realization is both father and mother to accusations of wrong doing on the part of someone else. That the Stockton Terminal & Eastern Railroad has so far not been a profitable enterprise is unquestioned, but the same may be said of the Western Pacific and other ventures where stockholders had had no other returns than experience.

He concluded by removing the restraining order sought by Prater, which meant the judgments of Davis, Dietrich and McCormick against the bonds were upheld, but the banks still had possession of the bonds.

Shortly after this, Adams ran out of money and left town with his wife and daughter.

Prater had kept the minutes of the board meetings up to December but none of them was ever signed after Nesbitt's and Adams' letters were entered into the minutes back in October. The last minutes were entered in the books under a date of December 9, 1916. Tucked in the back of the book were notes written on S.T. & E. envelopes and a scrap of paper. These were dated Stockton, April 26, 1917. The meeting had been called for morning, but adjourned until mid-afternoon. Adams presided over the session, with Prater, Turner, Nesbitt, Churchill and Scott present. Although Adams was conducting the meeting he presented a resolution, written in his handwriting on the back of a portion of an I.C.C. form: "Resolved that this board of directors elects to consider J. Nesbitt guilty of Misfeasance, Non Feasance and or Malfeasance in office and that we hereby declare his office of director vacant for the reasons mentioned herein."

The notes say that the resolution carried unanimously, but it is difficult to believe that Nesbitt voted for it. It is a mystery that will remain unsolved for there is no way to determine exactly what occurred. However, the rest of the notes confirm that he was removed as director. Adams declared a nomination by Nesbitt out of order and a vote for a new director was retaken when it was discovered that Nesbitt had cast a ballot.

The bond company's audit report, requested earlier, showed that minor corrections needed to be made in the company books but did not uphold Adams' accusations against Nesbitt.

With all of the sloppy operations of the U. I. Co. and the S.T. & E. Railroad over the years, we could find no proof that any of the men were crooks. Even the $45 in cash that a sailor claimed to have sent to Burns for stock could have disappeared before ever reaching the company office. If there was a leak in the pot it was in the sales of the stocks and bonds. Both the Railroad and the Blue Sky Commissions pointed out that the cost of stock and bond sales were excessive. The working men on the road also tended to agree; they suspected that "salesmen made pockets of money for themselves." There had been too much salaried management and we did find evidence of greed, arrogance and an unbelievable head-in-the-sand attitude by directors of the company. There was a lack of ethics by today's standards, but not necessarily by those of that day. It must be remembered that business practices of the time were so loose that one state commission after another was organized to protect the public. The problems of the S.T. & E. were mainly a case of too little too late—too little money to complete the road, and too late to reap the bonanza of the railroad years.

CHAPTER IX

RECEIVERSHIP UNDER DIETRICH

The life's breath of the company seemed to be coming in gasps by now and death seemed imminent for the S.T. & E. Railroad. No one was working on the road except 18-year-old John Hewitt. He drove the Mitchell on the rails to Bellota each day, delivering bread and hauling light freight. He towed the trailer in which to haul the freight just in case he had a few stray passengers, but almost no one depended on the railroad for transportation any more.

Hewitt took in cash, bought the necessary fuel, lived in the bunk house at the company yards and bought groceries enough to feed himself. He kept a cash record of all transactions, but received no wages. He was the railroad during the winter and spring of 1916-1917. He later said, "I didn't know anything about the company finances; it was my job to keep the railroad running."

By spring the railroad tracks were overgrown with weeds and the rails were getting rusty since only the little auto-car traveled the line. Engine #1 was still in the S. P. shop and if the money had been paid to get it out, there was no one left to run it. Citing the interruption of service, the Wells Fargo Company applied for permission to discontinue its agency in Linden.

Mrs. Muriel Stroup Saunby recalls, "We children sang, Slow Tired and Easy and Stop Talk and Eat cruelly about the S. T. & E."

Farmers who lived along the line became concerned when it looked as if there would be no way to get their produce to market during the upcoming harvest season and filed a complaint with the Railroad Commission. On May 27, 1917, a second complaint was filed charging that the road did not maintain its schedule, that it lacked funds, its employees had not been paid for four months, it had no gasoline and the lone engine was in the S.P. shop. The Commissioners finally decided to make an investigation.

At the same time the Mercantile Trust Company of San Francisco filed a notice of default on the first deed of trust held by them. The company stated that the S.T. & E. had defaulted on the bond coupon payments. With both payments and principal now due, the railroad owed $166,000. The trust company requested, through its attorney Thomas S. Louttit, that F. J. Dietrich of Stockton be named receiver. This was done in Judge Buck's chambers of the Superior court on June 12, 1917. Louttit represented both the Trust company and a group of bondholders.

The next day a man appeared at the S. T. & E. depot and office on Union Street. He looked around and found no one but the young redhead, Hewitt. He asked many questions but did not say who he was or why he was there. Hewitt was evasive and finally lost his temper.

"What the hell do you want? I have work to do. I have to go to Linden and get back before dark." The lights on the Mitchell were out of order and Hewitt knew it was too dangerous to travel the track in the dark.

The stranger told Hewitt that a receiver had been appointed and served some papers on him.

"You will have to hand over the money you have on hand."

Hewitt remembers it was only about $12.00 since he had just bought a tank of gasoline. He finally got started to Linden as the man left with the cash.

In the meantime Dietrich had gone to San Francisco and closed the office there. He moved the business records to his own real estate office in Stockton.

On July 14 the California Railroad Commission held a hearing in Stockton to investigate the conditions on the railroad. Dietrich was present and agreed that the hearing would be continued. Commissioner Alexander Gordon's first question was concerning the whereabouts of Adams. On being told he was in Humboldt County, the commissioner commented, "He has taken a strange time to be absent."

The first to take the stand was W. J. Hanford, a traffic expert for the railroad commission who had

The "MILK TRAIN" ON THE STOCKTON TERMINAL & EASTERN R.R. ABOUT 1910.

A Ralph Yardley cartoon shows the only operating rolling stock on the railroad when it went into receivership in 1917. John Hewitt, S.T. & E.'s only employee at this time, used the Mitchell autocar to deliver bread and towed the trailer to haul any light freight. (Mrs. Myrtle Seymour)

This was used as a trailer behind the Mitchell to haul light freight. (S.T. & E. collection)

knowledge of the S.T. & E.'s problems. He testified that he had asked Adams for a financial statement and was told he was unable to give him one. Hanford found the books in "chaotic condition" for they had not been written up for more than four months. He said he found a deficit of more than seven thousand dollars for the six months period ending December 31, 1916. He recommended that the passenger service be discontinued and the road overhauled to handle the upcoming crops.

Louttit, representing a group of the bondholders, said the foreclosure proceeding had been taken with a view to taking care of this year's freight service. He added that some of the prospective shippers might be willing to advance part of their freight costs to get the road back in shape and get Engine #1 out of hock.

Hunt Brother's orchard employees later agreed that their company would help out in this way, as did other farmers.

Nesbitt was then called to the stand. As usual he testified as to the financial history of the road. When asked what had brought the company to its present state, Nesbitt replied, "Improper use of the money earned."

Gordon pricked up his ears and asked if Nesbitt could produce the records showing the meetings at which he had, as a director, voted against such use of funds. Nesbitt replied that he doubted if he could obtain possession of the books as he was no longer an official.

The hearing was called off at noon. The Commissioner accompanied Dietrich over the route and promised to give a quick decision on the railroad commission's position in the matter of getting the road in operation.

Years later B. C. Wallace wrote that "the town rocked with laughter" when they read of the

hearings that night. The next morning Dietrich sent a crew of men out to clear the tracks of dry grass, for this was apparently the most urgent need according to the railroad commissioner. Within four days the promised decision was delivered. The Commissioner suggested, "Shippers and property owners adjoining the right of way of the railroad cooperate with the receiver in the matter of eliminating the fire hazard caused by the presence of dry weeds and grass."

The commission also authorized the discontinuance of all passenger service until further orders, but requested the operation of a daily freight service for carload shipments until the close of the present crop season.

With all the bad publicity and the undependable reputation of the little railroad, the Stockton newspapers were supportive. The *Stockton Evening Mail* summed up the situation and tried to explain why the railroad could or should be saved:

The company's liabilities are problematical, the manner in which they were able to contract indebtedness will excite the wonder of businessmen who pay more careful attention to their bills. For instance Standard Oil holds a claim of $700 against the company. Any company or firm that can get credit to the amount of $700 from Standard has to be gilt-edge to say the least. In fact banks, bondholders and creditors generally have exercised a rare degree of restraint in pressing their claims. The only explanation must be in their anxiety to assist an enterprise which ought to be, under normal circumstances, a success.

The newspapers reflected a general confidence in Dietrich and one mentioned his characteristic energy in acting promptly. Dietrich was to be an influence in the S.T. & E. Railroad much longer than he apparently realized or even desired. He had been involved with the railroad when it had

Freight Traffic.
New settlements along the right of way.
This job paid over $300 to the railroad.

This house was given away as a real estate promotion by the Davis Bros. who sold off all but 35 acres of the Archer place. The picture was taken from the S.T. & E. right of way and the note probably refers to the railroad's fee for delivering the lumber used in the house. (Mrs. Myrtle Seymour)

JOE DIETRICH USED TO MOW DOWN THE GRASS SO HIS TRAIN COULD PASS

THE STOCKTON TERMINAL AND EASTERN R.R.

Stockton citizens laughed when the California Public Utility Commission ordered the tracks cleaned up before the train could run, when Joe Dietrich took on the job as receiver. Ralph Yardley could chide him publicly because Dietrich loved a good joke even if it were on him. (S.T. & E. collection)

been in its most active building period. Being a real estate man, from the beginning he had recognized the value of the road and the land through which it passed. After he, Davis and McCormick had been pushed aside by other directors, he had continued his land development. As early as 1912 his firm had advertised in a Navy magazine, stressing good loam and water in "the Linden Country traversed by the Jenny Lind Railroad where the sea breeze comes from the Golden Gate."

The following two years the firm concentrated heavily on lands along the tracks, in the Kipple tract, Archerdale community, the Wooten and Davis subdivisions. Dietrich apparently took a leaf from the railroad stock selling book and sold land with as little as 1/48 cash down payments—three dollars down and three dollars a month.

Perhaps this would be a good time to learn about Dietrich the man, and the boyhood that led him to become the single guiding light of the S.T. & E. Railroad.

He was a man of medium height, a little rotund, often referred to as "jovial Joe," a good natured man who could be depended on to do his share of any job that came along. We suspect that he had a little stubborness that gave him a stick-to-it-ive quality, with an overriding sense of humor that pulled him through rough spots. We found that he was well-liked and that his employees were always

loyal to him. In later years, local cartoonist Ralph Yardley frequently found him a ready subject. He wrote:

His last name is Dietrich and his initials are F. J. "Nobody ever asks what the F. stands for; everybody calls him "Joe" and he's just the likable sort of a fellow whom you would expect to call Joe, too. The name fits him perfectly. He's genial, kind-hearted, easy of approach though always busy, a fine story teller and appreciative of a good joke, even when it's on himself."

Caroline Messler of Germany had married Joseph Carl Weber in New York City in 1858. They came to California the same year by way of the Isthmus of Panama. In 1872 her half-brother Theodor Carl Dietrich arrived in Stockton from Germany. Two years later he married Margurethe Sophie Meger who had been born in France. They had five children, Theodor, William, Caroline, Otto, and Joe.

Dietrich once wrote about the time he ran away from home at the age of two:

Uncle and Tanta (Caroline Weber) raised me from when I ran away from Mother's home in fall of 1877. Victor Hichk, a friend of the family, driving a grocery wagon for Hedges Buck found me at Catholic Church on Washington St. traveling west and south, and took me to the Cool Corner, where after my ardent entreaty I was allowed to stay.

The Cool Corner was a business established by

Advertisement in the magazine Our Navy, *run during 1912 and 1913 by Joe Dietrich to sell some of the land around the S.T. & E. tracks. (F. J. Dietrich III collection)*

Linden loam land for sale near the S.T. & E. Railroad 1912. (F. J. Dietrich III collection)

his Uncle and Tanta Weber. Little Joe had an independent spirit even at the age of two. The baby, Otto, was ill and Mrs. Dietrich was apparently unable to handle both children so he stayed on at Tanta's. As strange as this may seem, at the time it was not uncommon for a relative or a friend to take on the job of raising another's child. Tanta was the mainstay of the family, the one to whom everyone went with their problems. She also raised and educated Lena (Caroline) Dietrich, Joe's sister. But let us go back to Dietrich's reminiscence:

I never left the Weber's and actually was given their name as my third—Francis Joseph Weber, except about 1882-83 when my father conducted the San Joaquin Hotel at San Joaquin and Weber Ave., when I lived there and went to Washington School for several months and got diptheria. On recovering was again allowed to live with Uncle and Aunt Tanta.

After graduating in '93 from High School I went to study art at Mark Hopkin's Art Institute in San Francisco, about September '93 until June '94.

At the art school, he was in the same class as Rube Goldberg. As he later put it, "I left when I saw I had enough, and they were right."

After Uncle Weber died in '95 I went into County Clerk's office under Otto Grunsky to read law and act as office help for the privelege (no pay). Soon earned money, became a deputy and actuary after being Registration Deputy Clerk.

While a deputy clerk he worked in the marriage license department and became known among his friends as "Cupid." Because he loved to tease and was a great practical joker, friends were always looking for a way to get back at him. Dietrich even got married a day earlier than planned to outsmart his friends who had planned to reciprocate some practical jokes on his wedding day. He married Henrietta Flora Mann on October 6, 1902.

About 1902 Otto Grunsky retired from public office and Joe went with him. They formed a partnership under the name of Grunsky and Dietrich and began selling real estate. They occupied the only five foot wide brick building in Stockton, a little one-story structure squeezed in between two larger buildings.

Joe and Henrietta had four children, F. J. Jr., born in 1903, Margarethe, 1906, Steven Mann, 1908 and Henrietta Caroline, 1913. Now a family man with much responsibility, Dietrich worked hard in the real estate business. His company developed the Oaks, Brookside, Bours Park, Mossdale, Northcrest, Burkett Acres and North Oaks in Stockton; Green Colony in Lodi; Manteca Colony; Escalon Colony and Ripon Supplement. Dietrich was a major influence in the construction of the Elks building, just as Leistner was in the Stockton Hotel. The company was involved in the building and was an agent for rental in Stockton's first skyscraper, the Commercial and Savings Bank Building located on the northwest corner of Main and Sutter Streets.

This was the man who had taken over the railroad in 1917 and there was little doubt that he had the energy to make it work, but the problem remained—was there enough business to make it a paying proposition?

Because the Stockton banks were unable to make Davis, Dietrich and McCormick pay the notes signed by them as officers in the Railroad Corporation in 1912, they now forced public sale of the gold bonds they held. The sale was held on the steps of the San Joaquin County Courthouse in Stockton on July 30, 1917, and the three men bought the bonds for the amount owed. This gave the banks their money and the three men legal possession of the bonds.

69

The Grunsky, Dietrich and Leistner real estate office on San Joaquin Street in Stockton. F. J. Dietrich (left front) was active in the operation of the S.T. & E. Railroad at the time this picture was taken in 1912. Written on the back of the picture in Dietrich's handwriting is the following description: "Roy Potter-looking, Truitt-posing, Norman Devlin-thinking, Bill Ferguson-deliberating, George Leistner Jr.-studying and Joe Dietrich-working." (F. J. Dietrich III collection)

Before long the Stockton newspapers were telling of the revival of the railroad. One paper headlined the story:

BANKRUPT ROAD NOW LIVE WIRE — In the hands of an energetic receiver it is doing well. From idleness and rust and a fast approaching state of chaos, the Stockton Terminal and Eastern Railroad has...

The paper gave the credit to the energetic and common sense methods of receiver Joe Dietrich. Another called it a little home "dosing."

The farmers along the route had cooperated by cleaning the tracks, and the road bed had been declared in good condition. Peaches were being moved daily. The train left Stockton at 10:15 each morning and Bellota at 4:30 each afternoon. F. B. Wooten had been put in charge of the office.

By the end of July 1917 Dietrich had applied to Judge Plummer for permission to issue receiver's certificates, in exchange for money borrowed at 6% interest not to exceed $500 per month. George Leistner, confident in his real estate partner's ability, took up a certificate and continued to do so

as additional money was needed. By the end of the fruit and grain season, Dietrich had come up with a gravel contract; so the railroad did not close down.

During December of 1917 rumors were flying that the government would be taking over the operation of all railroads in the U. S., since they were such an important part of the war effort. A Stockton newspaper proclaimed, "One Railroad Head is Happy. Governmental Control is not worrying Receiver Joe Dietrich."

This, however, was only one of the many times to come that Dietrich would look forward to, but not succeed in, getting rid of the S.T. & E. Railroad.

The new year of 1918 arrived with the railroad showing a loss of only $55.18, as it chugged along. It was now truly the Slow Tired and Easy Railroad for there was no need to hurry any more. Old bills were being filed with the court and current expenses were being taken care of by the modest income. Dietrich presented his first report to the court in June 1918. It showed only $45.85 dif-

F. J. Dietrich, as he was depicted in a Ralph Yardley cartoon, showing his numerous real estate subdivisions and the S.T & E. railroad. Yardley called him "the man who made the trains stop and go." (Mrs. F. J. Dietrich Jr.)

71

ference between the receipts and disbursements, that sum being cash on hand. Hewitt was still with the road and being paid. The courts allowed Dietrich $250 a month for his salary. In July the Mercantile Trust Company secured a judgment against the railroad and the final process was beginning to roll.

The change in public attitudes towards transportation was being revealed in newspapers by September of 1918. It was reported that in thousands of instances the motor truck was proving to be a better transportation method than the railroads. It was stressed that the retailer could deliver more goods in less time and could extend his area of delivery without increasing his overhead. Another paper pointed out that "a farmer can maintain his own schedule and not be dependent on undelivered goods. The truck came to the railroads' rescue in helping to clear congested freight depots." But the truck was also taking the revenue.

November 8, 1917 was set as the date for public sale of the S.T. & E. Railroad. A Stockton news reporter was less than formal when he wrote about the event: "Well, Well, Well! If they haven't gone and sold 'Joe' Dietrich's railroad!"

Auctioneer Joseph Gall was surrounded by a gathering of bankers, big · businessmen and capitalists and many curious onlookers on the San Joaquin County Courthouse steps at 11:00 A.M. that morning. The bidding began promptly with Morris Davidson, wholesale junk dealer, opening at $40,000. After a few anxious moments when it seemed the little railroad might end up on a junk heap, E. F. Davis raised the bid by a thousand dollars.

Davidson went to $45,000. Davis nodded and another thousand was added. The bidding continued back and forth between the two, as no one else seemed interested. Davidson went to $64,000. Davis nodded.

"$65,000," Gall continued. "All done? All done? Going for $65,000. Who will make it 70 and double your money?"

This time Davidson shook his head no and it was done.

"And sold for $65,000 to E. F. Davis."

Davis told the reporters that he had purchased the railroad for a group of the bond holders who had pooled their interests. He continued, "There will be no immediate changes in the operation of the road. We will continue to run it and Mr. Dietrich will remain for the present, at least, as manager."

The total due against the railroad at the time was $192,102.75, but everything was now wiped clean and the little railroad had a chance to start over. The original stockholders were all out and the bond holders were in.

The company books carry a list of all the bond holders and the bonds held by them. This now became their share in the new company. There was a total of $84,500 worth of bonds and together Davis, McCormick and Dietrich held $54,000 worth, which meant they were in control once again.

On November 21, 1918 the final funds under the receivership were accounted for, with Dietrich showing $2,155.89 cash on hand. On February 1, 1919 the deed was surrendered to Davis and his group. The Slow Tired and Easy Railroad had new owners and a new lease on life.

CHAPTER X

NEW CORPORATIONS

Now that the pressure was off the little railroad, Dietrich looked for experience to help him revitalize the company. At his request the Southern Pacific loaned one of its best men, Frank Odell. He was hired for a six month period "to see how it worked." After another harvest season the road was making money.

That Odell and Dietrich proved to be a good team is not surprising, when one knows their backgrounds. As children each showed a strong will, although Odell had less education and ran away from home when he was a little older.

Frank Odell was born in 1875 at Folsom Prison. His father, a stone mason, worked on the first cell block there. He died when Frank was seven, leaving two sons and a daughter for their mother to raise alone. She remarried and years later Frank wrote about his stepfather, "We had a very good stepfather, tho he believed in making my brother and I saw wood on Saturday and that never fit any too good."

The Odell boys once got into trouble over riding someone else's horse and their stepfather proceeded to punish them. Frank's brother got his licking first. Not wanting the same, Frank ran out of the house and away from home. He returned after several months but from that time on was his own boss. When he was 16 he lied about his age and became an S. P. railroad man. He worked up to conductor on two runs, one from Sacramento to Sparks, Nevada over the famous Sierra route, and the other from Oakland to Red Bluff. When he was loaned to the S.T. & E., he brought his wife and daughter to Stockton. His daughter, Florence, enrolled in school and remembers being asked what her father did for a living. She would reply that he was superintendent for the Stockton Terminal and Eastern Railroad. More frequently than not, the comment would come back, "Old Slow Tired and Easy. That's no railroad!"

She resented the remarks but when she mentioned it to her father, he would reply, "Don't

worry about it. They are just jealous."

Odell's daughter was not the only one who did not like the name Slow Tired and Easy. Hewitt devised a way to change the company image. He would answer the telephone in a deep voice saying, "Stockton Terminal and Eastern Railroad."

If the caller asked for information on freight rates, he would say, "Just a moment, please, I will connect you with that department." Then he would come back on the line with his normal voice, "Freight Department."

"I'll show them we are a big railroad with lots of departments and they won't call us the little Slow Tired and Easy Railroad," he would reply when Odell reprimanded him.

For a time Odell and Hewitt were the only regular employees of the company. The bond-holders committee which had taken over the railroad did not organize a set of officers but left things up to Dietrich.

In November 1919 a letter came from M. O. Lorenz, statistician for the Interstate Commerce Commission in Washington, D.C.

We have been unsuccessful in getting any late information as to what disposition has been made of the property of the above named railroad.

We have, however, received some unofficial information that operations had been discontinued, but as to the date of the final disposition of the property we have no record.

Dietrich's reply was short and to the point:

I am in a position to state that any rumors that the operation of this railroad has been discontinued, are false.

I am operating the road for a number of the bondholders who bid the property in at the foreclosure proceedings and have been keeping it in operation since this sale, pending reorganization.

Lorenz and Dietrich were to exchange much correspondence in the future. Dietrich's attitude toward the I.C.C. was slow, tired and easy, to say the least. As each I.C.C. report became due and

A view at the corner of Weber Avenue and Sutter Street in Stockton around 1918, looking south. The building on the left foreground is the Elks building which was new when the S.T. & E. R.R. engineer W. H. Newell opened his office on the third floor in 1908. The railroad's office had been moved to Dietrich's real estate office by the time this picture was taken. Dietrich and Leistner acted as agents for "Stockton's first skyscraper" seen in the background. (Stockton Chamber of Commerce)

was filed, usually late, letters came requesting an answer to a previous request. Dietrich would eventually get around to settling the matter. A prime example of this was the case of a matter relating to corrections to be made on the 1918 report. Lorenz sent the original request in April of 1919. Dietrich replied promptly but the letter went astray in the halls of bureaucracy. In March of 1920 another letter came to Dietrich followed by others in June, September and November. Apparently the letter writing was getting no results. In June of 1921 an examiner from the Bureau of Accountants found a rough copy of an answer in the S.T. & E. files, but this did not suffice. In December another request arrived in the company office, followed by two let-

ters in January, one in February and another in April of 1922. The company sent the information out again in April but soon a letter came back pointing out mistakes in the information sent. Two more letters to the railroad in July and August were necessary before the matter was finally settled. It took three years and four months to complete the correspondence on this one matter.

During 1919 the company did not make any profit but had an overall loss of a little over $500. 1920 proved to be better, for the company hired enough crew to ballast the main track from East Street to the Diverting Canal. A new single pen corral with a double deck loading chute was added at Bellota. The traffic over the road was heavy, with sand, gravel, crops and livestock producing most of the revenue. Even after spending more than $3,000 to overhaul and rebuild Engine #1, or the "One Spot" as it was referred to by the company men, the S.T. & E. still showed a net profit of $1,192.08. The bondholders must have been enheartened, to say the least, for this was the first time in more than ten years of operation that any profit had ever been shown for a full fiscal year.

The Diverting Canal bridge was replaced during the summer of 1921. The company improved the Bellota corral and doubled the tonnage of animals shipped. The Ryburn Brothers, Brad and Bob, received 17 carloads of cattle late on Thanksgiving night. The Bellota gravel pit was closed down, however, and the company finished the year with a $9,000 loss.

Because 1921 had been such a poor year, profit wise, the company spent almost no money on the road during the following year. This, coupled with the fact that the gravel pit at Bellota was back in operation, cut the loss down to less than $200.

Most of Dietrich's time on railroad business was spent writing letters to the I.C.C. He had learned to duplicate almost everything and in some cases there were several copies of letters and reports ready to be sent off again and again, if necessary.

People who lived along the line became accustomed to the sound of the train but not all were overjoyed with the whistle. Many houses had the track almost in their parlors and even if only a driveway crossed the tracks, the "One Spot" whistled a warning of its approach. One new mother went out and asked the train crew to stop blowing the whistle because it woke up the baby. Hewitt told her that it was a crossing and the law said that they had to blow the whistle.

The train crews took time to pick berries in the summer and hunt mushrooms in the fall or gather free fruit in the orchards along the way. Occasionally they even took their guns along to hunt rabbits. One day the crew left Old #1 idling and went rabbit hunting in a field near Fine Road. The men were intent on the hunting when the engine started off down the tracks, as if to say, "Enough of this foolishness."

The train crew ran after it, but it was much too far away. They rushed out to Fine Road, guns in hand, and flagged down a passing automobile. The carload of men raced down Fine Road to Linden Road and turned west. By now the train was merrily chugging along toward Stockton. The railroad men urged the driver to go faster and finally passed the train near Potter's ranch. They piled out at Wall Road and caught the engine just before it went rolling into Linden. From then on the crew was more careful about leaving Old #1 unattended.

It seemed that money was spent on the road every other year and 1923 was one of those years. The company constructed a spur to serve the Linden Lumber Company which had located on property leased from the railroad for fifty dollars a year. Cross ties were added from Fine to Bellota to bring the road up to the standard 53 ties per 100 feet of track. The company spent more than $4,000 overhauling the "One Spot" again. All of these expenses brought the loss to more than $5,000 for the year.

The bondholders must have decided to get rid of the road, for twice during 1923 and 1924 Dietrich signed options for the sale of the property. But it was not going to be that easy for Dietrich and the others to get rid of old Slow Tired and Easy Railroad.

During 1924 little improvement was done and the company almost doubled the operating revenues, which resulted in a profit of more than $5,000. The following year the company spent large sums of money in replacing trestles, bulkheads and piers. They added 3,000 feet of track including spurs at Bellota and Stockton. They junked the three flat cars, used during the construction of the road, and the two track automobiles. They added another pen to the Bellota stockyards, abandoned the spur at the Diverting Canal, replaced the hand car with an S.H. motor car and still came up with a profit of almost $12,000. If this kept up, the poor little railroad just might make it after all.

In 1924 Samuel Kahn, vice president and general manager of the Western States Gas and Electric Company of Stockton, had been a member of the Stockton Chamber of Commerce industrial committee. This group took on an extensive project of making an industrial survey of the town. The report contained a map showing the S.T. & E. Railroad with potential industrial areas on one or both sides of the tracks in Stockton. Although the report was designed to find industrial sites in the city, it also advised the Chamber to stimulate agriculture and related businesses for it would "be good for Stockton."

In 1925 Kahn became president of the Stockton Chamber. Serving on his executive committee was George Leistner, Dietrich's real estate partner and an investor in the railroad. So it is little wonder that Kahn became interested in the S.T. & E.

Samuel Kahn purchased controlling interest in the Railroad in 1926. (Stockton Chamber of Commerce).

Railroad. Here was a road which served agriculture and had the potential of serving more than 20 blocks of industrial and packing shed property adjacent to its tracks. He was interested enough to have a complete valuation and prospective earnings report of the railroad made. The report was completed in late March of 1926 and early in May articles of incorporation were filed with the California Commissioner of Corporations for a new corporation, The Stockton Terminal and Eastern Railroad Company. This company had only three directors, Samuel Kahn, Clifford A. Smith and Miss A. Cattermole. Smith and Cattermole were employed by Kahn, so it was his company. The new corporation intended to issue 3000 shares of capital stock at $100 per share. A total of 220 shares was subscribed by the directors, with Kahn holding all but two shares. Kahn was elected president and Smith secretary.

Within a month the corporation received a formal offer from Dietrich, Frank Guernsey, and George E. Catts, representing the bond committee. In return for all of the S.T. & E. property and the

assumption of approximately $75,000 in debts, the new corporation was to issue and deliver all qualifying shares of the capital stock of the new company to the bond committee. The conditions were naturally subject to the California Railroad Commission and I.C.C. approval. By mid-July the first setback came in the form of a decision from the California Railroad Commission. The commission directed the company to issue only 2250 shares of stock instead of the 2997 requested and to do it within six months. Later developments were to prove that this was a most generous decision.

An interesting sidelight to this event was that Thomas S. Loutitt was serving on the Railroad Commission at this time. He was the attorney who had represented Dietrich in past dealings with the Railroad Commission and had served as vice president of the Stockton Chamber of Commerce under Kahn. Three attempts had been made for approval by the I.C.C., with no results and the Railroad Commission's deadline looming ahead, so Kahn appealed to U.S. Senator Samuel M. Shortridge for help. A month later a telegram came from Washington saying the Senator had lost the letter. Kahn promptly sent a copy of the original letter and waited.

Disaster struck again! The I.C.C. ruled that the railroad company would be allowed to issue only $92,000 worth of capital stock. It had used the bondholders' purchase price back in 1918, plus improvements and cost of reorganization, as the basis for the decision. This was termed the upset value, being what the road would bring in a foreclosure sale. It meant there were not shares enough to either include or take out the bondholders unless Kahn could come up with cash. This called for new tactics so the men got together and came up with one more corporation! This time it was organized under Nevada law and named the Stockton Terminal and Eastern Railroad Company, hereafter referred to in this book as the S.T. & E. Nevada Corporation. Kahn's attorney, K.W. Cannon, made all the arrangements and Dietrich met him in Reno on January 8, 1927 to complete the deal. The newest company was organized with 847 shares of preferred stock at a par value of $100 and 150,000 shares of common stock at no par value. The California corporation was designed to own and operate the railroad, but the Nevada corporation was to own the stock of the California corporation.

The original bondholders relinquished the railroad property for $92,000 worth of stock in the new California corporation. They now exchanged

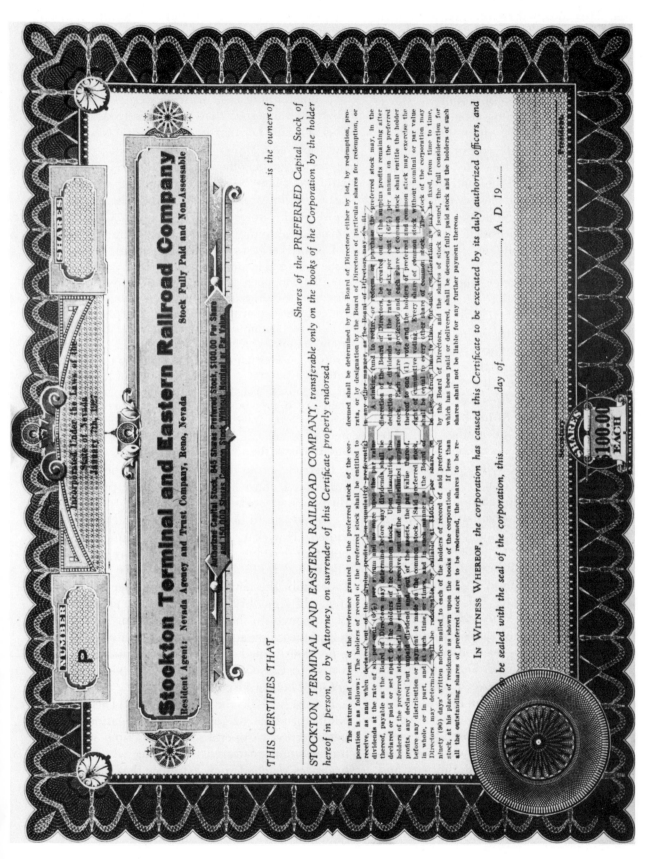

A copy of the preferred stock certificates issued by the Stockton Terminal & Eastern Railroad Company of Nevada under Kahn's direction, 1926. The common stock was issued at no value but soon raised to $1.00 a share. (S.T. & E. collection)

these for $84,500 worth of preferred stock and 4,225 shares of common stock in the new Nevada corporation. This meant that for each $1,000 in bonds held, an individual received ten shares or $1000 dollars worth of preferred stock and 50 shares of common stock. This left Dietrich, Davis and McCormick, for example, with 540 shares of preferred and 2,700 shares of common stock. Kahn took all the remaining common stock, 145,772 shares, for himself. All preferred stock was made collectable by the corporation on 90 days notice for $105 per share. Each stock share was given a vote so Kahn had the controlling votes.

Despite Dietrich's apparent desires to get out of the railroad business, which obviously did not happen, he was named vice president and general manager. Kahn elected duplicate officers in both corporations before long.

The company needed money and almost immediately a note was issued to Rosalind Kahn, Samuel's wife, for $10,000. The note was apparently to be repaid out of the company revenue.

The next significant move was a change in the articles of incorporation of the Nevada corporation. All the subscribed capital stock had been taken up so the common shares were assigned a value of one dollar. Now Kahn had $145,772 in stock in exchange for accepting the company's liabilities, which he was paying for with money given in return for a note to his wife — a good deal for him, there is no doubt.

Perhaps now is the time to learn about Samuel Kahn. He was a native of Texas, born in San Antonio in 1882. He earned a Bachelor of Science degree from Purdue University in 1903. From then on he moved up as a successful executive. By 1925 he was vice president, general manager and a director of the Western States Gas and Electric Company, with an office in Stockton, He was also vice president and director of the Sierra and San Francisco Power Company, president and director of the El Dorado Power Company and a director of the Standard Gas and Electric Company of California. All of these companies eventually became a part of today's Pacific Gas and Electric Co. Kahn moved from Stockton in 1926 to become president of the Market Street Railway Company of San Francisco. He had an office in that city and a home in Burlingame. The Stockton railroad was only a sideline.

The Slow Tired and Easy Railroad was not out of trouble yet, as there was still a need for cash, so

Kahn came up with more and received a note in return. By September 1927 the railroad had borrowed more money from Mrs. Kahn, Dietrich, Leistner and a Stockton bank. But the I.C.C. chastised the company again about these particular notes. The company was warned that only notes of less than two years and not to exceed 5% of outstanding securities were permissible. Dietrich suggested that the notes to Mrs. Kahn, Dietrich and Leistner be made to the Nevada corporation and shown in the railroad company's books as an account payable to the Nevada corporation. The Nevada corporation would then issue the notes to the holders, but this eliminated most of the notes as far as the I.C.C. was concerned. Kahn jumped at the suggestion:

I favor the idea of having the Nevada corporation issue notes and lending the money to the California corporation on open account. You will recall that we discussed this procedure some time ago, but at that time we concluded that in carrying out this plan Interstate Commerce Commission might endeavor to make too many inquiries regarding the Nevada corporation. From a businessman's standpoint, I don't see how the Interstate Commerce could direct any of its inquiry to or take any jurisdiction over a holding company and therefore, to preclude the necessity of a lot of correspondence with the Interstate Commerce Commission, I am in favor of taking the change of having the Nevada corporation issue the notes.

Dietrich wrote to the I.C.C. and the reply that came back must have delighted the two men for the plan had worked.

The issue had been sidestepped and the file was closed. However, the I.C.C. continued to be a constant irritant. Apparently it was not always Dietrich's fault that reports were late; Wm. Lipscomb, the new company bookkeeper, seemed to need frequent reminding. Dietrich used his sense of humor to do this on one occasion. A tough letter arrived, demanding additional information for a previously filed annual report; Dietrich penciled a note to Lipscomb: "Bill—What about this, let's get it off before we go to jail!"

It must have been difficult for both Dietrich and Kahn to adjust to government regulations., Both had learned to operate during a time when the businessman answered to no one, when business practices reached such extremes that laws finally had to be passed to protect the general public. They were men of their times and their plight was no less difficult than that of the frontiersman facing the advance of civilization.

CHAPTER XI

SURVIVING THE DEPRESSION

During the "roaring twenties" the Slow Tired and Easy Railroad was not breaking any records but it had begun to roll merrily along. The Graham Brothers Truck Company occupied a long unused factory on the railroad in east Stockton. Trucks had long been blamed for taking business away from the S.T. & E. Railroad, so it seemed appropriate that the road now derived some revenue from the trucking industry. A spur track agreement for the new business was signed in November 1927.

The long-predicted great potential from Linden agricultural products also was being realized. The San Joaquin Valley Walnut Growers Association signed an agreement with the company, allowing four lots along the tracks east of Linden to be turned over by the railroad to the association. To be used as a plant site, the lots were given in exchange for ten dollars and the freight haul to and from the plant.

The walnut haul soon proved to be the most lucrative on the road, for the association shipped nuts from the Linden plant to the California Walnut Growers Association plant in Los Angeles. The revenue from this was figured as a local rate, with the S.T. & E. getting about 20% of the total. In addition to this, if the walnuts were shipped on to an eastern point within one year, the rate would be refigured as a reconstructed transcontinental rate. The local road got only 12% of this rate and sometimes took a weight loss if the nuts were cracked, but it was not unusual for the reconstructed rate to be four times that of the original one. Although it was slow coming in, it was responsible for putting the railroad in the black. Profit making became a monthly instead of a seasonal occurrence for the first time.

The prosperity of the railroad had always been linked with the times and when the roaring twenties came to a crashing halt in 1929 the Slow Tired

One of the few snowfalls to ever lie on S.T. & E. tracks. This picture was taken east of Linden in the late 1920s. (Lloyd Potter)

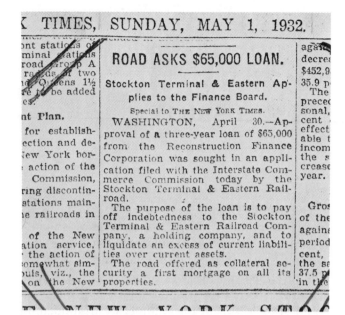

ROAD ASKS $65,000 LOAN.

Stockton Terminal & Eastern Applies to the Finance Board.

Special to THE NEW YORK TIMES.

WASHINGTON, April 30.—Approval of a three-year loan of $65,000 from the Reconstruction Finance Corporation was sought in an application filed with the Interstate Commerce Commission today by the Stockton Terminal & Eastern Railroad.

The purpose of the loan is to pay off indebtedness to the Stockton Terminal & Eastern Railroad Company, a holding company, and to liquidate an excess of current liabilities over current assets.

The road offered as collateral security a first mortgage on all its properties.

The New York Times *carried an article about S.T. & E. application for financial relief from the R.F.C. in 1932.* (S.T. & E. collection)

and Easy Railroad fell back to a slower pace again.

The following spring Dietrich took over both Davis's and McCormick's stock. Leistner died the same year, leaving Dietrich without a partner in his real estate business and more responsibility than ever.

The next two years almost finished the railroad and the company threatened to shut down if they could not get help from the government by a loan from the Reconstruction Finance Corporation. The I.C.C. had approved the loan, but the application was turned down in October of 1932 for lack of sufficient security. On January 6, 1933, Dietrich appealed to U.S. Senator Hiram W. Johnson to intervene, but he only referred back to the letter already received from the R.F.C.

Dietrich began to feel desperate when the company compensation insurance was cancelled for lack of money to pay the premium. He wrote that he was praying that the R.F.C. would "grant us relief to tide us over until things become more normal."

The next week a letter did come from the R.F.C. saying that careful consideration was being given to a request for reconsideration of the loan application, but the loan was once again turned down. Kahn continued to try, by writing that the railroad would settle for half of the money requested in the application. However he lost his patience in the last paragraph:

It has been rumored that one cannot get anywhere

with the Reconstruction Finance Corporation unless he had a "pull." I refuse to believe that a government agency of your caliber is operating in that fashion but am beginning to believe that there is an element of truth in the rumor.

Rash words, indeed, but not persuasive ones. The reply came back that the application was turned down again. The letter concluded with a reference to his doubts:

With respect to the rumors which you state have come to your attention, the Directors are confident that you will realize that all applications are considered by them entirely on their merits and that the rumors to which you refer are unworthy of comment.

This time Kahn accepted the results and almost immediately suggested that the city of Stockton buy the railroad. The city had money for a new deep waterport and he suggested that the S.T. & E. might tie in with it. Dietrich replied that the city had no money left either. Kahn was acting like a desperate man and asked the I.C.C. officials if they could not force some other railroad to take over the road. Again the answer was "no."

About this time Kahn wrote to Dietrich about the Washington scene. He concluded with, "The NRA has put a damper on business as responsible heads do not know which way to turn."

Dietrich was no longer the daring young man who helped Stockton boom in the early part of the century. He was a conservative, substantial businessman, sitting with his hands practically tied, like others about him, in the midst of the terrible depression. His reply to Kahn, dated September 29, 1933, reflected his concern:

I have long wondered whether man's tinkering with what might be called the laws of nature isn't a dangerous undertaking, the rules and theories of economics are probably perfect on paper but there are so many apparently unimportant elements that enter into these matters that any innovation like a new invention will not work properly without years of experience and readjustment.

The Slow Tired and Easy Railroad moved peaches but the government shut down the canneries early and the company figured it lost 200 cars of freight. The walnut crop was short so this too meant less tonnage. It seemed that even nature was against the railroad. One bright light appeared when part of the former Graham plant was leased to a vegetable shipper. As bad as everything seemed, by the end of the year revenues were up slightly. All expenses were paid although the company bank account was almost non-existent.

In February 1934 the train crew had a good

S.T. & E. #1. This picture was taken in Stockton in 1935, after 21 years of service on what was by then known locally as the Slow Tired & Easy Railroad. (Gerald M. Best collection)

scare. It was about 7:30 A.M., a typical cold winter morning, when the locomotive was backing across Wilson Way with its bell ringing a constant warning. A heavily loaded truck was traveling south, the driver engrossed in conversation with a woman in his cab. He saw the engine too late and attempted to swerve but hit the tender, hard. The trucker tried to blame the train crew, but Odell filed a report and nothing more was said until an attorney contacted the company. Fortunately for the poor little railroad, nothing more ever came of the incident.

During the spring Dietrich was overjoyed to report that a cherry packing shed would be opened in Linden. Subsequently cherry shipments proved to be good until prices dropped suddenly when the bottom fell out of the market.

The city of Stockton had Civil Works Administration money with which they took up the unused S.T. & E. Railroad tracks on Union Street between Flora and Miner Avenue. The city and railroad split the rails equally.

During August 1934 Dietrich received Order Number 1 of the National Mediation Board in Washington. It included a request for acknowledgement of the order and a copy of the orders as posted on the company premises. Dietrich's reply said in part:

I am afraid, like a great many laws and regulations, this has been passed to fit railroads that have a considerable number of employees. We have only one train crew, hardly any business and no money to spend on surplus notices.

Dietrich could see one more government agency requiring more paper work and expressed his opinion on the subject in a letter to Kahn:

These Government Bureaus are inclined to run wild on the reports and while they may be necessary in larger railroads, there is no sense putting us to the expense of hiring someone to put down a lot of figures when we haven't the money to maintain a track crew.

Dietrich developed his own special way of handling the bureaucrats. He gave them the old slow, tired and easy, "We are just country folks" routine. A classic example was a letter he sent to the Federal Mediation Board:

Your request for this information, as far as I can find, had never come to my attention. I can report, however, that we have no contracts whatsoever with any employees.

This road, while dignified under the classification of a railroad, is in reality a long freight switch (approximately 17 miles) and our entire crew consists of four men. The road operates one freight train every other day, except during the fruit season in the summer months, when we operate a daily train. We carry no passengers and we have no set of printed rules or outline of working conditions.

The crew is simply a sort of happy family, each doing

81

his part, knowing that they must remain sober and on hand when there is work to be done. The pay of the men at present averages monthly as follows; Engineer $120, Conductor $120 and Fireman $75.

We also have a part time section crew of from two to four men who now receive $.25 an hour, and we furnish them houses, water and fuel. We do not expect to enter into any new contracts with any class of craft as every man knows his duties and is satisfied with his work.

Apparently the explanation did satisfy the federal board for they did not bother to reply.

During the summer of 1934 Cal Pack, which had been one of S.T. & E.'s best shippers, started using trucks for shipping during the peach season. The railroad men did not take this action lightly and used the only leverage they had to protect themselves. Dietrich served notice that the railroad scales, packing sheds, and loading docks could not be used for loading trucks. This forced some shipments back to the road, but due to government agricultural control the season was cut short and the tonnage was not as great as expected.

In September, Dietrich sent five monthly reports to Kahn with an apology: "These reports, until the August one, have been so bad that I did not think you would get any pleasure out of seeing them."

He included a check for interest on Mrs. Kahn's note and added that it looked as if there would be a good walnut crop, which was almost ready for shipment.

Kahn soon replied: "The August report and check is the first ray of sunshine that I have had so far as the road is concerned for several years. I hope that from now on your troubles and mine will be reduced in geometric proportions."

Lettuce shipping increased along the road and Massie Harris took a lease on a part of the old Graham plant, which meant the possibility of eastern freight. A cannery leased all of the remaining space. All of this new activity resulted in the Slow Tired and Easy Railroad's greeting the new year of 1935 with a net profit of more than $1700.

After the first of the year, the company built cattle pens and loading chutes on a small peice of ground near Broadway in east Stockton, with the promise that the Orvis and Clinger slaughterhouse would make use of the facilities. By the utilization of secondhand material the whole project cost less than $450. Although the slaughterhouse was located at Linden Road and the Diverting Canal, some distance from the railroad, it was convenient most of the year. The cowboys used the bottom of the canal as a lane and it became a simple task to drive the cattle between the two points.

By this time Dietrich had learned that local shippers produced the best revenue and he welcomed their business so he bought ten lots near the Magnolia Street shed for the railroad. He built a shed on one of these and leased it to the Pacific Ice Company, which sublet space to others. The new shed cost the railroad less than 50 cents a square foot.

As usual, before long another problem arose. This time it was the cherry shipments that appeared threatened. A new cooperative association was organized which eliminated the former packing concern. Dietrich worked hard to keep the shipping on the line but failed. He wrote to Kahn, "If it isn't one thing it is another."

Kahn questioned the increase in costs for labor and Dietrich reminded him that 1934 had been their "zero hour," when they had paid the crew only for the time they actually ran. He pointed out that the men had agreed to this only on a temporary basis and he used Odell as an example in a letter written on May 17, 1935:

I continued to pay him only $125 and I probably could not replace him for twice that as he knows his business thoroughly, and pays no attention to ours. He never complained as he knows the traffic has been slim, but when this builds up, I will have to put him back to at least $175.

The lettuce market collapsed in the east and shipping stopped. Cabbage, carrots and celery started again after the first of the year, but it was the cattle shipments out of Clinger station that kept the road going during the winter of 1935-36. By June the company showed considerable improvement by having handled twice as many cars as the previous year.

The Slow Tired and Easy Railroad showed so much profit by the end of 1936 that there was concern about having to pay taxes on excess profit of anything over 7% of the investment, so the directors declared a salary of $3,000 a year for Dietrich and Kahn. The two men did not get the cash but were simply credited with it. The money was then used to pay interest and other bills. This practice was later questioned by an I.C.C. auditor but his warning came too late. Dietrich had already found that he had to pay income tax on the money even though he had not actually received it.

The railroad had been doing well but a hard freeze hit the area during January of 1937, with the drastic result that only four carloads of vegetables moved during January and February. The storms were especially hard on the railroad

Above: F. J. Dietrich Sr. (left foreground) and F. J. Dietrich Jr. upon opening of new real estate office on Weber Ave. in Stockton, 1937. Below: The S.T. & E. Railroad business office was tucked in a corner of Dietrich's real estate office. Superintendent Frank Odell is in the far left rear. (F. J. Dietrich III collection)

John Hewitt directs the train from the front of Old #1 in East Stockton. The boys on Roosevelt Street called him "Whistling John" because he whistled if a crossing was clear. He went to work for the road in 1915, one year after the locomotive was purchased by the company. (Leonard Covello collection)

crews because when the Diverting Canal reached flood stage they worked long hours on flood watch. The men spent many nights watching the trestle and removing trees and logs before they jammed against the pilings. As soon as the rain ceased they had to go to work on the waterlogged roadbed.

All of the problems of the railroad did not come from the weather. During the spring of 1937 one of the stockholders wanted out. Kahn was quick to reply to E. C. Stewart, president of the Union Safe Deposit Bank in Stockton about the matter:

I have your letter of May 12th, relating to the Slow, Tired and Easy Railroad. I note that you would like to get your money out of it; so would I but the prospects are not very encouraging at the present.

Dietrich moved his real estate firm in Stockton. It was now F. J. Dietrich & Company and included his son F. J. Dietrich Jr. The railroad office was located in the back of the new establishment.

The S.T. & E. Railroad's business was picking up again in spite of the fact that most canneries were establishing local loading areas where the farmers could bring their fruit to be weighed and graded before being loaded onto trucks and delivered directly to the cannery yard. The railroad was

compensated for this loss by Stockton Packing which shipped cases of canned goods over the line, much of it to eastern markets.

The Slow Tired and Easy Railroad had an attraction of which the company officials were not fully aware. It was "One Spot," the locomotive which everyone took for granted. It continued to chug along, doing its job with only an occasional rest during its annual checkup in the Sacramento S.P. shops. During 1938 the curator of a Los Angeles museum wrote asking if there were a possibility of acquiring the engine. This finally alerted Dietrich to its possible age and he was quite prepared when two men arrived to look it over for an exhibit at the upcoming New York World's Fair. He told them the company could not part with the engine unless it was replaced by a similar one. So Old #1 never left California.

It was at about this time in its history that the Slow Tired and Easy Railroad lived up to its name one more time. Elwood Juergenson, the new Linden High School agriculture instructor had purchased a refrigerator in Sacramento and ordered it shipped to his home, which faced the railroad tracks in Linden. The doorbell rang late one af-

Locomotive #1 on a freight haul to Linden, 1940. (Guy Dunscomb collection)

ternoon and when he answered one of the railroad men told him they had a delivery for him and that the bill was $1.90.

"Can you pay it?"

"Yes, I think I can," he replied and proceeded to do so. About that time he looked up and there was Locomotive #1, a flat car with the refrigerator tied in the middle of it, and a caboose with three crewmen—a full train for one delivery at $1.90 with most of the money going to the connecting railroad.

The company bookkeeper, Lipscomb, had not been well for some time and seemed to get farther and farther behind in his work. Dietrich finally laid him off. In the meantime a friend of Dietrich, Dewey Bowen, had been telling him of a girl friend in southern California who would make a good bookkeeper. Dietrich hired her by telephone for his real estate business. He added, as if it were unimportant, that there were also some books to keep for a small railroad company and said he would add $25 per month for the extra work. Years later she recalled:

He didn't mention that there was a drawer full of notices, letters, etc. from the I.C.C., Public Utilities Commission, (the former California Railroad Commission) and the Board of Valuation for reports etc., that had to be taken care of.

Leah Wilson proved to be a jewel and took much of the burden of dealing with the bureaucrats from Dietrich.

In the summer of 1938 Dietrich wrote that it was necessary to renew the note at the Stockton Savings and Loan Bank again, adding, "The darn banks only make notes for 90 days now but I understand after July 1st, the National Administration is going to allow longer time loans.

Although the company had finally had a good cherry season, he worried about the peach shipment and continued in his letter to Kahn:

I am not looking forward to much of a peach movement as the canners have not even indicated as yet that they are going to buy peaches and no one knows what price peaches will be. It seems the canner's warehouses are still full of last year's canned stuff. Of course, in the end they will buy peaches but they are laying low so they can make a price that will not net the farmer much.

The National Mediation Board continued to be the target of Dietrich's homespun humor. In a reply to a request for labor relation information, he first apologized for apparently treating the government circular as an advertisement and throwing it away. He went on to explain that they were a "tea pot" railroad with one crew, and concluded with an explanation:

There are no written agreements since each one realized the dealings are among men and not chiselers and I am glad to be able to say that everyone is extremely happy operating as one big family, under the leadership of Superintendent Odell who is their "Daddy."

By the end of 1939 the railroad declared a dividend to Kahn, Listner Estate and Stockton Properties in order to disburse the surplus from the

85

year's income. Joe Dietrich Jr. had been made assistant treasurer of the S.T. & E. by this time, so that he could take over more of his father's work.

Business was slow during the first of 1940. On top of this, spring rains ruined the early fruit and by late May the railroad had shipped only one carload of cherries, so the spring report was dismal. By November, 1940, however, Dietrich wrote a letter to Kahn, starting it in a tongue-in-cheek manner:

I have your letter of the 15th. It must have been mental telepathy, as I have for several days been preparing to write you about an unfortunate circumstance.

Miss Wilson informed me last week that the books would show that we would have a profit and I have been wondering ever since how to lose it since we still do not know what the income tax rate will be but do feel that they are going to sock it to anyone not in the red. I am still further bothered because we need every cent earned to pay off overdue debts.

Kahn's reply arrived by return mail:

I am just in receipt of your letter of November 19 relating to the "unfortunate circumstance." I can hardly believe that the Road will show a profit of over $7,000 this year but I am perfectly willing to be bothered with troubles of this kind.

The two got their heads together with a couple of good accountants and discovered an item for back rent due on property owned by the Nevada Corporation. The local agent of the Internal Revenue Service gave a temporary OK to the entry and all was well. They had overcome another "unfortunate circumstance."

The Slow Tired and Easy Railroad had finally survived the great depression and by the end of 1940 the light of prosperity was finally visible at the end of the tunnel.

CHAPTER XII

THE RAILROAD GROWS

Asparagus shipments increased traffic early in 1941 and the cherry crop looked good. Dietrich wrote that it looked like the "prodigy is about to materialize," when the cherry growers' marketing association officials agreed to use the company sheds. More than 90 cars of cherries were shipped and there would have been more if a windy rainstorm had not eliminated about a third of the crop.

Business looked so good that Dietrich suggested the railroad employees' salaries be raised. Kahn replied that the matter should be considered only after the year had elapsed and proved to be profitable. Before long Dietrich tried again but Kahn said they should at least wait until the current month showed a profit rather than a loss. The raise was too slow in coming, however, and the fireman quit. Dietrich pressed Kahn again and he finally agreed.

Business picked up enough that the two executives once again became concerned about taxes and Dietrich also began to think of a new locomotive. His plans were interrupted when he got a leg infection and, in all, spent more than two months in bed during the winter. His health was failing him.

After the Japanese attacked Pearl Harbor on December 7, 1941, the government once again took special interest in the railroads. An order came to set the clocks up for daylight savings time. Dietrich pondered this fact and decided they could only do it if they went out and bought a clock.

When Dietrich was able to return to work in the spring of 1942, he almost immediately began to press Kahn to get a new locomotive. He investigated several but found none suitable, so the search continued.

On August 14, 1942 a devastating fire hit the railroad. A crew of men and women were packing tomatoes in the Magnolia Street packing shed leased by the Independent Produce Company. Flames burst through the floor at one corner of the frame structure and spread rapidly throughout the

building and to box cars parked on the nearby siding. A carload of lumber fed the flames and more cars would have burned without the efforts of the volunteer firemen and nearby residents who flocked to the scene. The local fire warden took charge and the bystanders hand-pushed three more cars out of the way. Three boys were later picked up for questioning. The newspapers called it a $70,000 fire but the shed was insured for only $5,000 and the S.T. & E. Railroad had to settle for that. There was a governmental freeze of building materials so Dietrich acquired some used corrugated iron to reconstruct the shed. He was able to do this only after priorities on structural lumber had been approved by the local War Production Board.

Peach season was in full swing but pickers were short so a "Harvest Camp for Victory" was established in Linden. City boys of 15 and 16 were hired to pick the crops. Before long Linden area farmers were calling for the importation of Mexican farm labor for the next year's crop. As a good-will gesture the S.T. & E. Railroad loaned vacant ground in Linden to the Walnut Growers Association to allow them to build bunkhouses for 300 Mexicans, to be used during the next harvest season.

January of 1943 showed the S.T. & E. on the upswing again. A report prepared for the previous year revealed an interesting development. It was the first clue to the future real success of the railroad. The report showed the average carload returns to the company from different commodities. Canned goods from Wilson Cannery headed the list, with walnuts next, followed by cherries and shipments from the LeTourneau machinery plant.

Early in 1943 the S.T. & E. officials were approached about locating a bean processing shed in Linden, where the Bean Growers' Association planned to process beans for seed. Most of the seed would go to New York and net the railroad more than $40 per car. The existing shed east of Linden

S.T. & E. #1 at the S.P. Sacramento shops in 1943, following boiler repairs and overhaul. S.P. shop men moved the locomotive outside so Gerald M. Best could take this picture. (Gerald M. Best collection)

was to be used for a season, until the association remodeled and moved into the old brick building at the corner of Front and Mill Streets in Linden. It still produces the most carloads out of Linden today, even though it is only a drop in the bucket of the road's overall business.

The rolling stock of the Slow Tired & Easy Railroad had always been in short supply and was now becoming short in performance. The company men were desperately trying to find a replacement, but the war shortages made this an impossible task. The "One Spot" blew a plate in the fire box and had to be sent to the Sacramento repair shop one more time. The repair bill exceeded $6,500 and the company had to make arrangements to pay it off in installments. While the engine was in the Sacramento shops, Gerald M. Best, railroad historian and author, went to look at it and the S.P. men moved the engine outside so he could take its picture.

In February E. C. Stewart of the Union Safe Deposit Bank in Stockton once again pressed to get out of the Slow Tired & Easy Railroad. He wrote, "I believe there was a time when a junk dealer offered the company enough money to pay off all the notes outstanding, but same was not accepted."

But once again his request was refused. The company management reminded him that the bank was only a stockholder like the rest of the former bondholders.

Other skeletons were rattling in the closet and one of the original stock and bond salesmen, Grover Herring, showed up on the scene. He arrived at the Stockton office and made inquiries about the road. Dietrich reported the event to Kahn:

This chap I believe is the promoter type although he tells me he himself invested $15,000 in the stock of the original company besides selling $4,000 or $5,000 worth of the bonds to his mother or some other relative. He asked me if you would sell the road and I told him I thought you would but did not know at what price.

Herring attended the annual stockholders meeting in 1943 and stated that it seemed that now was the time to dispose of the railroad. He proposed to facilitate the sale by making a concerted effort to increase the earnings within the next six months. He suggested he be given the opportunity to take over the management of the company, "to get some real money for the stockholder." He returned to Stockton to look the road over and had "considerable palaver" with Dietrich but did not produce any money. Sometime later Dietrich wrote to Kahn:

Just had your letter about Grover Herring. I feel like you. He has grandiose ideas but he is a small time operator. I would not think of turning over the management of the railroad to him who has had no experience whatsoever in this line. It would simply give him a seat in the saddle.

Dietrich once again thought he was going to get someone else to run the railroad when on December 27, 1943 the U. S. Government, by executive order, took over all railroads. But if this was his hope, it was short-lived, for not even the govern-

Locomotive #1 near the engine house. The hooded headlight was used during World War II as a blackout precaution, late 1943. (Guy Dunscomb collection)

ment wanted the Slow Tired and Easy Railroad. Within three weeks a release was sent to be signed, but typical of government policy that once is never enough, soon an amended release had to be processed.

Prosperity was coming to San Joaquin County again so business once again reflected confidence. The Diamond Match Company, which now occupied the old Linden Lumber Yard, purchased the property from the railroad. Pollock's shipbuilding company sent out a feeler to see if the railroad was for sale. Dietrich and Kahn agreed they would sell for $150,000 cash, but the sale fell through when Pollock missed a big government contract and did not need the railroad and the Bellota gravel.

The road traffic increased as Kelly and Barosso were expanding their Independent Fruit Company and again asked for more room. The nearby railroad spur was lengthened but in the spring of 1944 cars still had to be loaded on the mainline.

Two out of every three years the Central California Traction Company showed an interest in purchasing the S.T. & E. Railroad. This occurred because of the Traction Company's tri-ownership by W.P., S.P. and Santa Fe. White, the Traction Company manager, had talked more than once of purchasing the road but the S.P. men had always put the damper on any serious negotiations. In the summer of 1945 it was a Western Pacific man, Mettler, who called on Dietrich. George Covert, a shipper, also showed an interest in buying it.

The S.T. & E. men agreed that they should sell the Nevada corporation to avoid legal complications. They also raised the sale price to $175,000 but still no deal was made.

Both Odell and Dietrich were ill during the winter of 1945–46 and Leah Wilson ran the business. Trouble developed when the company was filling an order for 100 cars of gravel. It proved to be too much for the tracks, between the bad ties and the soft roadbed, and gondolas of gravel were off the tracks almost at once. Miss Wilson and Hewitt diverted the last 50 cars to another railroad.

Without Dietrich and Odell, others in the company looked for an easy solution to their problems and the seed was planted for abandonment of the east end of the line.

Dietrich was 70 years old with the vital mind of a man 50 years younger and must have had little patience with the confining illness that seemed to strike him down each winter. He was not ready to give up on the railroad, however, for as soon as he returned to work he ordered new ties and rails to rebuild the worst sections of the road. He also signed a 20-year lease with Kelly of the Independent Fruit Company.

When Odell got back to work, he found the section crew was not getting the work done to his satisfaction so he fired them all, including the foreman. This time he hired Mexicans to do the job. The men were paid for eleven hours work even though they worked only nine, the extra two hours being paid at time and a half. He was following the

Loading onions in late May of 1945. (S.T. & E. collection)

lead of the S.P. and W.P. railroads which used the practice to keep crews, since the law allowed the railroad to pay only 62½ cents an hour for regular time and section men refused to work for this amount. Contractors were asking $1.75 an hour for the same work.

New businesses were building along the railroad. Don Blair Lumber Company, located on the north side of Linden Road in Stockton, was one of them.

During 1945 one-fifth of all walnuts shipped by local walnut growers' associations in California were hauled by Locomotive #1. This amounted to more than 15½ million pounds of nuts. The *Diamond Walnut News*, the California Association publication, carried an article about Old #1 and said it would soon go into retirement. Dietrich was making inquiries into locomotives and salesmen were appearing frequently with cost figures.

1946 turned out to be a bad year because of a national railroad strike which once again stopped eastern shipments. Dietrich wrote to Kahn:

This strike, I think, is uncalled for, but I'm afraid the labor leaders know they have our amiable Mr. Truman's goat, and while they are having fun making this white livered mouse dance, they're really raising

the devil with the American economy and with every citizen of the country.

Dietrich and Company purchased the Estep property, 20 acres of land near the engine house, for industrial development. He confided to Kahn that he would put in a drill track along the south side of the property which joined the S.P. right of way. This would prevent S.P. from putting in spurs and save all the traffic from the property for the S.T. & E. Railroad.

Winter came and Dietrich was ill again, but he concentrated on the problems of another locomotive anyway. The situation became critical when the government turned down the company's application for a time extension to put new flues in the "One Spot." On top of this S.P. refused to take the locomotive into their Sacramento shops, using the excuse that they did not have time for their own work. Fortunately W.P. agreed to do the work in their Sacramento shops. In the meantime, the company was using a Tidewater Southern locomotive which was due for inspection also.

The company found an engine but could not buy it without a priority even though they had the cash. They finally made the purchase by paying a

90

Top: Superintendent Frank Odell and F. J. Dietrich went out to "look over the line" during the cherry season, 1945. Above: The bags on the truck contain rock salt to be added with the ice. Odell and Dietrich are walking away from the camera on the right. (S.T. & E. collection)

commission to E. J. Mahoney, a former Army Colonel, who could get a priority as an exserviceman. Dietrich had to make the company a loan to pay the $25,000 purchase price and $2,500 commission.

It was mid-November 1947 before the locomotive was repaired and delivered. In the meantime the company had lowered and reroofed the old roundhouse to receive S.T. & E. Engine #10.*

About this time a man arrived at the Stockton railroad office looking for a job. Odell had been talking of retiring and the word was out that his

*See addenda note #5

job would be available. The new man knew about diesels so he was hired instead as traffic manager. He was soon trying to undermine Odell and when he got nowhere with Dietrich he went to Kahn. Dietrich wrote to Kahn, "While I think he is a good railroad man, I think he had accumulated some very bad habits and unless he forgets them we may have to replace him."

The company soon had another traffic manager who proved to be just as bad and he too was fired. Next a retired railroader was hired, but he soon found the job too much for him and quit. Finally a younger man with S.P. experience was interviewed. Orville Muehlberg had just purchased a house and had no automobile, so Dietrich agreed

Top: Frank Odell and F. J. Dietrich look on as a Union Ice Company truck delivers ice to refrigerator cars spotted on the S.T. & E. main line in East Stockton, 1945. Above: Blocks of ice were lowered by hand into the refrigerator cars in preparation for shipping cherries to eastern markets. (S.T. & E. collection)

Locomotive #1 parked at Stockton Station, 1947. (Guy Dunscomb collection)

to buy him a used car and take payments out of his salary if he would come to work for the railroad. He proved to be satisfactory and the traffic manager problem was finally solved.

In February of 1948 Odell fell and broke a rib. Complications set in and he developed pneumonia, which put him in the hospital. The doctor diagnosed high blood pressure and hardening of the arteries. He came back to work but was still weak and unable to do much. Dietrich wrote about his concern for Odell and speculated on the future: "I am afraid we will be looking for a new superintendent if his condition will not improve."

He praised Hewitt's ability to perform Odell's duties, but added that he was needed as conductor. He felt that Hewitt knew more about the intricate diesel machinery and its "vast electric installation than the engineer who operated it."

Hewitt was a valuable man for the road, but often lacked tact and at times was incorrigible. Naturally a railroad that had gone into receivership and had a reputation of being slow, tired and easy, never got much respect from the Linden residents. The tracks were considered part of the street for many people who used them as a convenient parking strip. One day when the train arrived in Linden, there was a car jacked up on the tracks with the wheels off. During the peak of walnut season, trucks were often lined up on the tracks at the Linden plant waiting to be unloaded. Occasionally a trucker would get tired of waiting

and would pull his keys and leave. On several occasions the train had to wait almost an hour for trucks to be removed.

Naturally none of these conditions helped make good relations between the townspeople and the crew, but probably the worst feeling existed between the railroad crew and the men at Lee's Garage. It all started when one of the railroad men walked into the shop. Because he had come out of the bright sunshine, he could not see in the dark building and stepped between two automobiles parked over a pit. He fell into the pit, directly into a bucket of crankcase oil. He was not hurt but the oil splashed and he was "oil clear to his collar," according to a witness. The men in the shop got a big laugh out of it and continued to razz the train crew. This had happened when the garage was in the present bean plant, but eventually the garage moved across the street just south of the tracks. There was just enough room between the tracks and the side of the garage to park autos at a right angle to the building. Frequently someone would not pull in close enough and the train would have to halt while the tracks were cleared. It finally got so bad that on days when the train was going to Linden, someone in the railroad office would call and tell them to clear the tracks. One particular day as the train arrived at the garage, the tracks were blocked again. Hewitt went inside and asked them to move their cars.

"One of these days we are going to mess up some

93

cars if you don't keep them off the tracks," he warned.

The autos were moved and the train went up to the walnut plant. In the meantime a pickup truck drove up to the back of the garage and parked on a slight diagonal. Before long the train came back, traveling west. An eye witness later reported that the engine came to a stop about 12 feet from the pickup, whose bumper extended out too far. Hewitt signaled the train to come on, waving his arm in the appropriate circular motion. The engine eased forward and proceeded to push until the wheels of the locomotive spun and all nine automobiles were in a heap. When the garage men heard the crash they knew what had happened. The pickup owner went running out waving his arms and shouting, "It's all my fault! It's all my fault!"

Fortunately only five of the autos suffered damage but after the story got around, most Linden residents were more careful about parking on the railroad tracks.

In spite of his reputation Hewitt had a good side. The children all along the line knew him. On Roosevelt street the kids all called him "Whistling John" because he rode the front of the engine and whistled if the street crossing was clear. Many a young boy got his first ride on a train from Hewitt, and several caught rides home regularly.

There must have been occasions when Dietrich looked back at the "good old days" in Stockton when he was a young man and a businessman could make a profit without government directives and the high cost of labor. During the spring of 1949 he wrote to his friend and business associate, Kahn, about a forced pay raise for the men, "I remember when I first started on the road we paid section men 25 cents an hour; now they receive $1.03."

In spite of this, Dietrich was neither a dishonest nor a stingy man. He once paid out $10,000 rather than fight over a real estate deal with a relative, although a lawyer consulted by another member of the office staff said there was no legal way the money had to be paid. Dietrich closed the issue: "If he says I owe it to him, I owe it to him." He paid it and the subject was closed.

In the spring of 1949 Dietrich began negotiations for a sugar beet haul from Comstock Station to the Spreckels Sugar Company in Manteca. S.P. had no desire to share a rate because they already had two available stations at Walthal and Holden, south of the S.T. & E., so they held out for a rate higher than their own. Fortunately the W.P.

could also service the sugar company as a connecting railroad and were happy to cooperate. The two railroads and the sugar company finally agreed on five cents per hundred, although Dietrich and Kahn had privately decided to go as low as four and a half cents. The final agreement netted the S.T. & E. $18 for each minimum carload of 40 tons and would mean an additional $20,000 a year in revenue.

The sugar beet deal must have had an impact on someone in the S.P. organization, for by early June a representative of the company approached F. J. Dietrich Jr., questioning the availability of the road. Kahn also interested A. D. Schader, using the sugar beet contract as a strong selling point. The two men traveled to Stockton and Dietrich accompanied them on an inspection of the property.

Schader's original intent had been to buy the road to scrap it and he discussed the possibility with T. K. Beard, the Superintendent of the Modesto Empire & Traction Company line, who had worked for him in dismantling the Yosemite Valley Railroad. Beard reminded him that it was getting more and more difficult to abandon railroads since it took only one customer on a road to block the action. In the meantime, Schader had seen what the Beard family had done with their Modesto line and could see the potential of the Slow Tired and Easy Railroad. Beard and Arno B. Appel, his traffic manager, arrived to inspect the road for Schader.

Beard, who little dreamed he would one day be president of the road, appraised the physical property while Appel investigated the economics. Beard reported to Schader, "It would cost too much to bring it out of the mud."

He estimated it would cost $250,000 to put the road in safe operation. Schader either did not take the advice or did not inform Kahn of his decision, for two months later Dietrich was looking for three to four hundred acres of land on the road for Schader.

Early in August Kahn inquired as to how many miles of track could be removed from the east end of the line. He pointed out that it served no useful purpose. Dietrich delayed several weeks in answering. He was having a love affair with the Slow Tired and Easy Railroad, for it had made a railroad man out of him. No doubt it pained him to abandon this track for it was under McCormick's, Davis's and his direction that this portion of the road had been constructed in 1912. He attempted to interest a rubber plant in locating at Bellota but

S.T. & E. #10, purchased in March of 1947, was the first diesel electric locomotive ever owned by the company. (S.T. & E. collection)

to no avail. He finally wrote to Kahn saying that Fine Station, which Charles Anderson used for loading walnuts, was the last pickup point in use on the line.

On August 31, 1949 Kahn suffered a slight heart attack in his San Francisco office. He was confined to bed for more than four weeks and it was late in October before he returned to work. But it was not Kahn's health that was to fail first; Dietrich was about to be taken from his beloved railroad. He wrote his last letter to Kahn on December 6, 1949. He covered the problems encountered when Kelly put improvements in the packing shed and wanted the railroad to pay for them. He was concerned with Odell's health and wrote that he hoped Schader would once again become interested in buying the road.

Dietrich could have written this letter in 1939, or 1929 or 1919, for it showed the same concern for his employees, the sharp business sense, and his continual interest in selling the Slow Tired and Easy Railroad.

On December 10, 1949 shortly after noon, Dietrich entered his real estate office on Weber Avenue. He greeted the staff with a cheery "Merry Christmas," walked to a nearby desk, collapsed and died.

Three days later private funeral services were held in Stockton with inurnment in the Park View Crematorium. Kahn, still recuperating from his heart attack, wrote to Leah Wilson that he would miss his friend very much, and he was not alone in that feeling. The Slow Tired and Easy Railroad would not be the same without congenial Joe Dietrich, the man who, although he was not a railroad president, made the trains stop and go.

CHAPTER XIII

THE ERA OF DR. HISS

In mid-January of 1950 Samuel Kahn called a meeting of the S.T. & E. Nevada corporation to appoint F. J. Dietrich Jr. vice president and treasurer, to fill the vacancy left by the death of his father. Joe Jr. had inherited his father's railroad responsibility. He reported to Kahn on the company's financial condition, concluding that there was going to be money available for reduction of debts:

Miss Wilson assured me the record clearly shows that my method of hoarding cash sins on the side of conservatism. Before disbursing more than the interest, however, some accelerated attention to deferred maintenance may be preferable to debt reduction.

The railroad had always been the elder Dietrich's baby and was a standard joke in his family, so no doubt Joe Jr. felt that he did not need the Slow Tired and Easy Railroad to manage, along with a successful real estate business. Although he indicated this outwardly, his daughter Helene believes that he was afraid of the railroad, "afraid that if he got involved, he too would be hooked," as his father had been for those many years.

Dietrich immediately sent a letter to the I.C.C. in Washington inquiring into ways to abandon the track from Bellota to Fine Road. He reiterated that the eastern 2.7 miles of the road had produced no revenue for the past two years.

C. E. Stewart of the Union Safe Deposit bank in Stockton was once again prodded by a notice from the corporation. Joe Jr. went to see him and reported to Kahn in a letter dated January 25, 1950:

I frankly told Mr. Stewart of the financial conditions of the railroad, of its 1949 operations and of his status as a stockholder. In the latter connections, I assured him that the Dietrichs were even more interested than the Stewarts in the possibility of liquidating an investment, and there is no plan preferential for his account as against any other stockholder.

Our meeting was very pleasant, and I feel it answered the purpose.

Joe Jr. remembered the lesson of slim months during the first part of each year, so he hung on to the cash reserves. The road traffic was up over the previous year, and Odell was replacing ties as fast as the weather permitted.

In May 1950 Joe Jr. was on a trip, so he sent his proxy for the annual meeting of the California corporation. In spite of his absence, he was elected director, vice president and treasurer of the corporation. Kahn was retiring so he replaced his people on the board of directors with Dietrich's people. Control seemed to be returning to Stockton where the railroad was located. History proved that this had always been good for business on the Slow Tired and Easy Railroad, but would history repeat itself?

Early in November Joe Jr. took time to bring Kahn up-to-date, reporting on increased revenue and maintenance. Included almost as an afterthought was the first indication of a new business that would prove to be extremely important to the future of the railroad, the forerunner of many such businesses that might someday change the image of the Slow Tired & Easy Railroad:

Dietrich & Co. is negotiating with Richmond-Chase Co. for a five acre site on the S.T. & E. Railroad, which Richmond-Chase proposes to use as its shipping warehouse. If this materializes, the location of this new industry should result in a greatly increased volume of profitable eastern shipments originating on our line. In connection with this project Mr. Muehlberg, in cooperation with the industry and others, succeeded in obtaining a new tariff permitting stopping in transit to complete loading. This makes us competitive with other roads in this respect through elimination of the switching charge, which heretofore we had to add to the stopover charge.

Regardless of what might be, the railroad had firmly established its reputation and name in Stockton. It was on December 22, 1950 that the company received a check from John C. Maurer & Sons, made out to "The Slow Tired & Easy Railroad." The bookkeeper deposited the check along with others but made a copy to keep in the files.

Frank Odell, superintendent of the road for 35 years, stands beside Old #1. (S.T. & E. collection)

Before the year's end a note to Rosalind Kahn was paid in full, the first indication we have that the company was finally paying off its old debts.

Dietrich again wrote to Kahn in early February of 1951 about the Richmond-Chase deal:

There will be two kinds of traffic. The first and most important will be that of cars originating from East Stockton. Mr. Richmond estimates this annual shipment will be from 400 cars up. The second class will be cars which originate in San Jose and which are stopped over at East Stockton for top-loading. Based on past experiences, Mr. Richmond believes this may run in the neighborhood of 100 cars a year.

He went on to explain that the first classification would bring the company from $65 to $95 per car. Richmond-Chase bought ten acres, giving themselves room for planned expansion. Before long the property was transferred and the railroad installed tracks to accommodate the new facilities.

Dietrich once again reported to Kahn and added a little something extra, something that would be of vital importance to the railroad. A Dr. J. M. Hiss had come to look the railroad over with the possibility of buying it. Dietrich wrote:

From talking to Dr. Hiss, I feel that his interest is chiefly that of a "railroad buff" and that he does not seriously mean to buy a railroad property; unless he would acquire such on a "plaything basis." From what he said, I think he would be chiefly interested in polishing up the brass parts of old No. 1 and running her up and down the line.

However, from the information I have Dr. Hiss apparently is quite well-to-do, so we don't know what may develop. However, I do not think that I should send him our statement until convinced that his interest is other than indicated to date. Possibly it was a mistake to let this man ride the engine, as I am not at all sure that this is a permissable practice.

As casual as F. J. Dietrich Jr.'s letters seemed they were the results of a long, often slow, process. While his father had written frequently and off the top of his head, he might take as long as a week to make sure a letter was "just right," much to the chagrin of his own son, F. J. Dietrich III.

Dr. Hiss came back to look over the road again. In August 1951 Kahn wrote, "I was disturbed to learn that Dr. Hiss is taking liberties with our property and train crew and I hope Mr. Odell's order to the crew is most emphatic. I have heard nothing more from him."

The track abandoning papers were progressing, for the city of Stockton issued a purchase order buying the trestle located at Bellota. The order was for $300 and noted that the trestle was to be removed by the city.

By the end of the year the company had paid half of its obligations which left only about $8,000. However within a month three new promissory notes, totaling almost $13,000, were issued by the Nevada corporation.

By June of 1952 there was still no word from Dr. Hiss. The financial condition and revenue of the road was so good that Kahn predicted it would be a record year for the company. Dr. Hiss had gone to Ohio and when he got back reached an agreement with Dietrich and Kahn. On July 15, 1952 simultaneous meetings of the California and Nevada Stockton Terminal and Eastern Corporations were held in Stockton. A resolution was

JOHN C. MAURER & SONS

GROWERS & SHIPPERS

CALIFORNIA VEGETABLES

CAR LOT DISTRIBUTORS

STOCKTON, CALIFORNIA

No. 2690

DECEMBER 22, 1950

PAY TO THE ORDER OF _____ SLOW, TIRED AND EASY RAILROAD _____ $ 139.55

REPLIONS$139and55cts

ENDORSEMENT OF THIS CHECK ACKNOWLEDGES PAYMENT IN FULL OF THE ACCOUNT AS STATED ON THE VOUCHER PORTION HEREOF.

JOHN C. MAURER & SONS

TO STOCKTON SAVINGS & LOAN BANK
90-103   STOCKTON. CALIFORNIA   90-103

BY _____

The company officials took much kidding about the name Slow Tired and Easy but did not seem to mind if it was on a check. Someone took the time to make a copy of this one and put it in the company files. (S.T. & E. collection)

Above: Loading an excursion train, powered by Old #1, in the early 1950s. Right: Picture-taking stop near the Diverting Canal. (John Hewitt)

Frank Odell, superintendent of the Slow Tired and Easy Railroad, shown here about the time he retired in 1952. (Mrs. Florence Grant collection)

passed giving four directors the power to carry on the company business. Both Kahn and Dietrich resigned as officers and directors. Dr. John M. Hiss was elected president, O. H. Muehlberg, executive vice president, Clifford Bourland, Hiss's son-in-law, was also named vice president, and Leah Wilson was named secretary-treasurer. Dr. Hiss had acquired 146,000 shares of the Nevada Corporation stock, taking out the Dietrich interests completely and most of the Kahn interests.

Within two weeks a Stockton news story told of Frank E. Odell's retirement. He had finally gone home to stay, to sit and listen to his radio. Calling

him the sparkplug of the Slow Tired and Easy Railroad, the article told of the increased traffic of the road and concluded with a dash of sentiment: "It's tough to raise a child, or a railroad, from a little sprout and see it walk alone."

Retirement had finally come to Frank Odell but it must have been a sad day, indeed, for a man who had known little else outside of railroading for most of his life.

The new Slow Tired and Easy Railroad president, Dr. John M. Hiss, was a southern California man and the control of the company had once again left Stockton. Who was this man and was he serious about running a railroad?

Dr. Hiss was a successful chiropodist with several clinics. He appeared to be a man of great energies, with a quick sense of humor, a rather complicated man who might overwhelm one person with his enthusiasm and make another uncomfortable with his shyness. His father had been a Columbus, Ohio cabinet maker with a desire to have his son learn the business. He taught John to work with tools and helped him develop hands and fingers capable of doing precise work.

Instead of following in his father's footsteps, however, young John went to Kirksville College of Osteopathy in Missouri and graduated in 1914. He returned to Columbus and became an assistant to Dr. John T. Morris, an eminent bone surgeon. He soon became fascinated with feet and discovered that often surgery was not the answer to a foot problem, that many times the problem was caused by bones that were out of place. He developed a medical theory and realized that a man with a desire to spread a new idea must have an M. D., so he decided to go on to school. He finally enrolled at Rush Medical College at the University of Chicago and completed his study at Ohio State University. Dr. Hiss opened a foot clinic in Columbus in 1922 and designed a shoe which was later marketed through chain stores. He began publishing some of his theories in medical and scientific journals and before long was recognized as an expert in the field, eventually writing a textbook on the subject. He was asked to lecture at medical conventions and universities throughout the country. However, his dynamic energies were not consumed by his medical interests, as zealous as he was, so he threw himself into hobbies, painting, printing and railroading.

Dr. Hiss had already qualified for a locomotive engineer ticket on the New York Central Railroad. Was the Slow Tired and Easy Railroad a new toy

Above: S.T.&E. #3, at speed, crossing the Diverting Canal trestle. Dr. Hiss is at the throttle for this excursion trip, June 6, 1954. (Gerald M. Best collection) Right: From top to bottom, Dr. Martin Hiss, F. J. Dietrich Jr., Walt Willmette and Fred Boler. The occasion was an excursion trip in early 1950s. (Mrs. F. J. Dietrich Jr.)

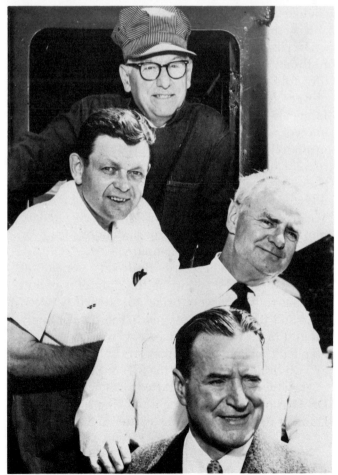

Business developed by Dietrich on the north side of Miner Avenue. It was serviced by an S.T. & E. spur track. (S.T. & E. collection)

or would he make it work? Would he be an absentee owner, who would come up and play with his train when he had nothing else to do? The answers were not long in coming. Every Tuesday night he rode a sleeper into Stockton from the southland city. John Hewitt met him at the S. P. depot and took him to the railroad yards where he kept his own private caboose.* There he would change into striped overalls and cap and climb aboard the engine.

Dr. Hiss was in complete control of the S. T. & E. Railroad. He had put his employees on the board of directors of both corporations, and naturally employees have a tendency to agree with the boss. John Hewitt was added as a director of the California corporation in October 1952 and was immediately instructed to hire S. M. McGaw to rebuild the tracks from Sargent Street to Golden Gate Avenue in east Stockton. Hewitt was also directed to proceed with the installation of the new Miner Avenue industrial spur. Hiss delegated to himself the job of looking for a standby steam or diesel locomotive for the company.

The Bay Area Electric Railroad Association showed an interest in buying the right of way and existing rails that were being abandoned between Fine and Bellota. Hiss offered to sell the company interest in the property. An escrow was opened and Stephen Dietrich, the attorney son of F. J. Dietrich, Sr., was hired to represent the S.T. & E. Railroad.**

The new year of 1953 started with new plans, as Dr. Hiss proposed building a packing shed for the Dumont Packing Co., at the corner of Sargent and

Magnolia Streets, for approximately $30,000. The Nevada corporation borrowed the necessary money from a Stockton bank.

Hiss located a Baldwin steam locomotive at Scotia, California and purchased it for $3,000. It was towed to the Stockton W. P. shop to be brought up to operational specifications. It was not a practical purchase but gave Dr. Hiss another steam locomotive for a toy. No doubt he justified his choice for buried in the company files is an article written at the time which states that steam engines make good switch engines on roads of limited service.

The new locomotive already carried the number 3 which was retained on the S.T. & E. Railroad. This time, at least, the number fit, because it was the third steam locomotive ever owned by the company.***

With a new steam locomotive, Dr. Hiss donated Locomotive #1 to the Los Angeles Traveltown Museum. In October, 1953 Old #1, the true epitome of the Slow Tired and Easy Railroad, was towed away after 39 years with the road and 89 years of service in California. The railroad would never be the same again.****

By the end of the year the operating revenue was up by $10,000 over the year before, but the profit was down due to the fact that more than $8,000 had been spent on road maintenance alone. Revenues at the end of 1954 were up another $11,000 and with the maintenance cost down, the net income went to the highest level ever.

With more money on hand, Hiss decided to pur-

*See addenda note #6
**See addenda note #7

***See addenda note #8
****See addenda note #9

102

Top: This is the builder's photograph of the 1922-built Baldwin locomotive, construction No. 55248. A prairie type locomotive, it received #3 for the Humboldt Northern Railway and carried the same number under succeeding ownership by the Dolbeer and Carson Lumber Co., the Pacific Lumber Co. and the S.T. & E. Railroad. Center: Locomotive #3 at the Miner Avenue yards after it was purchased from Dolbeer and Carson Lumber Co. at Scotia, California. Bottom: Locomotive #1 under steam at the Diverting Canal on an excursion run to Linden before retirement in 1953. (S.T. & E. collection)

103

S.T. & E. #11 was an Army surplus locomotive purchased by the company in February 1955. It was a rare off-center cab model and one of only five to reach the West Coast. (S.T. & E. collection)

chase another diesel locomotive. Hewitt went to the Bamberger Railroad shops in North Salt Lake City to inspect a 45-ton General Electric Cooper Bessemer engine. Dr. Hiss advanced the money for the purchase and took a note in return for 6% interest. The new locomotive received the S. T. & E. Number 11.*

By the end of 1955, the gross operating revenue was up another ten thousand dollars, but so was maintenance and equipment expense, bringing the net income down again. A pattern was developing that indicated Dr. Hiss was not interested in making a profit even though the railroad was growing in volume.

During the past two years the company had begun to deal in real estate, a practice which had been reserved for the Nevada corporation or Dietrich's interest, in the past. Parcels were sold to

*See addenda note #10
**See addenda note #11

Hughes and Devencenzi in Linden and the Bacigalupe interests in Stockton. The corporation had also purchased several acres from Garibaldi in East Stockton.

1956 had proved to be such a good year for the railroad that operating revenues were up almost $28,000 over the previous year and the company showed a net income of more than $27,000.

The final three miles of track repair work was let out on contract to S. M. McGaw and there was still some money left.

Hewitt went to Seattle to inspect yet another diesel locomotive for $33,500. When it was ready to be moved, some three months later, Dr. Hiss once again put up the necessary cash and received a note in return. This was to be S.T. & E. Locomotive #22.**

During 1957 the California corporation purchased several lots of Block 9 in El Ricado Terrace from the Nevada corporation which in turn purchased more land.

During the 1950s, under the leadership of Dr. Hiss, the company purchased a portion of the Garibaldi property in East Stockton along the tracks. This event was given very little attention at the time but would play a key role in the expansion of the company. This picture was taken at the height of the rainy season to show that the property had no drainage problems. (S.T. & E. collection)

Being a railroad fan, Dr. Hiss had been generous in allowing excursions on the road. Steam Locomotive #3 had replaced the "One Spot" on these trips and had its picture taken almost as reverently by the enthusiastic rail fans.

By 1957 Dr. Hiss' interest in the railroad was beginning to diminish. It had apparently served his purpose twofold, as a tax advantage and an avocation. It had outlived its usefulness in the former instance when it began to consistently show a profit. He also seemed to have satisfied his desire to play railroad on a grand scale, and had acquired a new yacht that was beginning to consume much of his spare time and energy.

Labor problems were brewing; the company had been operating on an eight-out-of-twelve-hour schedule, making a split shift for the train crew. The Switchman's Union of North America was trying to get a straight eight hours which would require a second crew to meet the switching schedules. During the labor negotiations Dr. Hiss even offered to sell the railroad to the union. He was offering to sell to almost anyone who came along, so the word was out that the Slow Tired and Easy Railroad was for sale. Its past record, however, was not such that people were waiting in line to buy.

During the Christmas holidays in 1957, T. K. Beard II, known as Tom, vice president of the Modesto & Empire Traction Company, had lunch in Stockton with Art Hammond, district freight representative for the Chicago Burlington & Quincy Railroad. During their conversation, Hammond prodded Beard, "Why don't you buy the S. T. & E. Railroad?"

"Is it for sale?" questioned Beard.

Tom Beard was not a stranger to the Slow Tired and Easy Railroad, for he had investigated it for A.

D. Schader before Hiss had purchased the road. Before long, Beard contacted Muehlberg, who set up an appointment for him with Hiss.

In the meantime Dr. Hiss had transferred his Nevada corporation stock to Alexander Haagen and had taken back an option. In turn Haagen had found a possible buyer in an S. Andy Seligman.

On January 8, 1958, Tom Beard arrived on the West Coast train and was met by Hiss at the Glendale station. They went to the Ham & Eggs Breakfast Club before proceeding to the doctor's office. When they finally got around to talking about the railroad, Hiss stated a price.

Beard said, "OK."

"Don't you want to dicker?"

"No, the price is right," Beard answered.

So they shook hands and the deal was closed between the two of them. Dr. Hiss could now pick up his option or sell it to Beard.

At almost the same instant a meeting of the Nevada corporation was being held in Stockton. Haagen was named a director and officer, but because of the option Hiss was renamed president. Seligman was also named an officer in the corporation.

Hiss must have boarded a train that very evening, for at 10:00 a.m. the next morning he was present in the Stockton office for another special meeting of the board of the Nevada corporation. Haagen and Seligman, both Los Angeles men, had stayed over for the meeting. Hiss was close-mouthed about his new agreement with Beard, only telling Miss Wilson to give Beard any information he wanted, as he was interested in buying the railroad.

During late March and early April of 1958 the Stockton area was deluged by a continual series of storms. The flood waters reached a peak at the

Left: An S. M. McGaw dragline backs onto the Diverting Canal trestle during high water. The trestle had special planking to accommodate the heavy equipment. Forrest Wyman of that company, right, is pictured here talking with the unknown dragline operator. Right: The dragline lifts debris from the upstream to the downstream side of the S.T. & E. trestle on the Stockton Diverting Canal. (S.T. & E. collection)

Diverting Canal trestle on April 14. A dragline was moved out to the approach to the railroad trestle, where it was used to pick up debris lodged against the structure. At one point a tree was dropped directly on the trestle, knocking it off its foundations. It once again floated on the pilings. There was some consideration given to blowing up the bridge entirely, but that would only compound problems for similar structures downstream.

Much of the time at the annual S. T. & E. California Corporation stockholders' meeting held in May, 1958 was taken up by a report on the problems created by the spring floods. At this meeting, Seligman held Haagen's proxy for the controlling stock shares. Grover Herring once again appeared on the scene and reported on another 300 shares.

By now it was apparent to the company employees that Seligman intended to purchase the railroad when the option held by Hiss expired. He also told anyone who would listen that he was not interested in operating a railroad. He intended to use the company to own railroad cars to be leased out to other lines. The company people were very concerned for their little railroad, so when "real railroad men" showed an interest they gave them full cooperation. Leah Wilson refused to cooperate with the Los Angeles interests. She recalls receiving a telephone call from Seligman in which he told her that he was going to buy the railroad and she would be fired.

"You won't have to fire me, I will have already quit," she retorted.

In the meantime Tom Beard and his father,

George, had organized a new corporation, the Stockton Terminal Company. They were the only stockholders in this new corporation formed for the specific purpose of purchasing the road. The two men had kept close tabs on the railroad operation, but it was June before they started the necessary paperwork to acquire the company. They finally purchased all but approximately 1,000 shares of the S. T. & E. Nevada corporation stock.

The transaction was finalized late in July. However, official action was not taken until August 7, 1958. That summer afternoon Dietrich's real estate office on Weber Avenue, still the official place of business of the railroad, was the scene of another special meeting of the stockholders of the Nevada corporation. Present were Muehlberg, Wilson and George Beard. Beard presented certificates showing that 580 shares of preferred and 148,625 shares of common stock had been purchased by the newly organized Stockton Terminal Company. He stated that, as president of the new controlling corporation, he was voting the stock. The resignation of the directors was accepted and new ones elected. This time Wilson, Muehlberg and George Beard were named directors. Leonard Hardaway, Jr., a Beard employee, was authorized to sign the company checks and directed to supervise operations in Stockton.

The transition was made with little apparent outward change, but by November a dividend of $1.00 per share was declared on the rail stock, the second time for a dividend in the history of the road. Things were being accomplished by the new management of the Slow Tired and Easy Railroad.

106

CHAPTER XIV

SUCCESS AT LAST

George and Tom Beard brought expertise from the Modesto & Empire Traction Company, which operated in Stanislaus County, approximately 30 miles south of Stockton, and was owned by the Beard family.

George Beard's father was T. K. Beard, the son of a Stanislaus County pioneer farmer, Elihu B. Beard. In the early 1900's T. K. Beard had organized a construction company with Walter, another son. This company did grading work for railroads, among other jobs, which eventually led Beard to invest in an interurban railway between Modesto and Empire in 1909. The road had been constructed to connect Modesto to the Santa Fe tracks at Empire. In 1915 this shortline, like the S. T. & E. Railroad, was also in trouble, so Beard bought the road. His son Walter closed down the construction company and became president of the newly organized railroad company.

When the first T. K. Beard died in 1926, his son George also joined the company business. George Beard had named his only son T. K. Beard II. The boy, commonly known as Tom, grew up in the family-owned railroad business. At the age of 13 he worked for the railroad after school and on weekends, as a swamper on freight pickup and deliveries. He progressed to office work, doing bills of lading and learning office procedures. He moved into the operating department by the time he was 16 years old, and went to the shop and maintenance of way department before becoming a fireman on a steam locomotive and finally a yard master. By this time he was going to Modesto Junior College, was playing varsity football and was president of the Associated Men Students. He left the family business and transferred to the University of Oregon in the spring semester of 1941.

Tom Beard left Oregon university in September of 1942 to enlist as a private in the Army. In December he was sent to Officers Training School at Ft. Belvoir, Virginia. He graduated as a Second Lieutenant in March of 1943, as a member of the Corps of Engineers. He next went to Ft. Hamilton, New York, to await assignment. At this time the Transportation Corps was being organized and he was sent to England to work in the new corps. He was involved in troop movements in Southern England, for "Operation Overlord" at the time of the Normandy invasion. Within a short time he was in Normandy, one of those directing troop movements across the beach. He later became coordinating officer in charge of delivering material, particularly gasoline, to General Patton's fast moving 3rd Army. He was next transferred to the Paris Command Headquarters of the European Theater of Operations and placed in charge of transportation of all perishable foodstuffs coming into the European theater.

Tom Beard returned to the States and received his discharge in January of 1946. His military career had expanded his lifelong interest in railroading. He found employment with A. D. Schader Company and immediately got involved with the dismantling of the Yosemite Valley Railroad. He had proved he could make it on his own, so before long his family asked him to return to their company in Modesto. He became vice president of operations in June 1946, and eventually added the responsibility of being vice president in charge of traffic. George Beard became president of the family-owned business in 1954. These were the men who were going to change the Slow Tired and Easy Railroad, and there was no doubt that they could do it.

The Beards knew where to get expert help. Leonard Hardaway, the man supervising in Stockton, was one of their hand-picked men. He had been born and raised in Tennessee but as a child had vacationed in Modesto with a grandmother. His father was a railroad man, and he followed him into the Lewisville and Nashville Railroad. Len, as he was known to his friends, enlisted in the Navy during World War II. Having

Above: An aerial view of the S.T. & E. office and packing sheds on Broadway in east Stockton. The building in the front center is Foppiano's, built in 1962. The one directly above is Baxter-Pacific built for Mid-Valley Produce in 1959. The one to the left of this was built for Chinchilo's, 1959. A locomotive is shown in the extreme right and two business cars sit on a siding near the railroad office at the top of the picture. Below: A close-up of the general office building constructed in 1959 at the railroad's Broadway Street crossing. Because of the continued growth of the company, there have been two additions to the building since then. (S.T. & E. collection)

Business Car #21 was purchased from A.T. & S.F. Railraod Company in November 1958. It sits on a siding near the main business office of the S.T. & E. Railroad. (S.T. & E. collection)

long before decided to live in California, he came west after he got out of the service. He was determined not to get involved in railroading again. However, the Beards convinced him to go to work for them as a rate clerk. He later transferred from the traffic to the operating department.

After purchasing the S. T. & E. Railroad, the Beards immediately made Howard Hutchison, an experienced auditor, an officer in the new corporation. Bert Schneider, bringing experience from the S. P. and the M. & E. T., and Chet Packard, an experienced Modesto warehouseman, would also be moving into the Stockton office before long.

When Tom and George Beard took over the Slow Tired and Easy Railroad in 1958 it still deserved its name. After 48 years the company had only a handful of customers. The one major canning company, now Wilson Cannery, which had brought the railroad through many lean years, was still a major shipper. Richmond Chase's warehouse, which had become the major customer during Dr. Hiss's years with the railroad, was going through a transition period. It would evolve into California Canners and Growers and would have a major impact on the railroad's future success. Other customers at the time included Jewel Tea Company, Breuner's Furniture warehouse, Montgomery Ward's warehouse, two small lumber yards, a few packing sheds and two agricultural growers' associations.

A comparison of employee statistics between 1958 and the early 1970's tells what has happened in the intervening years. The railroad had only 16 employees in 1958, including three executives, one clerk, 9 maintenance of way men and 4 train crewmen, operating on an 8-out-of-12-hour split shift. In 1974 there was a total of 53 employees with only four executives but 19 clerks, 13 in the maintenance of ways department and 17 train crewmen. The train crews had to operate five 24-hour days, one 16-hour day and one 8-hour day a week to keep up with the traffic. An employees' profit-sharing plan was established in 1966, when a trust agreement was set up by the S.T. & E. Railroad California Corporation. The company agreed to place in trust up to 15% of the total annual wages paid to the employees, the sum to be over and above the said wages. The trustees then either purchased or built buildings that were leased back to the railroad. By 1974 the participating employees owned the railroad office building on Broadway and the engine house and shop on Shaw Road in east Stockton.

The railroad handled 3,119 carloads of freights in 1958. In 1973 the total had gone to 19,043 carloads, multiplying more than six times in the intervening years.

In the same period the gross operating expenses went from $120,444 in 1958 to $1,089,244 in 1973. The gross operating revenue showed an even larger increase, going from $214,589 to $2,108,972.

Since 1958 the S.T. & E. Railroad has been responsible for the construction of the packing sheds and warehouses in the foreground, the refrigeration company in the center and the warehouse in the upper right. Here the tracks cross Broadway with the company office at the upper left of the intersection. They continue over the top of Highway 99 and eastward across the Stockton Diverting Canal. (S.T. & E. collection)

Top left: The Chinchiolos, (front to back) Phil, Andy and Jim, face Superintendent Leonard Hardaway and a Kopper Company representative during a discussion of building progress on their new packing shed in 1959. Top right: Superintendent Hardaway and a representative of the Kopper Company, builders, look over the pole construction of the new packing sheds. Center: Tracks were laid into the Mid-Valley Produce, Chinchilo, and Zuckerman packing sheds in 1959. The property was the Garibaldi ranch purchased by Dr. Hiss for the railroad. Bottom: An aerial view of the first packing sheds built by the S.T. & E. Railroad under the direction of the Beards, 1959–60. (S.T. & E. collection)

111

Upper left: A view looking north out of the company yards toward Miner Avenue in East Stockton, 1968. Upper right: A lead frog with guide rail near the engine house. Left: Old engine house and yards near Miner Avenue. (Richard A. Cowan collection)

In 1958 the company owned only 33,715 square feet of building space, most of which was in packing sheds on a single block of Roosevelt Street, including the Magnolia Street packing shed rebuilt by Dietrich after the 1942 fire. Up to the beginning of 1975 the company was responsible for building more than one million square feet of space, mostly warehouses.

In a 1958 news release, George Beard had declared that the name of the railroad would be changed to the Swift, Tenacious and Energetic Railroad, but the change did not occur overnight. It was a long slow process. In 1960 George moved to San Francisco to open an office to generate more business for the railroad. Coinciding with this, Tom Beard began to devote his full time to the S. T. & E. and moved into the Stockton office. The Institutional Warehouse Company was organized under the Nevada corporation and the first major warehouse was built on the road.

In the meantime the S. T. & E. Railroad had applied for and received permission to handle storage in transit traffic under existing transcontinental tariffs. The company decided it would offer a special service between west coast shippers and eastern buyers. Fortunately Stockton's strategic location proved to be an added asset. Because of the city's deep-water port, the railroad also received ocean shipping rates, whether the cargo was unloaded in Oakland or Stockton. This made it advantageous to Hawaii and Alaska shippers. In the past buyers who wanted less than a carload lot of canned items had to pay a high initial freight rate and if a car going east stopped in more than one place, to have other items added, the costs went up more. The Institutional Warehouse has become a single stopping place. Producers send full carloads of single items to the warehouse where it is unloaded and reloaded in broken lots. Sometimes as many as ninety different items are loaded in one car, allowing a carload of these mixed lots to arrive at the retailers for the same traffic rate as a full carload of a single item. Institutional Warehouse Company collects a warehousing fee and the S. T. & E. Railroad receives a share of the freight revenue. The producer finds he is able to sell more goods and the retailer receives convenient size lots for less overall

Above left: This was the first of many warehouses to be constructed by the S.T. & E. parent corporation. This 50,000 sq. ft. warehouse, constructed in 1960, was turned over to the newly-organized Institutional Warehouse Company, another division of the corporation. Right: The interior of the first Institutional Warehouse Company building. Although company officials worried about filling the building in the beginning, this would be a rare sight today. The warehouses are kept full from incoming carloads of single items which are reloaded into cars containing as many as 90 different items. (I.W. Co. collection)

Left: On November 18, 1961 fire completely destroyed an S.T. & E. owned packing shed. A shed in the same location burned to the ground in August 1942. Right above: This view shows the tar blackened, second-hand, galvanized iron used by the Slow Tired and Easy Railroad officials to build this shed in 1942. Building materials were under war restrictions and this type of material was all that was available at the time. Right below: Although the fire was within the Stockton Fire Department's jurisdiction, an Eastside Fire Department pumper laid the first hose line. (Richard Cowan collection)

Top: The S.T. & E. Nevada Corporation built this 50,000-square foot warehouse in 1962 for Institutional Warehouse, a division of the corporation. Above left: El Solo Packing shed handled market tomatoes during the early 1960s. Above right: A new customer built industry north of Miner Avenue in East Stockton. This picture was taken in 1963. (S.T. & E. collection) Below: The tank near the right corner of the building is the original well on the Garibaldi property. It served the I.W. Co. and packing sheds on the property until 1964. An S.T. & E. maintenance-of-way motor car is in the foreground. Additional ballast was being added to the spotting track at the time this picture was taken. (I.W. Co. collection) Bottom: The Institutional Warehouse division of the company constructed a new office building in 1965. A duplicate of the S.T. & E. office, it was located on Golden Gate Avenue, near the S.T. & E. tracks and warehouses in East Stockton. The building suffered extensive fire damage in late 1974. (S.T. & E. collection)

Above: Another Institutional Warehouse, at Golden Gate and Harding in East Stockton, was built in 1965; still another was added in 1970. Here a Matson Line cargo container is shown being unloaded. (I.W. Co. collection)
Right: I.W. Co. receives and ships by truck or box cars with equal ease. (S.T. & E. collection)

cost. This practice also saves the retailer the necessity of maintaining high cost warehouses near his outlet.

At the time I. W. was organized there was only one other such warehouse service on the west coast. It was located in a high cost area and was doomed to close down. The policy of I. W. is service. The company officials take pride in the fact that orders are on their way within three days of placement. The company figures that two men, working with highly sophisticated fork and squeeze lifts and slip-pack machines, can unload a car of single items and reload the same car with 30 to 90 different items in a five-hour work period. The company also finds it an advantage to operate on a shortline railroad, for the minute a rail car hits any of the mainline roads, it is on the way to its destination as a foreign service car. This practice assures the buyer of a more accurate timetable for receiving the goods and enables close figuring of inventories. With I. W.'s dependable and fast service, many customers have been able to reduce out-of-stock items by fifty percent.

The I. W. Company received national recognition in 1969, during the Union Pacific Railroad's centennial year, when it received a U. P. award. This was given "in recognition of

progressive contributions to freight loading and industrial development."

As the I. W. Company continued to grow it became unwieldy in sheer size and was in danger of overwhelming the parent S. T. & E. Corporation, so company officials convinced several major shippers to save money by operating their own consolidation warehouses. This also freed the I. W. men to carry on the building program within the company and to generate more business for the railroad.

The Carnation Company became the biggest shipper on the S. T. & E. Railroad when it set up its own west coast shipping consolidation warehouse. The company brings carloads from the east coast and other areas to distribute in broken lots to its west coast outlets. This also gave the railroad a much needed supply of empty cars that could immediately be reloaded and sent on their way.

Although the S. T. & E. Railroad and Institutional Warehouses are both divisions of the Stockton Terminal Company, each has a completely separate management. It is an established policy that the railroad treats I. W. equally but with no preference over any other customer on the road.

Overall, the S. T. & E. Railroad gained only 2.03

Above: The S.T.&.E. Nevada Corporation built this 168,000-square foot tilt-wall-construction building in 1967. Carnation Company moved their west coast consolidated warehouses into the building as soon as it was completed. Below: This picture, taken around 1970, shows the Carnation Company warehouse upper left and undeveloped property purchased by the Railroad for future development. Shortly after this picture was taken new S.T. &. E. shop buildings were constructed just in front of the building at lower right. (S.T. & E. collection)

track miles between 1958 and 1973, but the figures are deceiving. The company had abandoned more than a mile and a half of unproductive track on the eastern end of the line and added more than three and a half miles of high revenue producing switching and siding tracks in East Stockton. As of 1973 the shortline railroad consisted of 13.79 miles of main line track, 1.75 miles of passing track and 6.77 miles of yard and switching track.

When the Beards acquired the railroad, the locomotive power included steam locomotive #3 and two diesel locomotives #11 and #22; an out of service report had already been filed on #10. The new Company soon added locomotives #12, #25, #505, #506 and #507.* Two others, #1000 and #1001 were purchased and traded for two of the above engines.** Three locomotives #11, #12 and #22 were scrapped during the summer of 1974, leaving #25, #505, #506 and #507 in operation.

During the years of Beard's control of the S. T. & E. East Stockton has taken on a new look. The in-

*See addenda notes #12,13,14,15,16

**See addenda note #17

The Stockton Terminal Company office built in 1973 contains 4,080 square feet of office space with a central patio. (S.T. & E. collection)

dustrial development has broadened the tax base, provided investment income and created hundreds of much needed jobs in the area. A most attractive new feature is the small modern office building of the Stockton Terminal Company in early California Spanish style, near the interchange of California Highway 26 and U.S. Highway 99, now California Highway 99.

The metamorphosis of the S. T. & E. made it a profitable operation, there is no doubt, but the prosperity had all come to the western terminus of the line. Linden was still prime agricultural land and the town was still small. In the 1960's, when urbanization reached its peak, it suffered like many rural areas in the country. Because the community had stood still it was suddenly falling behind. The business district was unable to compete with nearby urban business and one store after another closed. It looked as if another ghost town was in the making.

In 1972 a town meeting was once again held in Linden. In attendance were some of the children and grandchildren of those who had attended that important meeting at which the community pledged stock to the S. T. & E. Railroad in December of 1909. The railroad men again came with an open hand, this time offering to give rather than take. Tom Beard, S. T. & E. president, was the major speaker of the evening. He offered suggestions for remedies of the seemingly insurmountable problems facing the town. He talked of establishing a railroad museum and offered to run excursion trains to Linden if and when there was a demand for the service. He offered to help the community in any way but added, "The im-

George Beard was still active in the Railroad when this picture was taken in 1975. (S.T.&.E. collection)

petus of any tourist attraction or other development must come from within Linden to be a success."

The people of the community responded. A development committee was organized under the direction of the Linden Peters Chamber of Com-

117

Thomas K. Beard II, President of S.T. & E. Railroad, 1976.

merce. Within a year the trend had been reversed and Linden was beginning to look more prosperous as new businesses opened.

The local Community Day and F. F. A. Fair was changed to a Cherry Festival in 1973 and the S. T. & E. ran an excursion train, the first in many years.

The company is still collecting old rolling stock and railroad paraphernalia in anticipation of establishing an extensive railroad museum. Today the company owns a steam locomotive, two business cars, four passenger cars, a diner and a caboose.

The S. T. & E. Railroad has become a modern successful shortline railroad and a key link in the country's food distribution chain. It receives many California-produced canned food products but more than half of its inbound freight comes from outside the state. In turn this is sent into the nation's food distribution system. It has earned the name Strong Tenacious & Energetic but does not intend to rest on its laurels, for the company has purchased additional property and plans a continuing expansion program following its established successful pattern. However, if the town of Linden achieves its goal of attracting people, the S. T. & E. Railroad could have yet another name. It may one day be known as the Swift Transport & Excursion Railroad.

Superintendent Leonard Hardaway (left) and president Tom Beard. (S.T. & E. collection)

ROSTER

S.T. & E. STEAM LOCOMOTIVES

NUMBER	TYPE	DRIVERS	CYLINDER	WEIGHT	BUILDER & DATE	SERIAL #	ADDENDA NOTE
2	4-4-0	57"	16x24	?	Baldwin 1882	?	#1, 2, & 3
1	4-4-0	63"	16x22	31 tons	Norris-Lancaster 1864	?	#4 & 9
*3	2-6-2	44"	17x24	63 tons	Baldwin 1922	55248	#8

S.T. & E. DIESEL ELECTRIC LOCOMOTIVES

NUMBER	TYPE	DRIVERS	HORSE POWER	WEIGHT	BUILDER & DATE	SERIAL #	ADDENDA NOTE
10	B-B	34"	460	65 tons	Midwest Locomotive Works October 1933	7196	# 5
11	B-B	33"	300	45 tons	General Electric 1941 Schenectady, N.Y.	13162	#10
12	B-B	33"	380	44 tons	General Electric December 1943 Erie, Pa.	18154	#12
22	B-B	36"	500	80 tons	General Electric August 1942 Schenectady, N.Y.	15672	#11
**25	B-B	33"	380	44 tons	General Electric December 1946	28339	#13
1000	B-B	---	1000	100 tons	E.M.D. October 19, 1939	889	#17
1001	B-B	---	1000	100 tons	E.M.D. May 16, 1940	1000	#17
**505	B-B	37¼"	660	100 tons	American Locomotive Co. April 1942	69686	#14
**506	B-B	37¼"	660	100 tons	American Locomotive Co. April 1942	69687	#15
**507	B-B	37¼"	660	100 tons	American Locomotive Co. May 1942	69691	#16

*This locomotive is still owned by the road but not in operation.

**This locomotive is still in operation on the road.

S.T. & E. PASSENGER CARS, ETC.

NUMBER	TYPE & DESCRIPTION	ACQUIRED	CONDITION
?	Mitchell autocar - seats seven	1909 - new	retired
?	Combination coach and baggage car - seats 24	1910 - used	retired
#100	Hall-Scott Gasoline motor car - 4 cylinder, 110 HP, 31 feet long, wood body and steel underframe	1912 - new	retired
?	Garford Studebaker autocar - seats seven	1913 - new	retired
#532	Coach - seats 44; former U.P. #532	May 1972 - used	storage
#2202	Streamlined coach; former S.P. 2202 - seats 122	October 1972 - used	storage
#2297	Streamlined coach, former S.P. 2297 - seats 48	October 1972 - used	storage
#3302	Streamlined coach; former S.P. 3302 - seats 77	October 1972 - used	storage
#21	Business Car; former A.T. & S.F. #21 & M. & E.T. R.R.	November 1958 - used	storage
#125	Business Car; former U.P. #12	August 1966 - used	storage
#5016	Diner-lunch counter type; U.P. #5016 in 500 series	April 1972	storage
----	Caboose; former Y.V. Railroad and C.C.T. Co. caboose	1952 - used	storage
#2	Box car, wood body and underframe, 50,000 lb. capacity	1910 - used	retired
#5	Flat car, wood underframe, 50,000 lb. capacity	1910 - used	retired
#7	Flat car, wood underframe, 50,000 lb. capacity	1910 - used	retired
#9	Flat car, wood underframe, 50,000 lb. capacity	1910 - used	retired

Locomotive #2 pulled the first train through parts of the Feather River of the Western Pacific line before it came to the S.T. & E. Railroad where it was the first engine on the road but carried the number 2. (Gerald M. Best collection)

Locomotive #1 switching in East Stockton in December of 1937. (S.T. & E. collection)

Slow Tired & Easy's #1 in December 1937. The locomotive was 73 years old when this picture was taken and was the only locomotive power owned by the railroad. (S.T. & E. collection)

Locomotive #1 approaches Stockton Station, after picking up cars from W.P. tracks in the background, 1947. (Guy Dunscomb collection)

Locomotive #1 at Stockton Station on Roosevelt Street, 1947. (Guy Dunscomb collection)

Old #1 with a borrowed coach, crossing Highway 99 on an excursion trip, 1948. (S.T. & E. collection)

S.T. & E. #1 at the Glendale, California Station in October of 1953. It was on the way to its final resting place at Traveltown Museum in Griffith Park. Before Dr. Hiss donated it to the museum, he added a flashy paint job and changed the pony truck wheels back to the type used on the locomotive when it was C.P.'s second #31 and #1193. (Gerald M. Best collection)

S.T. & E. #1 as it looked in 1974 at Traveltown, Los Angeles. A headlight of the type used when it was S.P. #1215 was donated by Gerald M. Best and remounted on the locomotive. A new paint job also made it more nearly resemble its old self when it had been a Central Pacific engine before the turn of the century. (Gerald M. Best collection)

Locomotive #1 in Travel Town Museum, Los Angeles, California. (S.T. & E. collection)

124

S.T. & E. #3, Baldwin #55248, built in 1922. Dr. Hiss purchased it from Pacific Lumber Company in February 1953. Here he is in the cab with Mrs. Gerald Best on an excursion trip, June 6, 1954. (Gerald M. Best collection)

The Stockton Station at the corner of Roosevelt and Union Streets was built in 1910 and served the company until 1959. (S.T. & E. collection)

A locomotive pulling into the engine house yards near Miner Avenue. (S.T. & E. collection)

S.T. & E. #22, built in 1942, was a little-used Army model that was reported to have only 500 operating hours of service before it was purchased by the company in 1957. (S.T. & E. collection)

S.T. & E. #12 was an A.T. & S.F. R.R. engine which had been used on the San Diego division before coming to S.T. & E. in 1961. (S.T. & E. collection)

S.T. & E. Locomotives #22 and #1001 parked near the engine house in January 1966. (Richard A. Cowan collection)

S.T. & E. #'s 1000 and 1001 were purchased from Union Pacific but were soon traded to Western Pacific for two of their switcher engines in 1969. (S.T. & E. collection)

Locomotive #22 sandwiched between #1000 and #1001 in the yards. The two big E.M.D.'s which had been purchased from Union Pacific would soon be traded to the Western Pacific Railroad for two A.L. Co. engines, 1968. (Richard A. Cowan collection)

S.T. & E. #505 came to the company on a lease purchase from Western Pacific in 1968. (S.T. & E. collection)

S.T. & E. Locomotives #12, #11 and #22 on their way to Levin Metals Co. in Stockton, June 1974. (P. A. Panos)

ADDENDA

NOTE #1

For many years there was much confusion over the early locomotive power of the S.T. & E. R.R. The company books hid the information of when and how the construction engine had been acquired and whether it was locomotive #1 or #2. As early as 1922 a company official had written to the I.C.C. that the company records were incomplete. Add to this the misinformation perpetuated by news articles and company letters and it seemed the puzzle was much too difficult to solve. So we will deal here with the evidence that was finally established with the expert assistance of Mr. Gerald M. Best, vice president at large of the Railway and Locomotive Historical Society Inc. and author of many railroad books. Utilizing his expert advice and opinions we re-examined the company books and the pieces began to fall in place.

One of the most confusing facts was that the first engine on the road was always identified as the construction engine. It was the only company-owned locomotive in operation on the road for at least four years, and it was Locomotive #2. Every picture taken of the road locomotive during the early years reveals this fact. The pictures of the locomotive pulling the construction train taken by Potter, the ones taken in Linden during the celebration and the one of the freight train at the Linden Station are all of the same locomotive. A voucher book entry shows that a locomotive was purchased from Norman B. Livermore Company in July of 1910, although the engine was probably in the company's possession when the rail laying was commenced in May. The $2,400 entry was made under construction costs, which meant this was charged to the United Investment Company. Later two entries were made for "rent of Engine #2" but this was eventually followed by another entry that stated that the other two had been erroneously made. The rent entry was probably an attempt by a bookkeeper to charge the railroad company rent for freight hauled while construction was still under way. The company was later criticized by the California Railroad Commission for charging too many expenses to the construction rather than the operation of the railroad.

Locomotive #2 is identified in the early pictures as a former Oregon Railway and Navigation Company engine. About 1902 that company, under new management, sold many locomotives of this type. It carried the Union Pacific type boiler installed on all the O.R. & N. locomotives during the 1890s. The headlight, with the engine number on the panel mounted above the glass, and the characteristic mounting of the whistle in the exact center of the steam dome, plus the sandbox shape with the flat lid, make it unmistakable to locomotive experts.

Although this locomotive has never been positively identified as to the O.R. & N. number it carried, one expert believes that it was one of the O.R. & N. #30-39 class. Of these engines, #37, #38, and #39 were all sold to a secondhand dealer, A. J. McCabe in 1902 and 1903. There is considerable speculation that it might be one of these. #37 went to the Oregon-Washington Power Company as their #107, #39 went to E. English Lumber Co., Mt. Vernon, Washington, in May 1902, and #38 went to the Columbia River & Nehalem Railway, May 1903.

We also have a picture of #2 at the Linden station that says it is "Old 93." We have not been able to dismiss this entirely either, but what #93?

The Oregon Historical Society attempted to connect it with O.R. & N. #93 but was unable to do so. This information is included in the hopes it will enable others finally to unscramble the complete story of this particular locomotive.

The only clue as to the whereabouts of Locomotive #2 between the time it left the O.R. & N. road and its arrival in Stockton through Norman B. Livermore, are pictures taken of the construction engine and first trains to run on portions of the Feather River Canyon route during the construction of the Western Pacific Railroad. The pictures show two and three business cars and Engine #2 with the number very clear on the front number plate. This brings out another possibility as to the engine's whereabouts, for it could also have been the Boca & Loyalton Lumber Company Engine #2. This lumber company owned all sorts of second-hand engines before it sold out to Western Pacific, who actually purchased the road for its right of way. The W.P. kept three of the B. & L. locomotives, renumbering them to the W.P. numbering system, and sold the rest.

We do know that #2 was the number on the engine when it arrived on the S.T. & E. Railroad, and it was the first and only locomotive owned by the road for several years. Any extra motive power needed was rented from other railroads.

NOTE #2

A fire that would cause such damage to a locomotive must have been severe but we were unsuccessful in finding any details of it. We know that locomotive #2 was used to haul freight and to pull the small yellow combination passenger and baggage coach until late 1911 or early 1912. We also know that by March of 1912 the S.T. & E. Board of Directors' minutes noted there was $141.80 due from Aetna Insurance Co.

Even though Cameron had declared it beyond repair it may have been repaired, as almost $200 was charged to steam locomotive repairs between June 1912 and June 1913.

NOTE #3

This time it was Master Mechanic Stone who declared Locomotive #2 unfit for service. The board members voted to sell it for $475 and authorized the executive committee to do this. It could not have been done immediately for there is a 1913 Poor's report which shows one locomotive on the S.T. & E. Railroad. The company rented locomotive power for a considerable time because from June 1913 to June 1914 $1,821.64 was spent for lease of equipment and only $24.24 for repairs.

NOTE #4

Eight years later F. J. Dietrich would try to fathom the history of the S.T. & E. Locomotive #1 in order to meet government regulations on a specification card. He was not sure when it had been purchased or even from whom it was acquired. He did, however, come up with the annual locomotive inspection and repair report made on the Palmer McBride & Quayle Construction Company Engine #1, dated May 28, 1914. Using this as a concrete piece of evidence, and with the assistance of Gerald Best, we were able to unravel the history of Engine #1. Both Dietrich and S.P. records agreed that this was the former S.P. #1488 sold by that company on January 6, 1909. This is verified by S.P. Revised Classification and Assignment of Locomotives reports still in existence. This was shortly after S.P. had electrified its East Bay commute line and many small local steam engines no longer needed by S.P. were being sold to contractors, shortline railroads, or being scrapped.

But let's start at the beginning. Engine #1 was built by Norris-Lancaster in 1864. It was shipped around the horn and arrived in San Francisco to become Engine "G" and named the *Mariposa*, of the original Western Pacific Railroad of California. After Central Pacific took over the Western Pacific it was one of eight engines shipped to Sacramento. During the winter of 1867–68 these were stored in the dead-line at Sacramento waiting for construction to begin on the eastern end of the Western Pacific line. This work was postponed and the stored engines were turned over to the Central Pacific. The *Mariposa* was given the Central Pacific's second #31. The first #31, the *Klamath*, had exploded near Elko, Nevada on March 30, 1869. This was to cause confusion later, when Southern Pacific Company officials informed Dietrich that Engine #1 was the *Klamath* instead of the *Mariposa*.

The Central Pacific Railroad was extending its line to the north to meet the Oregon & California R.R., which was building south. The tracks were laid north of Redding to Soda Springs near what is now Shasta Spring, where Locomotive #31, piloted by Engineer Ketty, pulled the first train in from San Francisco. Fortunately for us a photographer recorded the event.

The locomotive was renumbered to Central Pacific #1193. In 1891 the engine went into the Sacramento shop for another overhaul, and received a new boiler with a new steam dome and sand box. Shortly after this engine had its picture taken again, this time at Biggs, California.

Southern Pacific engineers claimed it was the fastest engine on the west coast up until 1900. It was also reputed to be the first engine on the Sacramento Division to receive an electric headlight. Southern Pacific renumbered it again, making it the second S.P. #1215. It went to the shops again in 1904 for another complete rebuilding. This time it was converted to burn oil and received a new silhouette, with the installation of a new smoke stack and steel cab. The fenders were removed and new pony truck wheels added, and the tender got a new frame and trucks.

In 1907 all of the S.P. engines left in the 1200 series were renumbered so #1215 became S.P. #1488. It had by now been pressed into commuter service as a local out of Oakland. Sometime during 1908 S.P. #1488 was derailed near Oakland Estuary bridge to Alameda. The late Robert H. McFarland took a picture of the locomotive before it was righted and returned to the shops for repair.

After #1488 was repaired it was sold to Erickson & Peterson Contractors, who used it in the construction of the Los Angeles aqueduct and water works.

A letter written by Dietrich in 1922 stated the engine had been sold to the Norman B. Livermore Company and this could be true, happening either before or after its being in the possession of Erickson & Peterson. Or Dietrich could have assumed this because Locomotive #2 had come from the Livermore Company when he had first been a company official. We do not know what number it operated under at this time but we do know that it eventually went to the Palmer Mc-Bride and Quayle Construction Company and was given their number 1.

This brings us back to the inspection and repair report dated May 28, 1914. The company books show that regular payments of $300 a month were made between August and January. With all the costs included, there was a total cost of $2,181.75 for Engine #1. The reason Dietrich could not find the information was probably the same reason the author had difficulty finding it, because the Railroad Commission had cautioned the company bookkeeper about putting operating costs in the construction ledger—exactly what had been done again.

NOTE #5

Locomotive #10 had been built by the Mid West Locomotive Works in 1936 for the Chicago, Burlington & Quincy R.R. and given their number 9121. It was sold to the U.S. Army Quartermaster Corps, then transferred to the U.S. Army Transportation Corps, where it became #7196. It was used at the Sacramento Signal Corps depot in California.

An out-of-service report was filed on #10 on March 31, 1958. The engine was sold for scrap to an Oakland junk dealer. The company had agreed to a sale price of $3,200 but received only $100. A collection agency was not even successful in getting the rest of the money.

NOTE #6

The company had purchased an old Yosemite Valley Railroad caboose from the Central California Traction Company and parked it in the company yard to be utilized as quarters for Dr. Hiss when he was in Stockton.

The caboose is still in the possession of the S.T. & E. Railroad as part of their collection.

NOTE #7

In August 1953 permission to abandon the track came from the I.C.C. and the club continued negotiations. Most of the right of way had never been deeded to the company so clear title could be given only to property described as parcels I, II, and III. The club members began to gather rail cars and planned to use the track as a museum. The money was still in escrow by October of 1954, so the railroad officials issued an ultimatum that if the escrow was not closed before November 1, the deal was off. The escrow was closed but the Railroad fan club created problems for the land-owners near Bellota. The farmers retaliated by filing trespassing suits against the club representatives, Wolf and Laflin. The court settled the matter by dismissing the charges but giving the club until September 1, 1957 to remove the steel rails etc. or let it all revert to the property owners. They managed to remove the rails and ties before the deadline.

NOTE #8

The third and last steam locomotive owned by the S.T. & E. Railroad was purchased by Dr. Hiss in February 1953 and became S.T. & E. #3. It had been built by the Baldwin Locomotive Works in Philadelphia, Pennsylvania in 1922, for the Humboldt Northern Railway Company. It was numbered H & N #3, then transferred to the Dolbeer Carson Lumber Company as their #3. This company was taken over by the Pacific Lumber Company, who later sold the locomotive to the S.T. & E. The tender tank was exchanged for the Mc-Cloud River Locomotive #2 tender tank in 1955. The 2-6-2 steam engine was more of a toy than a working engine after it came to the S.T. & E. and was out of service by December 31, 1955. It was in operative condition up to the day it was parked in the old S.T. & E. engine house in Stockton, where it still stands today as part of the company's collection of old rolling stock.

132

NOTE #9

Dr. Martin Hiss donated Locomotive #1 to Traveltown, a transportation museum under the auspices of the Los Angeles Parks and Recreation Department. In October 1953 Old #1 left Stockton and arrived at the Glendale Station in Southern California, where Gerald M. Best once again took a picture of it. By now it had a flashy paint job and the solid type pony truck wheels used on the engine when it had been a Central Pacific locomotive. Some time later Best donated a headlight of the type that adorned it as S.P. Engine #1215 and this was added. The paint on the engine was once again modified to make it look more like it had before the turn of the centruy.

NOTE #10

Locomotive #11 was acquired by the S.T. & E. Railroad in February of 1955 from Walter H. Wilms of Los Angeles, a dealer in locomotives. It had originally been built in General Electric's Schenectady, New York, plant in 1941. It went directly to the Savanna Ordnance Depot in Savanna, Illinois and was given the number 05. It was transferred to the Army Transportation Corps and finally shipped to the U.S. Arsenal at Ogden, Utah. From there it went to the Bamberger Railroad shops in North Salt Lake City where John Hewitt inspected it for the S.T. & E. It became S.T. & E. #11 and was put out of service on February 12, 1970. It was a rare off-center cab model and one of only five ever to come to the west coast. It was sold to Levin Metals Corporation in Stockton, California for scrap in June 1974.

NOTE #11

S.T. & E. Locomotive #22 was a diesel electric built in the Schenectady, New York General Electric plant in 1942. It went directly to a G.E. Corporation project in Hanford, Washington and later was moved to the Transportation Corps of the Army and became USA #7385. It was shipped to a small army camp, Camp Atterbury, Indiana, in 1945 and placed in storage. In 1953 it was moved to the Transportation Corps facilities at Ogden, Utah for more storage. It must have been transferred from there to Seattle, Washington as that is where John Hewitt picked it up for the S.T. & E. Railroad. The company had purchased the engine from Walter H. Wilms & Sundfelt Equipment Co. of Seattle. It was reported to have only 500 hours of actual service on record. Hewitt picked up the engine on January 7, 1957 and rode it home to Stockton. The engine was out of service by February 1970 and was sold to Levin Metals Company of Stockton in June 1974. It was transferred to their Richmond yards for an evaluation and was operating in the yards as of April 1975.

NOTE #12

Diesel Electric Engine #12 was originally built for Atchison, Topeka & Santa Fe Railway and given their number 466. It was used in the San Diego, California division before being transferred to Fresno. It was acquired by S.T. & E. in 1961 and received their number 12. It was out of service as of May 2, 1971 and was sold to Levin Metals in Stockton in June of 1974 for scrap.

NOTE #13

S.T. & E. Locomotive #25 is a diesel electric built by General Electric in Schenectady, New York in December 1946. It eventually became California Traction Company's number 25. The number was retained when the S.T. & E. purchased it from that company in April 1971. It is still in operation and the company uses it primarily to haul light loads to and from Linden.

NOTE #14

S.T. & E. Locomotive #505 was built by General Electric Company's American Locomotive Company at Schenectady, New York in April 1942. It eventually became Western Pacific's Switcher #505 and came to the S.T. & E. in September of 1968 on a lease purchase, retaining its old number. The company was so happy with the performance of this particular locomotive that they wanted more of the same model. This locomotive is still in operation on the S.T. & E.

NOTE #15

S.T. & E. Locomotive #506 was built by the American Locomotive works in 1942, the next one off the line after #505. It became W.P. Switcher #506 and came to the S.T. & E. in a trade with W.P. for U.P. and S.T. & E. #1000, in 1959. It is still in operation on the S.T. & E. today.

NOTE #16

S.T. & E. Locomotive #507 was also built by the American Locomotive works, being completed in May of 1942, a month later than S.T. & E.'s #505 and #506. It had received the W.P. number 510 and was the last SL Switcher owned by that company. It was changed to S.T. & E. number 507 and is still in operation on the road.

NOTE #17

S.T. & E. Locomotives #1000 and #1001 were built by E.M.D. in 1939 and 1940 respectively. They had been purchased from U.P. on a sales contract and arrived in August 1966. The company repainted each a light yellow, with red trim and black below the decking. They retained the numbers already assigned to them. Both units were traded to Western Pacific Railroad for two of their locomotives, #506 and #510. A final S.T. & E. report for #1000 was made October 22, 1969 and one for #1001 on February 14, 1969.

BIBLIOGRAPHY

BOOKS

Abdill, George B., *Pacific Slope Railroads*, Bonanza Books, New York, 1959.

Best, Gerald M., *Iron Horses to Promontory*, Golden West Books, Alhambra, California, 1969.

Deane, Dorothy Newell, *Sierra Railway*, Howell-North, Berkeley, California, 1960.

Elliott & Moore, *History of Stanislaus County 1881*, (reproduction), Unigraphic, Inc., Evansville, Indiana, 1974.

Fee, Harry Thomas, *Essay on Early Stockton*, California Room, Stockton Library, Stockton, California.

Johnston, Hank, *Short Line to Paradise*, John & Howe, Long Beach, California, 1962.

Martin, V. Covert, *Stockton Album*, Simard Printing Co., Stockton, California, 1959.

Men of California, 1925, Western Press Reporter, Inc., Los Angeles and San Francisco.

Railroad Commission, California, *Books of Issues and Orders*, Volumes 1,2,3,4,5,7,10 and 11, San Francisco, California, 1912–1930.

Riegal, Robert Edgar, *The Story of the Western Railroad*, University of Nebraska Press, 1963.

Thompson & Butler, *Report on Valuation and Prospective Earnings of the S.T. & E. Railroad*, San Francisco, California, 1926.

Traffic Association, *The Valley Road*, Wheeler Publishing Co., San Francisco, 1896.

Wagner, Jack Russell, *Short Line Junction*, Valley Publishers, Fresno, California, 1956.

Who's Who in America, 1951–60, A. N. Marquis, Chicago, Illinois.

Who's Who in California, 1928–29, Armstrong, Los Angeles, California.

PERIODICALS AND NEWSPAPERS

Byron Times, Special Edition, 1910, Byron, California.

Linden Herald, August 3, 1974, Linden, California.

Literary Digest, "Blue Sky Legislation," April 26, 1913.

Literary Digest, "Jolt to Blue Sky Laws," February 21, 1914.

San Francisco Call Post, July 20, 1914, San Francisco, California.

San Francisco Examiner, April 7, 1915, San Francisco, California.

Stockton Daily Independent, 1908–1916, Stockton, California.

Stockton Daily Mail, 1908–1917, Stockton, California.

Stockton Daily Record, 1906–1975, Stockton, California.

DOCUMENTS AND BOOKLETS

Articles of Incorporation of S.T. & E. Railroad, 1908 and 1926, Archives, Department of State, California.

Award, Institutional Warehouse, Union Pacific Centennial, 1969.

Court Cases #11836 and #12524, Clerk's Office, San Joaquin County, Stockton, California.

Gold Bond, S.T. & E. Railroad, April 1911, Stockton Public Library, California Room, Stockton, California.

Maps, El Ricado Terrace, Vol. 10, page 57, and Vol. 6, page 4, Recorder's Office, San Joaquin County, Stockton, California.

Map, The Oaks, Vol. 1, page 66, Recorder's Office, San Joaquin County, Stockton, California.

Program, Linden Celebration, 1910, Stockton, California.

San Joaquin County, California, Booklet by Fisher, D. E., Sunset Magazine Homeseekers Bureau for the Board of Supervisors, 1913.

The Stockton Terminal & Eastern Railroad, promotional booklet, United Investment Co., San Francisco, California, 1910.

COMPANY RECORDS, S.T. & E. RAILROAD

Cash Book, September 1913 to May 1916.

Cash Book, May 1916 to June 1917.

Cash Book, January 1916 to December 1920.

Cash Book, 1927.

Cash Book, 1928.

Journal, October 1908 to September 1915.

Journal, October 1915 to August 1918.

Journal, January 1920 to December 1926.

Letters, F. J. Dietrich, Jr., 1938 to 1952.

Letters, F. J. Dietrich, Sr., 1917 to 1949.

Letters, Samuel Kahn, 1926 to 1952.

Locomotive Files, 1914 to 1975.

Ledger, Construction, September 1913 to December 1916.

Ledger, General, October 1908 to August 1910.

Minutes Book, S.T. & E. Railroad, Vol. 1, October 1908 to December 1911.

Minutes Book, S.T. & E. Railroad, Vol. 2, January 1912 to April 1917.

Minutes, Board of Directors, S.T. & E. Railroad, California Corporation, 1925 to 1960.

Minutes, Board of Directors, S.T. & E. Railroad, Nevada Corporation, 1926 to 1960.

Reports, Interstate Commerce Commission, 1919 to 1960.

Right of Way Maps and Documents, 1908 to 1960.

Voucher Abstract, February 1910 to August 1913.

INDEX